Taking Charge:

A Parent and Teacher Guide to Loving Discipline

Jo Anne Nordling

R & E PUB   ❖ SARATOGA, CALIFORNIA

Copyright © 1992 by Jo Anne Nordling

R & E Publishers
P.O. Box 2008, Saratoga, CA 95070
Tel: (408) 866-6303   Fax: (408) 866-0825

Book Design by Diane Parker
Cover by Kaye Quinn

First Printing 1992
Second Printing 1993
Library of Congress Card Catalog Number: 91-50982
ISBN 0-88247-906-7
Printed in the United States of America
10 9 8 7 6 5 4 3 2 1

"Discipline is the slow, bit by bit, time consuming task of helping children to see the sense in acting in a certain way."

James Hymes
(A founder of the Head Start program)

"I'm holding on with my heart."

Ricky (age 4, while swinging at Fanno Creek Children's Center)

"It takes a whole village to raise a child."

African Proverb

DEDICATION

To my sons, Dirk, Eric, Chris, and Craig, my husband, George,
and my parents, Dora and Verle.

Note: *All of the situations in this book actually happened. Names of
the adults and children involved have been changed to protect
their privacy.*

ACKNOWLEDGMENTS

There are so many people responsible for the development of this eclectic approach to child discipline, I cannot list them all. Here are some of the people I am especially indebted to:

The parents and teachers who used the material and asked so many productive questions throughout the development of this text;

Dr. Morris Tiktin, family counselor, who introduced me to the consequence and democracy concepts of Rudolf Dreikurs;

Jean Lawrence, founder of Fanno Creek Children's Center of Portland, Oregon, for her many sensitive insights into the behavior of children;

Sue Edmiston, parent trainer and family counselor, whose teachings sent me on the fruitful search for completing her idea of an appropriate correction for each misbehavior. I have elaborated and refined Sue's idea but the basic Adlerian core came from her;

Lorraine Heller, my partner at the Parent Support Center of Portland, Oregon, whose dedication and compassion has been an inspiration, and whose constant encouragement to complete this manuscript has been invaluable;

My teachers in the graduate counseling program of Lewis and Clark College, Portland, Oregon: Dr. Bob McIlroy, Dr. Jerry McCubbin, and Dr. Gordon Lindbloom. I would especially like to thank Dr. Don Nickerson, who helped me come to terms with some of the difficult experiences of my own childhood;

Sean, Lisa, Sharon, Ted, and all the children I worked with in play therapy, who revealed to me the awesome integrity and strength of every child's inner self;

All the caring teachers, counselors, and parents I have encountered over the past thirty-nine years. I learned from each one of them something of the astonishing capacity which exists in adults for loving commitment to their own, and to other people's, children.

I would also like to thank Ron Olisar, Louise Waitt, Jewel Lansing, Lorraine Heller, Derene Meurisse, and Betty Daggett who gave so generously of their time and talents in the final preparation of this manuscript.

TABLE OF CONTENTS

✳ The problem.

The A and C parenting and teaching styles.

Guidelines for forming your own "Taking Charge" discussion group.

✳ What a child needs for healthy emotional growth.

Behavior you pay attention to will continue.

Positive, neutral, and negative behaviors.

The importance of giving nonverbal attention at neutral times.

The four self-sabotages: Procrastination,

✳ Forgetting to pay positive attention,

✳ Talking and talking, and Negative scripting.

✳ The hidden self-sabotages: The unmet needs of the adult.

The role of anger.

Sometimes the negative behavior is not a misbehavior at all, but rather a problem area for the child.

Adult can help the child in problem areas by 1. Adjusting the environment; 2. Teaching assertiveness and negotiating skills; and 3. Listening to inner-reality feelings.

AUTHOR'S NOTE

As a multicultural and increasingly multiclass society, we have not developed a unified approach to child rearing. Happily, there are widespread attempts to overthrow the often cruel and repressive child rearing practices of our Victorian ancestors, but we cannot agree on what should replace the old "spare the rod and spoil the child" philosophy. We are in transition from what the Swiss psychiatrist Alice Miller calls the "poisonous pedagogy" to something new, but we are not sure what. The media illuminates first one point of view and then another. As a young parent who had four children in five years, and later as a beginning teacher, I myself experienced the confusion of trying to sort out these many "expert" voices. Each new book I read, each new workshop I attended, promised the answer. And while each was helpful in some way, no one approach seemed to be enough. I would go home, or back into the classroom, prepared to do what I had just learned, and discover that real life constantly presented me with new misbehaviors which did not seem to fit the current philosophy.

In particular, I remember my early immersion in the teachings of Rudolf Dreikurs. Dr. Dreikurs had the keen insight that children must be allowed to experience the consequences of their own behaviors if they are to grow into responsible adults. He was right, but my dilemma came when I tried using his ignoring and consequence approach for all misbehaviors. I discovered that logical consequences and ignoring did not work for every situation.

Then came my introduction to the insights of people like Carl Rogers and Thomas Gordon who taught the importance of listening to the child's feelings. This, I was positive, was the answer. I am still convinced that acceptance of a child's feelings is one of the most powerful positive influences we can bring to a healthy shaping of a child's life. But listening to feelings did not solve all the problems in the child/adult relationship. I once saw a mother trying to hold her eight-year-old boy at arms length while he kicked her repeatedly in the shins. She kept saying in a solicitous tone of voice, "Now, now. You must be really upset about something." He kept yelling and kicking her. Obviously, some other response was needed. I could not figure out how logical consequences or ignoring applied to this kind of situation. The only logical consequence I could think of at the time was for her to hit him back. But I was as positive then as I am now that hurting a child does not work either.

Many people still believe in hitting children for misbehaving. Some even believe that hitting kids is somehow good for them. But I have noticed that it is often the very child who teachers and parents advise "needs a good spanking" who is most frequently spanked at home. Aside from the deeper ethical consideration of whether it is right to deliberately hurt another human being, hitting children seems to create an escalating cycle of more misbehaviors.

Next I discovered the writings of Abraham Maslow. Dr. Maslow's philosophy of how human beings develop into emotionally healthy persons struck me as being absolutely true, but it took many years before I grasped how to specifically translate his hierarchy of needs concept into a concrete, everyday approach to parenting and teaching.

Haim Ginott's insights into the use of descriptive versus evaluating language, and Eric Berne's concepts of the importance of early scripting, were beacons of light for me as I struggled to develop a unified and specific approach to child discipline.

I did not like B.F. Skinner and the other Behaviorists. I was opposed to the manipulation of people of any age. It took me many years in the private and public school of hard knocks before I finally accepted that the Behaviorists, too, had some legitimate insights into child rearing, that you did not have to treat a child as though you were training an animal for a circus act in order to apply some basic Behaviorist principles.

The idea that the repressed feelings and humiliations we suffer as children provide the fuel driving a violent society, as expounded by Alice Miller and John Bradshaw, came too late to help shape my early thinking, but they are welcome corroboration as to the validity of this specific approach to child discipline.

Through thirty-nine years of parenting, teaching, and counseling I became increasingly aware that although children have a right to grow up as independent people in control of their own lives without being demeaned and humiliated by adults in the name of good discipline, adults have an equal right to expect certain kinds of behavior from children. An outcome of this personal struggle has been the gradual development of an approach to child discipline which allows adults to take specific initiative action to change the disruptive behaviors exhibited by so many children in this culture, while still respecting the dignity of the child. It is a unified pattern which incorporates all common childhood behaviors. The pattern can be learned and applied selectively to each unique adult/child situation. It is a pattern which works for me and for the vast majority of the parents and teachers in my classes.

This is not to say that the Taking Charge pattern of discipline is the answer for all the problems which can arise in the adult/child relationship. There are many extreme situations, for example, family members who are incestuous, drug addicted, or who have chemical imbalances in their brains. This book does not attempt to address these circumstances. But most adults who demean children with physical punishment, or who humiliate children in nonverbal and verbal ways, do so either out of a mistaken belief that this is how adults are *supposed* to discipline children, or out of a sense of helplessness and frustration at having lost control of their home or classroom.

A family or classroom in which the adult feels out of control, and in which many of the children feel unappreciated and unloved, can change to one in which the adult feels in charge and is able to direct children's lives with respect and concern for their individual needs. Of course the changes cannot become permanent after reading once through a book, or attending a few weeks of class meetings. It takes a long time to change old habit patterns so that under stress, we do not revert back. Most of us need at least one other person with whom to share ideas and feelings as we try to change old, ingrained attitudes and habits of human relationships. Many of the parents in my parenting groups report that things go much better at home for three or four days after the most recent class meeting. But if there is stress at home, and there often is, they begin to slip into the old patterns with their children. For this reason, the Parent Support Center of Portland, Oregon, offers a continuing drop-in group which is open to parents who are familiar with the *Taking Charge* material. The ongoing discussion group is there for those who may be feeling the need for emotional support or help in solving specific situations at home. Teachers and school support personnel have organized similar informal groups within their school buildings. In this same way, I hope that many readers of this book will form their own weekly discussion groups so that each reader can join with at least one other person and continue to build on the foundation begun in this book. If even a small discussion group is not possible for you, *Taking Charge* is always available as a reference source to use as you continue to work independently on establishing new patterns in your relationships with children.

Taking Charge shows the adult how to take charge of the adult/child relationship so that both adult and child can feel respected, secure, and loved. Most parents and teachers can use the basic principles set out here. There is no magic to the process. The pattern can be taught. It can be learned. It takes hard work, but the way is open.

Jo Anne Swenston Nordling
Portland, Oregon
November, 1991

1 Getting Started

Our culture has many different ways of disciplining children. As parents and teachers, we are a collection of individuals, each independently pursuing our own parenting or teaching style. We often disagree with our best friends about how to discipline kids. We have different rules for toilet training, weaning from the bottle, off-limit items, bed time, diet, school work, clothing, hair styles, curfew—the list is endless. Teachers within the same school building often disagree on how to discipline their students. Usually, even one's spouse was reared in an entirely different family setting and sometimes has almost an alien concept from ours on how to handle discipline of the kids.

Everyone agrees that children need to be loved before they can become responsible, strong, and caring adults, but we differ widely on just how to express that love as we guide them throughout the early years of their lives. Some parents and teachers believe in the old adage, "Spare the rod and spoil the child," while others insist that the rod referred to in the Bible is a shepherd's crook which was used not to beat the sheep but to guide them. Other parents and teachers believe that adults should get out of the way, just "stand back and watch them grow."

If you are an elementary school teacher, or a day care provider, you are well aware of how often you act as a parent for other people's children. As a surrogate parent, working with very young children who have been removed from their parents for six to ten hours a day, you are asked to provide many of their emotional needs during the time they spend with you. In fact, you probably spend more time with the children in your charge each weekday than most of their parents are able to do. The demands of earning a living mean that many parents have only a precious three or four hours each working day to spend with their children, and much of that time must be taken up in doing household chores. For this reason, if you are a day care provider, please regard yourself, also, as the parent referred to throughout this book.

Classroom teachers interact with the children in their classrooms much as they interact with their own children. Especially in the area of discipline, teaching style and parenting style are inseparable. Most school teachers agree that as they parent, so do they teach. It is clear that as teachers, day care providers, and parents we all begin at the same place; the way we were parented when we were children.

We either parent in the same way as our parents did, or we consciously bend over backwards trying not to parent as they did. If we try not to parent as our parents did, we are left in a vacuum, not having experienced any other kind of child raising methods. After all, you learn to be a parent by watching your own parents. Consequently, under stress, we tend either to fall back into our own parents' behavior patterns or withdraw from the scene altogether. Which of us has not been horrified at least once at our own behavior towards our children, "And I said I would never act that way with *my* kids!"

How can so many caring, concerned parents and teachers have so much trouble with kids? Parents who are responsible people in their own lives often have children who grow up to be irresponsible. Their children do not mind, they avoid chores, they misbehave at school. When they become teenagers, they are among those who smoke and drink, experiment with harder drugs, or have exploitive sexual experiences. They are often involved in stealing and lying. Many of these kids follow along with any peer group who will have them, no matter what the value system of the peer group and how opposite it is to that of their parents. It is such a paradox. Parent after parent expresses the wish to just quit and walk away. "I sometimes think we should give that kid away and start over." But of course, caring adults are too responsible to walk away. Most of them stick it out and suffer, totally bewildered and suspecting that maybe it is something inherited, something "in the genes."

Teachers, too, go through similar kinds of misery in their relationships with their students. Many young teachers start out in their profession buoyed up by the anticipation of how satisfying it will be, to make a difference in the world and to leave the world a little better than they found it. The reality of resistant, even hostile, students—kids who refuse to do their schoolwork, who sometimes will not even extend basic courtesies to their teachers—all combine to create a growing bewilderment in the young teacher, culminating in resentment and anger. Teachers are freer to walk away from their profession than parents are. Still, many teachers keep at it, even though they feel betrayed and wounded by the behavior of the kids in their classes.

Most parents and teachers fall into two general groups. The first group, parent/teacher "A", believes that adults know best what children need to do; that children are too inexperienced and too young to make their own decisions. There is no doubt in the A adult's mind that children should not be allowed to annoy adults and that children should know their place. Parent/teacher A experiences very little inner struggle over when to correct the child. It seldom, if ever, occurs to A adults that the child might not love them if they make too many demands on the child. The belief that the rights of the adult take precedence over the rights of the child enable A adults to feel comfortable as disciplinarians.

In spite of feeling comfortable with the act of discipline, however, A adults sometimes find themselves locked in a power struggle with the child. If the adult says YES the child says, or quietly does, NO. Some children are afraid to openly refuse any adult.

They agree with whatever the adult insists on, but they go underground with their opposition by passively resisting and doing exactly the opposite of whatever the adult says. This power struggle becomes especially intense as the child grows into puberty. As children's minds and bodies mature, they become more and more convinced that they are capable of running their own lives. A adults, on the other hand, regard the child as a dependent who ought to conform to the rules and values of the household which feeds and clothes him, or the school system which educates her. In spite of the fact that these A adults are loving and dedicated, they often find themselves in a bewildering state of perpetual conflict with the child. Other people say the child is spoiled and needs a good spanking, even though sometimes the child has often been spanked by both parent A and teacher A. The A adult comes to think of the child as irresponsible, ungrateful, and uncaring, a disappointment to the family and to all school personnel who work with him or her. The child in turn feels misunderstood, picked on, and unloved. The child's behavior consequently worsens as the downward spiral of defiance and punishment continues. Both adult and child feel deeply wounded by the other's apparent lack of love and respect.

Parent/teacher "C", on the other hand, experiences a tremendous amount of inner struggle over when and how to correct the child's behavior. C adults wonder whether they are allowing children enough room to express themselves. They wonder whether the child will still love them if they make too many demands on the child. C adults often ask themselves, "Do adults have the right, just because they are older, to tell another human being what to do?"

Parent/teacher C suspects that children have just as much right to decide how to live their lives as the adult does. C adults also have a strong belief that if they are kind, understanding, and fair, children will respond by behaving in a similar fashion. C adults suspect that adults only need to love children and then stand back and watch them blossom. Parent/teacher C is bewildered if the child begins to show signs of developing into a self-centered "me first" person who expects to always get his or her own way. No matter how often C adults defer to the child, the child seems to demand more and more. "Give that kid an inch and he takes a mile." Parent/teacher C is confused and hurt when the child avoids doing a fair share of routine chores, including schoolwork, demands a disproportionate share of attention in any situation, expects others to always play by his or her rules, and frequently has difficulty forming friendships with peers. As before, other people advise that this child is spoiled and needs a good spanking. Parent/teacher C usually does not spank unless pushed to the extreme. Instead the C adult has intense heart-to-heart talks with the child about becoming more responsible, more generous, more ambitious, and more considerate of others. But the more the C adult reasons and cajoles, the more the child remains the same. Here again, a power struggle between adult and child emerges, although this time it is disguised by the unwillingness of parent/teacher C to make direct demands on the child.

Of course, no one individual parent or teacher falls absolutely into either the "A" or the "C" category. People are too complex. There are always too many variables. Still, most parents and teachers can place themselves somewhere along this continuum line. Where would you place yourself? Your partner? Your co-workers?

Parent/Teacher "A" ---------------------------------------Parent/Teacher "C"
(Adults have absolute authority)   (Child has as much authority as adult)

There is nothing intrinsically wrong with having the basic assumptions of a parent/teacher A or a parent/teacher C. Each style has strengths. Each can learn from the other. One Head Start teacher who calls herself a C adult, says she is always grateful when she has an A adult working in her classroom as a teaching assistant, because she knows the A adult will keep reminding her that adults need to provide the security of routines, predictable rules, and firm consequences. An A type teacher says he is grateful that the C type counselor in his school is available to talk to his students, because the A teacher cannot get his students to share personal problems with him. It is hard for this A teacher to listen to his students because he is convinced if the kids would just just do what he tells them to do, all their problems would be solved.

It is interesting how often couples turn out to have opposite parenting styles. Perhaps, when we choose a mate, we recognize at some nonverbal level our need for an opposite, complementary point of view. It should not surprise you if your spouse tends to parent differently than you do. Unfortunately, the temptation for both spouses is to criticize, and try to change the other's parenting style. Try not to resculpture your spouse. You will not be able to do it anyway. All you will accomplish is to get your spouse upset and uncooperative. Besides, *fighting among adults over how to discipline children is guaranteed to cause even more misbehavior on the part of the children.*

Talk over your parenting style with your spouse, or your live-in partner, if that is the situation in your family. It does not matter whether or not your present spouse is the biological parent of the children. If he or she is living in your home and acting as a surrogate parent, he or she needs to be an equal partner in raising the kids. Try to respect and understand the other person's mind set. Talk together about the strengths and weaknesses of your respective styles. Neither of you needs to change your basic personality. Try to accept, at least in some measure, one another's differences. If you can do this, you will be able to work together to adapt the methods in this book to your own situation, thereby creating new and effective parenting skills for yourselves.

It would be helpful if you and your partner could have a weekly discussion meeting while you work your way through this book.

Or maybe you can find one or two friends who would like to get together once a week. If you are a school teacher, try to find two or three fellow teachers to meet with you on a weekly basis. It is difficult to learn about one's own parenting/teaching mind set without having another adult around to give you some feedback, to offer ideas, and especially to be there to listen while you think out loud. Trying to learn about yourself all alone is like an eye trying to see itself, or a tongue trying to taste itself. We are too close to ourselves to get ourselves in clear focus.

However, if your partner does not want to participate, and all of your friends are too busy, or if none of the other teachers are interested, try to accept their decisions and do the best you can on your own. As Rudolf Dreikurs advised, "Do what *you* can do."

Whether you tend towards the A or the C end of the continuum line, take heart. It is the aim of this book to help you learn some ways to stop the power struggles you may now be involved in with your children at home or school. The concepts and processes herein are certain to ease the pain you may now be feeling. It will not be easy or quick. You will have to devote a minimum of two solid months of focused attention to learning a new way of relating to children.

Loving adults, no matter how different their parenting philosophies, hold in common basic values and goals for their children and students. Every parent and teacher wants the kids in his or her life to grow up to be responsible, loving, creative adults. No one wants their children to grow up to be either bullies or door mats. We want our kids to be able to take on leadership roles as well as to be willing to cooperate. We want them to be confident in their own abilities. We want them to be willing to risk. We want our kids to hold themselves in high self-esteem while, at the same time, respecting the worth of other human beings.

You are a conscientious and loving parent or teacher, else you would not have bothered to read this far. Your values and goals for your children are important. To engage in the hard work of change, you do not have to change your values, only the way in which you teach those values. Parents are the primary teachers of their children's behavior and value systems. Teachers run a close second. If your children's behaviors and attitudes are presently a worry to you and indicate that they are not learning what you want them to learn, then it is time to change your parenting and teaching approach. This book is designed to help you do that. The principles and techniques described in the succeeding chapters work. They have worked for others over and over again, and they will work for you.

GUIDELINES FOR WEEKLY GROUP DISCUSSIONS

1. Read Chapters One and Two before your first meeting. After that, the book is organized for your group to read and discuss one chapter a week, but it is possible to do two chapters a week if you feel the need to go faster.

2. Read each chapter assignment at least 5 days before your discussion group meets. This will allow you enough time to do the exercise given at the end of each chapter before your next meeting.

3. Participants in the group can be from 2 to 8 people.

4. Choose a regularly scheduled time, once a week, when you can relax and enjoy one another's company.

5. Rotate leadership of the group each week.

6. *Each group member is to share his or her thoughts and feelings only to the degree he or she wants.* Do not expect or encourage people to bare their souls. This is not a personal therapy group.

7. *Help other group members to think out loud by listening to them. Do not argue with them because they perceive the world differently from you. Do not give advice unless someone asks you for it.*

8. *Take turns talking.* Decide on a way to insure that each person gets an equal amount of time to think out loud. You may need to use a timer in order to give each person equal time to speak. This tends to be more of a problem as the group gets larger but it is not uncommon that even two people need some such means of distributing time fairly.

9. Ten minutes before your regular closing time, go around the group and give everyone the chance to talk just in case they have something on their minds but have not had the opportunity to say it.

DISCUSSION IDEAS: CHAPTER 1: GETTING STARTED

1. Tell about a time you were disciplined when you were a child.

2. What kind of family did you grow up in? Tell what you most admired about the way your parents raised you and what you most disliked.

3. In what ways are you raising/teaching your children differently from the way your parents raised you? In what ways are you doing things the same?

4. Write a description of the kind of adult you want your child (or children you teach) to become. Take a turn sharing this with the rest of the group.

5. Make two lists: (a) The things about your child (or the kids in your classroom) you feel happiest about and (b) the things about your child which worry or anger you. Share these lists with the other members of the group.

6. Do you consider yourself an A or a C parent or teacher? Take a turn explaining to the group your reasons for placing yourself in a particular spot on the continuum line. Where did you place your spouse?

7. Using two large sheets of paper, make a list of the strengths and weaknesses of both the A and C parenting/teaching styles.

2 Paying Attention

To be totally ignored is a painful experience. Children will go to any lengths to be noticed. The young child can sometimes use words and ask to be noticed. Think of the times your own child has called to you, "Look at me, Mommy." or "See what I can do, Daddy." Or, how many times has one of your students run up to you on the playground yelling, "Watch this. Watch this." When children do not know how to verbalize their need to be noticed, they act it out. One of the things I used to do whenever I wanted attention was to clean the bathroom. I knew my mother would always stop whatever she was doing and praise me if I scrubbed that bathroom. My brother used a different method for attracting my mother's attention. He broke things. Each of us, in his own way, was saying, "Come pay attention to me."

This process of interacting with other human beings by paying attention to them and having them pay attention to you is called social reinforcement. Social reinforcement is the most powerful tool available to you for changing the behavior of your child, yet very few adults understand how to use it effectively. Social reinforcement is widely misunderstood and misused, sometimes even by professional educators and counselors. In order to understand the basic concepts of social reinforcement and how to effectively use social reinforcement to improve children's behavior, we need to examine three broad categories of behavior.

First, there is negative behavior. Negative behavior means the child is doing something the adult does not like. The child may be rude, continually bring home a poor report card even though he or she is capable of average work. The child may whine, steal, fight with siblings, avoid doing chores, and on and on. The adult feels irritation or anger at the behavior.

The second category of behavior is positive. Positive behavior means that the child is doing something which pleases the adult. The child may be a hard working student, be responsible about changing school clothes, or clean his or her room regularly. The child may play with younger siblings and generously share toys with them. The adult feels pride and pleasure at seeing the child behave in these ways.

The third kind of behavior is neutral. Neutral behavior neither pleases or displeases us. At these neutral behavior times we hardly even notice the child. The child may be reading a book in the school library, petting the cat, lying outside on the grass watching ants, or helping big sister build a model car. When the child walks through the kitchen as you are working at the sink, or walks into the classroom on the way back from the rest room, for example, he or she is engaging in a neutral behavior. There is nothing special about neutral behavior. At these times the child is neither a bother nor a help. The child is just there, alive and breathing, doing his or her own thing in the world. When adults do notice this kind of behavior, they do not feel much of anything about it. In fact, the child's neutral behavior is often taken for granted and generally ignored.

An important idea to keep in mind concerning these three types of behavior is that each of them, negative, positive, and neutral, are strengthened when we pay attention to them. In other words, when we socially reinforce any of these behaviors, whether negative, positive, or neutral, we encourage the child to continue in that type of behavior. Tricky, isn't it? As parents and teachers, we are responsible for teaching our children attitudes and behavior. We cannot ignore a child's negative behavior and still function as responsible parents and teachers; we must intervene at times to teach desired behaviors. Yet, the more attention we give to a child's negative behaviors, the more we strengthen his or her negative behaviors. We will return to this in detail later.

As parents and teachers, we pay attention to children's behaviors with positive and negative behaviors of our own. (We are also often neutral with kids, but then of course we are not giving them any attention.) Ordinarily, the kind of attention you give a child depends on how the child is behaving. If Rene ignores your call to come into dinner, your emotional response will be negative and so your own behavior towards him is probably going to be negative, too. "Rene, I said *you get in here this minute."* In this case, a negative behavior in the child has provoked a negative response in the parent. If, on the other hand, Rene immediately comes running to the dinner table and says, "Boy, am I hungry. This stuff looks really good." Your emotional response will be positive and your own behavior towards him will probably be positive also. Rene might even get a hug from you, or at least a big smile. The difficulty with this perfectly normal reaction pattern is that the child becomes the initiator of the adult's responses. The child acts, the adult reacts. Or, another way of putting it, the child controls the responses of the adult.

If the child's behavior is usually positive, there is no problem. Most adults are quick to respond to a child's positive behaviors by giving back positive verbal and nonverbal cues. Positive responses flow back and forth between parent and child until it becomes hard to know who started them. It does not matter who started this positive response cycle...who cares as long as everyone is happy. The problem arises when the child has somehow gotten into a negative behavior pattern. The natural reaction for the parent or teacher is to respond in equally negative ways. Since the adult is more powerful than the child, the adult is often able to get temporary control of the situation but eventually the child initiates new negative behaviors. This elicits more negative responses from the adult. Soon a full blown power struggle is under way, a power struggle which neither the adult or the child want, but which both are unable to stop. In order for parents or teachers to help the child break out of this downward spiral of negative behaviors, they must first learn to deal with the child's negative behaviors without giving the emotional attention which unwittingly encourages the very behaviors they are trying to prevent.

We can usually recognize a positive and a negative behavior when we see it in a child, but we are not always so adept at realizing when we are the ones giving a negative or a positive attention to the child. The reason it is important to learn to recognize our own positive and negative attentions is because they are loaded with emotional energy, and emotional energy is what the child needs from us.

Our verbal attentions to the child are easy to recognize. When we say, "Cut that out, Jackie," there is no doubt that we have just given a negative verbal attention. When we say, "What a careful job you did, Jackie," it is clear we have given a positive verbal attention.

On the other hand, when we give nonverbal kinds of messages we are often unaware of the nonverbal attention our bodies are giving to our children. The body speaks a language of its own. Children are extremely good at understanding body language. Even if we seldom express feelings verbally, our bodies usually give an indication of the feelings inside: The look on our face, the way we walk, the tone of our voice, the kind of eye contact we do or do not make, all reveal our inner state. Even when children are very young, they can interpret body language. When an adult says, because the adult has been taught as a child that it is wrong to express anger, "I'm not angry," but the clenched fist, flushed face, and tight voice, says, "I'm so angry I can barely control myself," children will know which of the two messages is true. After all, children spend the first year of their lives with very little command of a verbal language. Their first language is nonverbal. Nonverbal messages from you, whether negative or positive, are highly charged with emotional attention for the child. If you can develop a basic awareness of your own body language, you will not be fooled into thinking that words are the major way you pay attention to children.

These nonverbal attentions are extremely powerful, even when we are unaware we are giving them. A touch, a smile, a scowl, a hug, a sigh, can express myriad moods and emotional attitudes. When you smile at one of your students and make warm eye contact when he is listening to you attentively, you are communicating values and emotions you do not have to put into words. When you grab your child's hand in exasperation and pull her down the grocery aisle because she will not quit whining about wanting more expensive junk food, no words are necessary for the child to know how you are feeling about the behavior.

One family, who managed to raise five responsible and loving children, engaged in so little talk that a typical dinner time discussion consisted of, "Please pass the butter." Most teaching of values and behaviors in that family took place through subtle nonverbal cues. Observers of certain so called primitive societies, have commented on the fact that, compared to our industrialized culture, much less talking about discipline goes on between children and adults. Hard as it may be to believe, for those of us who love to talk, nonverbal communication is at least as effective as verbal communication for teaching behaviors to children.

Adults often ignore children's neutral behaviors altogether. Maybe we ignore neutral behaviors because we are afraid that if we intervene the child will stop being neutral and start being a bother to us, or maybe we see no reason to consciously reward an ordinary behavior that seems to deserve no reward. After all, when children are doing what they are supposed to be doing, why make a big deal out of it? *Yet, paying attention to a child's neutral behavior is a powerful tool for bringing about positive behavior change.* Asking you to concentrate on giving positive attentions to a child at neutral times may not seem to make much sense at first, but it is a fact that children blossom when parents and teachers made a concerted effort to pay attention to them at neutral times.

Karin was a first-grader who refused to answer when spoken to and passively resisted doing her schoolwork and chores. Yet, when she was with her peers, she was talkative and animated. If you have ever been around a child who will not talk to you, who even resists making eye contact with you, you will understand how frustrated her teachers and parents were. The parents developed a program of regular, positive, nonverbal contacts. The plan especially focused on touching because this little girl tended to be stiff as a board when any adult reached out to hug her. Her parents understandably felt rejected and discouraged by her refusal to hug and be hugged. Consequently they reached out to her less and less.

The parents' day was divided into three parts. During each time segment, one parent or the other, depending on which one was home during that time, was to touch Karin four times when the child was engaged in neutral behavior. The touching was to be light and undemanding. (Tickling was forbidden since tickling is an extremely demanding kind of touching, and can even be interpreted as aggressive.) They were to touch her hair, put an arm around her waist, or touch her hand when they gave her an object. If she pulled away from them, they were to let that happen without any kind of notice. They were to continue to be pleasant and try their best not to feel rejected by any withdrawal on her part. The parents were cautioned that it might take a month or more to begin to thaw Karin out. To everyone's amazement, within two weeks Karin's teachers were asking, "What happened to Karin? She is so cooperative and downright bubbly lately." The parents reported that their daughter was not only smiling and talking to them, she had even begun to lean against them and put her arms around them for hugs.

What was so powerful about giving this child attention during neutral times? To be sure, to be held and touched is a powerful human need. Yet they had tried touching her at positive times before and were usually rejected. The power of giving attention at neutral times comes from the fact that when children are attended to in a positive way only when they are successful or achieving they begin to doubt that people value them for themselves. As children grow older, they may even begin to suspect that the adult is using their accomplishments as a kind of parental or teaching trophy.

A father told about the time his sixteen-year-old neighbor earned an Eagle Scout badge. The father was then twelve years old. One day his mother talked to him about how wonderful it was that the neighbor boy had been awarded the Eagle Scout badge. She smiled at her son pleadingly and stroked his hair. "You can do it, too." He remembered the moment clearly. "But it takes years and years and hardly anyone gets to be an Eagle Scout," he said. "Do it for me," his mother said. Do it for *her*. He recognized that, at some nonverbal level, she was seeking to meet, not his needs, but her own. Within the year he quit the Boy Scouts.

When learning the concept of paying attention to kids at neutral times, one mother told about her favorite uncle. "Actually, I never really knew him very well. When he came to the house to visit my folks, I would sit and listen to the grown-ups talk. Nobody paid much attention to me except him. Once in awhile he would look over at me and give me a grin and a big wink. I've always had this feeling that he loved me best, that I was his favorite. I think I just realized why."

Nothing bolsters our sense of self-esteem so much as knowing we are loved not because of what we have achieved or will achieve, but because we are here and alive, because we are who we are—just because. By paying attention to children at neutral times, adults convey a sense of unconditional love. The knowledge that we are unconditionally loved is a prerequisite for healthy, positive behaviors. The knowledge that we are loved just because we are loveable makes it unnecessary for us to seek out attention in other, more negative ways. The withdrawn, resistant first-grader, for example, had learned how to get the attention she so badly needed in her busy family by retreating into herself and hiding behind a mask when she was with adults. It was another form of the hiding game children play when they want an adult to find them. When she began to get attention just for being alive, she had no need for her old negative withdrawal behaviors.

But, you may ask, why should children ever want to accomplish anything worthwhile in life if they get all this attention for doing nothing special? People cannot just sit and pet the cat or read all the rest of their lives. Indeed, what is it that motivates human beings to learn and to achieve, to become the best they are capable of becoming? The psychologist Abraham Maslow, in his study of emotionally healthy human beings, proposed an answer to the question of what prompts a human being to become one of those people at the "growing tip" of humanity.

Maslow believed that all human beings have certain needs which must be satisfied before they are able to grow towards self-esteem and what he called self-actualization. Just as plants need water, sunlight, and nutrients to attain the promise of their genetic codes, so do people need certain basic requirements in order to grow toward the best they are capable of becoming.

The first thing humans need, like plants, is to have their basic PHYSICAL needs provided for. We need air to breathe, water to drink, food to eat, and shelter from the elements. Until we get these things, we have no time, energy, or inclination for thinking about much else. The need for food, shelter, water, and air are clearcut needs. Other physical needs, like the need for touching, are not as obvious. Yet being held and touched, especially for the very young child, is one of the most crucial of the basic physical needs. It is well known that many babies in orphanages sickened and died because they were never held and cuddled.

Sadly, western culture has been slow to recognize that all primate babies need to be carried snug and secure next to the mother's body until they begin to walk. In *The Continuum Concept,* Jean Liedloff tells of her experiences living in the jungles of South America with the Tauripan Indians, where adults keep children close to their bodies until the children choose to go off and do their own thing. *The Continuum Concept* is worth reading for an understanding of how far our western culture has strayed from a natural physical closeness with children.

As one need is met, another arises. Next comes the need for SAFETY. We need not only to feel physically secure, for example, to know that bombs are not going to drop on us, that the plague will not strike us down, and that we will not be beaten, we also need to feel safe emotionally. We need to know we will not be sexually harassed and intimidated. Children need to know that when they go to school their teacher will not humiliate them in the classroom and that bullies will not bother them on the playground or bus. Children need to know that Dad or Mother will not get drunk, or drugged in any other way, so that they neglect or abuse them.

Physical touching and holding by the adult is also a part of Maslow's safety need. Toddlers can be brave about going off and exploring the world on their own as long as there is an adult nearby who will hold and protect them if things get too scary. At many stages of childhood, children need to be able to run back to the parent and be picked up or hugged whenever they need the comfort of being close to their mother or father. Only in this way will children grow up feeling a sense of rightness and trust about life, a feeling of, "Hey, this is a great and secure world."

Adults and older children, too, never outgrow the need for someone to be there to support them with a hug or two when the going gets rough. A friend tells the wrenching story of when her husband died after a long illness. Two days after his death, she woke to find that every one of her five children, even the fourteen year old, had climbed into bed with her during the night. The security and safety needs for this family had been yanked out from under them. What better place to begin to rebuild a feeling of security than in the warmth and closeness of their mother's bed.

Equally important are the safety needs of children to be secure in the knowledge that adults around them are in control, that rules are clear and predictable, that the world makes sense. Children's security needs are threatened, for example, if they constantly hear their parents arguing over how to discipline the children. The need for security is also a reason young children thrive on routine and predictable outcomes. Anyone with a toddler knows how upset a child becomes if the daily routine is disturbed. Often, all a child needs who has trouble going to sleep at night is a regular, predictable bedtime ritual. Substitute teachers know that the younger their students are, the harder it is for them to accept a new person and a new way of doing things. Many a substitute teacher at the kindergarten or first grade level dreads to hear this constant refrain, "But our teacher never does it that way." And how many of you have moved into a new apartment only to have your youngster wail at bedtime that first night, "But I want to go *home.*"

As our PHYSICAL and SAFETY needs are met, at least in some minimum fashion, another need arises. We need to BELONG. We need to belong to some human society however small, even if only to one other person. We need to know that no matter what comes, this other person or persons will be there and will never leave us or cast us away from them. The need to belong is one of the reasons we join a church, the Elks club, Mensa, a hiking group, the Girl Scouts, the Cub scouts, fraternities, sororities, the Lions, the Eastern Star, and on and on. The need to belong is an important part of the reason so many teenagers join a gang.

A next step up this staircase of needs is the need to be unconditionally loved. Maslow called this unconditional love, BEING-LOVE. Children need to feel loved and accepted by at least one adult, just because they are alive, just because they are loveable. This kind of love loves us for no other reason than that we are who we are. We are loved even when we have not earned that love. Imagine how the six-year-old boy Rafer felt whose mother, whenever he was "bad," refused to wear the Cracker Jack ring he had given her. Rafer's father had already left the family. The mother's live-in boy friend had recently dramatically packed his suitcase and threatened to leave because the boy consistently did not hang up his clothes. Rafer's mother was the only person he could count on, and it seemed to him that her love, too, was conditional. "I will only wear your token of love when you are good. I will only love you when you are good." It is not surprising that Rafer exhibited almost frantic behaviors and that at school he was, incorrectly, perceived as a child with a physically based, attention-deficit.

Once the PHYSICAL needs are met, and the needs for SAFETY, BELONGING, and BEING-LOVE are met, at least to some degree, the human being is freed to step up to the next higher need, the need to be COMPETENT and to be RESPECTED for that competency. Every healthy human being has experienced the fun of learning some new thing. It may not be the thing others want him to learn. The boy who loves working on cars instead of his history and math lessons is a classic example. For each person there exists that excitement which comes with grasping some new concept, attaining some new level of mastery. Have you ever seen a first-grader who did not want to learn to read and count and write? There must be something in our genetic code, something in the makeup of our DNA, which elicits an intrinsic joy in learning some new thing. Maybe it is because the use of our minds has been the means of our survival as a species. Whatever the reason, the need to learn skills, and to feel competent in the application of those skills, is enormously important. It is a wise adult who can find a way for each child to feel not only that he or she is unconditionally accepted as a valuable member of the class or family, but that he or she is respected as a competent person learning important skills.

Finally, if all these needs are met, human beings blossom into what Maslow called a self-actualizing person. The self-actualizer has high self-esteem. The self-actualizer is self-motivated and self-confident. He or she learns for the joy of learning, builds for the joy of creating, trusts that the world is a wonderful place, and without even being aware of it, becomes a force for good in the wider community.

Many of us never make it to the very top step of this developmental staircase. Sometimes our PHYSICAL needs and our needs for SAFETY and BELONGING and BEING-LOVE and COMPETENCY are satisfied so meagerly that our character development is stunted. In this way we never achieve our full potential. We are like plants which struggle to grow in light so dim they can never really thrive.

Each one of us has experienced a falling back down the stairway of personal growth at some time in our lives. There have been times when we were hungry, maybe even homeless, times we felt abandoned, sick, unloved, inept, frightened, times when it seemed there was not even one other human being who cared about us. Any parent who has suffered through a divorce with a child, for example, knows the negative, age inappropriate behaviors which are manifested in both the child and the parents at this time. Parents, as well as their children, feel their needs for safety, belonging, Being-Love, and competency threatened during a divorce. You can probably think of times in your own life when the lack of one of these needs triggered some "childish" behavior on your part which now amazes you.

I clearly remember my own behavior as a fifteen-year-old high school junior. Because of my family's constant moving, I had lived in a state the year before which did not require a second year math credit. Since the state we were now living in required two years of high school math, I was forced to make up my missing second year of math by sitting in the midst of people a whole year younger than myself, all of whom (I was certain) thought I must be a stupid person who had flunked math the year before. Compounding the problem was my father's alcoholism, of which I was ashamed and trying hard to keep a secret from my new classmates. I sulked, argued with the teacher, avoided doing schoolwork, and talked to my classmates when the teacher was talking; yet in all my other classes I was a model student. The concerned and puzzled math teacher talked to me privately after class one day, "What's the matter, JoAnne?" I was unable to tell him. I was keenly aware of a whirling mass of painful emotions, but could not articulate the problem. From the vantage point of 41 years later, I now realize that my need for belonging to my new peer group was threatened, as was my need for competency and respect.

The fall back down the stairway is usually temporary, our character and emotional development is arrested only momentarily. Eventually, some basic level of needs is met, we realize again that someone does care, that we do belong somewhere, that we are competent, respected, loveable human beings. When this happens, growth up the staircase towards self-motivation and self-actualization begins once more. Each human being, if he or she has been nourished by having basic needs satisfied, at least to some minimum degree, continues up that staircase, pulled along by an inborn urge to learn and grow.

This, then, is the answer to the earlier question of why it is important to pay attention to a child at neutral times. Paying attention to a child "just because" satisfies the need to be loved just for being alive. Paying attention to a child at neutral times is an expression of that unconditional love which Maslow called "Being-Love." Not long ago, a teaching assistant who had been having problems during recesses with a second grade boy began paying attention to him at neutral times. She smiled at him in the halls. She made a point to greet him each morning when he got off the bus. Two weeks later she was telling us that not only was he not misbehaving with her anymore, but he was actually hugging her around the waist when he saw her on recess duty.

The need for unconditional love exists for adults as well as for children. In thinking of my own relationship with my husband, the times which most convince me that I am loved are not the times we make love, but those times when he touches my hair as he walks by or gives me the warmth of eye contact and a smile across a room crowded with people, unasked for, unearned, expecting nothing in return.

It is relatively easy to give positive attention to our kids at neutral or positive times, in spite of the fact that we often forget to do it. In these situations they are a delight to us and we are emotionally able to let them know we love them. The dilemma which arises for most of us is what to do when our children are misbehaving. What kinds of attention do we give them when their behavior is negative? Parents and teachers certainly should not give positive attention to a child during periods of misbehavior, yet positive attention is what a child needs in order to have the needs for security, belonging, unconditional love, and competency satisfied. It is hard to even like a child at negative times. What on earth is a parent or a teacher to do? Is it possible to be a strong disciplinarian and still not strip away a child's self-esteem and leave unfulfilled the needs for belonging, love, and respect? The answer to that question is an unqualified YES. The following exercise is the first step on the way to learning to be a firm disciplinarian while at the same time you help the child to strengthen his or her personal self-esteem staircase.

EXERCISE:

1. *The first thing you need to learn is to recognize the differences between the child's negative, neutral, and positive behaviors.* The following "Child's Staircase of Needs" chart has three boxes. Each box represents one of the three basic categories of behaviors. Set aside twenty minutes a day, for at least five days, to mark down checks or circles in the appropriate boxes, depending on the type of behavior you are seeing. Make a check in the negative box when you see the

child engaging in a negative behavior, and put a circle in the neutral or positive box when you see the child doing something neutral or positive. You can choose to observe only one child, preferably your "problem" child, if you have one, or you can observe any child at random. Do not put the observed child's name on the chart. If the children ask what you are doing, tell them you are learning some new things about being a parent or a teacher. "I am learning some ways to make things go better in our family (or classroom.)" Say nothing more about it. Some parents call this a refrigerator chart because they usually end up posting these charts on the refrigerator door. They are more apt not to lose it there. Teachers will have to find some other special spot so the chart does not disappear into the piles of papers on their desks.

2. *Do not try to change the child's behavior this week. Just observe and check off what you notice happening.* When you notice a negative behavior, make a check in that box. When you notice a neutral or positive behavior, make a circle in the appropriate box. Neutral behavior seems to be the tough one for many people to learn to recognize. A good internal clue to help you distinguish between neutral and positive behaviors is to remember that positive behaviors usually make you feel proud and pleased. You will not experience much emotion about neutral behaviors. Neutral behaviors are just there. Often you will not even notice them. Examples of neutral behaviors are when a child walks through the room, when he is sitting gazing out the window, or just watching television.

3. *Behavior which is neutral for one child might be positive for another.* If Gillian never just sits and reads in the classroom, and then one day you look over and see her sitting and reading, that is positive behavior for Gillian. After all, you feel mighty proud and happy to see her finally involved in a book. However, in Carlos's case, reading is a neutral behavior. When you look over and see Carlos just sitting and reading, you will

not have much emotion about the behavior because Carlos often sits and reads.

4. *Do not insist that your spouse or partner keep a chart.* Your spouse will resent it if you attempt to force him or her into participating. If your spouse does want to participate, that would be wonderful because change for children happens much faster if all adults are involved. But if the other adult does not want to take part in this, please respect his or her wishes. You can accomplish a great deal on your own. Keep in mind Rudolf Dreikurs' advice to stop trying to change your partner and instead just concentrate on what you yourself have the power to accomplish: "Do what *you* can do." You have no right to insist that your spouse or your fellow teacher or your friend do things your way (unless of course, they are actually abusing the children.) By the same token, you do not have to do what they tell you to do. If your spouse, or another teacher, tells you how you should discipline the children, and you can see that following their advice will make things worse instead of better, you can refuse to do what you are told. As long as you remember *not to argue about child rearing methods in front of the kids,* which will inevitably cause them to feel insecure and worsen their behavior, you are free to, "Do what *you* can do."

Child's Staircase of Needs*

What Human Beings Need for Healthy Emotional Growth

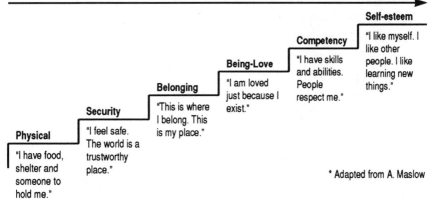

Self-actualization

Self-esteem

Competency
"I have skills
and abilities.
People
respect me."

Self-esteem
"I like myself. I
like other
people. I like
learning new
things."

Being-Love
"I am loved
just because I
exist."

Belonging
"This is where
I belong. This
is my place."

Security
"I feel safe.
The world is a
trustworthy
place."

Physical
"I have food,
shelter and
someone to
hold me."

* Adapted from A. Maslow

Total of Child's Behavior

Behaviors you pay attention to will continue

Positive	Neutral	Negative
(Pleases you—a joy for you)	(Child doing his or her own thing—not a problem for you)	(Angers or irritates you —a problem for you)

DISCUSSION IDEAS: CHAPTER 2: PAYING ATTENTION

1. Share the positive/neutral/negative behavior exercise which you charted throughout the week. Is everyone clear as to the difference between a neutral and a positive behavior? Did anything particularly interesting happen regarding the neutral behavior you observed?

2. Was there ever a special time of your life when any of the basic needs which Maslow outlined were not provided for you? Talk about that experience and what you remember about it.

3. Are you aware of any times in your child's life in which it has been especially hard for you to see that his or her needs are met?

4. If your spouse has decided not to participate with you in your attempt to learn some new parenting methods, talk about any feelings or thoughts you have regarding that decision.

3 How Parents and Teachers Sabotage Their Discipline

Many parents and teachers feel like failures as disciplinarians. Some read every new article and book on the subject that comes along. They take other people's advice and try getting tougher. They take other people's advice and try being more lenient. They even enroll in classes in child psychology, but nothing seems to help. Finally the day comes when they throw up their hands in bewilderment and say, in anguished tones, "I've tried *everything*. *Nothing* works with that kid." Usually the problem with these dedicated but ineffective parents and teachers is that they are sabotaging themselves. Without realizing it, they are subverting their own disciplinary efforts.

There are four basic ways to sabotage yourself. The first is PROCRASTINATION. Sometimes parents or teachers keep hoping that if they are patient enough or kind enough or reasonable enough, children will see the light and do what they are asked without so much fussing. These adults ask the child to do something once, a second time, then a third time, even a fourth time before they finally run out of patience and get upset enough to do something about it.

An example of this is the four-year-old boy who starts jumping on the couch when his mother is trying to visit with guests. Mother says, "Get off the couch, Aaron." Aaron ignores her and keeps on jumping. Mother says, "Aaron! You heard me." Aaron keeps on jumping, his eye on Mother. "Aaron. If you don't get off that couch, I'm going to get out the spoon and give you a spanking." Aaron keeps on jumping and at last responds, "Oh, Mom. Why can't I?" Mother, her voice rising to peak levels shouts, "Okay, young man. You asked for it!" She lunges at him but he leaps off the couch, and dashes outside. Mother shakes her head and complains to her friends, "I can't understand why Aaron is so naughty."

Unfortunately, Mother's procrastination is only teaching Aaron that it is okay to wait until the fourth time before doing what his mother says. After all, Mother never gets really serious about things until at least the fourth command. What Aaron is learning from this display of patience is that it is safe to ignore the first three or four commands. You could even make a case that Aaron has trained mother to ask four times before she acts. To avoid sabotaging yourself, you must *act the first time you see the misbehavior.* If you do not act at the first sign of misbehavior, and instead just keep on reminding and warning, you will only make yourself and your child miserable with your frequent threats. It is even possible that the kids will learn to simply ignore you. One mother said she overheard her ten-year-old daughter telling her new step-brother, "You don't have to pay any attention to mother when she threatens you. She never does anything."

Acting on the very first sign of misbehavior is extremely difficult for some parents and teachers, especially C adults who often have the sneaking suspicion that they do not have the right to make demands on the child anyway. Difficult or not, it is essential that you do, else you will not be able to teach children the behaviors and values which you know are important for them to learn. If the problem is that you do not know *what* to do about the misbehavior, be patient a bit longer. Subsequent chapters will answer those questions.

Besides teaching that you mean what you say the first time you say it, a further benefit of "act-the-first-time" is that if you act immediately you will not get so angry at the child. The longer children avoid doing what you want them to do, the more frustrated and angry you will become. Everyone gets angry occasionally. If anger is constructively dealt with, it poses no problem to any relationship. The problem with unresolved anger which builds over a long period of time is that it will not only sabotage your discipline and damage your relationship with your children, it will also undermine the building of their self-esteem staircase.

If you are the kind of person who lashes out with your anger, you will find yourself yelling at the kids, or hitting them, far beyond what you, yourself, feel happy about. Continual screaming at children and blaming them can be as destructive, sometimes even more so, than hitting. A mother in one of the parenting groups once said, "I would rather have been beaten than told the things I was told. My mother used to put her face up against mine and scream at me that she wished I had never been born, that it was my fault she couldn't have a happy life."

On the other hand, if you are the kind of person who deals with their own anger by withdrawing, rather than attack the child you will probably want to retreat. You cannot withdraw physically, of course, since as a parent or a teacher you must be with the child. The danger is you will withdraw from the child emotionally. A parent or teacher can be in the same room with a child and still ignore the child's presence. Positive behavior is ignored, neutral behavior is ignored, even negative behavior is ignored as long as possible. The nonverbal message sent by the adult is, "You are not a loveable person and I don't like being with you." We have already talked about how painful it is to be ignored by anyone, but it is especially painful to be ignored by someone as important as a parent or teacher. The only way the child has to gain the withdrawn adult's attention is to behave in more and more negative ways. Finally, the child's behavior becomes so outrageous that the adult explodes, directing pent-up rage at the child with abusive language or extreme physical punishments. Even the long suffering C parent and teacher can be provoked to this extreme. After the explosion, the adult again withdraws, refusing to acknowledge the child's presence until the child goads him into another explosion.

Pete was a quiet, reserved man who began his experience as a parent wanting to be a good father but not knowing what to do whenever his little boy misbehaved. Pete was determined not to repeat the mistakes his own father had made but he had no positive role models for interacting with his own child. As the years went by, his son escalated his negative behaviors in order to get his reserved father to pay attention to him. Pete grew increasingly puzzled and resentful of his son's negative behaviors. Since Pete's habit was to withdraw from people when he was angry with them, he not only ignored his son at negative behavior times, he began to ignore him *all* the time. With every misbehavior, Pete withdrew further from his son, ignoring the boy's existence until the boy would do something so outrageous Pete would explode. By the time the boy was a teenager, Pete and his son seldom talked to each other except with scorn and blaming. Both felt hurt and abused by the other. The boy continued his pattern of negative and irresponsible behaviors well into his adult life. As John Bradshaw, in one of his television talks, said, "If I am thirsty, I would rather have clear water, but if there is no clear water I will drink it muddy."

Repressed anger cannot be entirely hidden. If the adult is carrying around a heavy load of resentment and anger against the child, the child knows from the adult's nonverbal behaviors that somehow the parent or teacher does not approve of him or her. When the adult is forced to talk to the child or has to be with the child, there is no real affection expressed. The child is deeply hurt. The child is at first bewildered, then hurt, resentful, and angry. Inevitably, because children are so dependent on adult attention, they will continue their negative behavior, making the adult want to withdraw from them even further. In this way, the sad, downward cycle is continued in which the child's behavior worsens and the adult finds it harder than ever to look at him or her without feelings of resentment and anger.

On the other hand, there are few of us who have not whacked our children on the bottom at least once. Sometimes our patience cannot be stretched one millimeter further. I remember my own early parenting days when I sometimes yelled at my children and hit them on the bottom with my open hand. I still feel terrible inside when I remember those spankings. It is a common story whenever parents get together to share the difficulties of parenting, "I hit them and I yell and I feel so bad about it afterwards." Most of us feel badly about hitting and yelling at our kids because deep inside we know that hitting and yelling are demeaning both to the one who hits and the one who gets hit. Hitting and yelling tears down everyone's staircase of emotional needs.

If you find that you are doing a lot of yelling and spanking, or are often threatening to spank, do not give up. There are much better ways to discipline your children. Frequent spanking may help you to vent your own frustrations, but it will eventually rob your children of the self-esteem and dignity they need to grow emotionally and will cause them to become increasingly sullen and angry. Their misbehavior will not only continue, it will intensify. In our culture we use the word "spank" instead of "hit." Spanking is acceptable whereas hitting is not. It is against the law to hit another adult, but spanking a child is somehow socially acceptable. We often "spank" children for "hitting" another person. It seems ludicrous, even irrational, when we think of it in this way. Not all cultures approve of hitting children as a form of discipline. In Sweden, for example, spanking of any kind is against the law. Why is it okay to hit a child but not to hit an adult? The answer is that many of us simply do not know any other way to control our children's misbehaviors. Hence this book. Read on. There are many more effective ways to stop misbehaviors.

In the meantime, you need to learn some immediate ways to let your resentment and anger out without hurting your children. When the urge comes on you to hit the kids you could try going into the bedroom and punching a pillow. Try whacking your bed with a tennis racket a few times. It makes a satisfying thump and does not hurt anything except for raising a little dust. A counselor friend keeps a huge black pillow in her room at school for anyone, big or small, to come by and give it a few kicks when they had "had it."

A mother who had a violent temper and frequently hurt her children learned to punch a pillow instead of hitting her kids. She felt silly about it at first. She was embarrassed to have her preschoolers standing by, wide eyed, while she beat her fists against the pillow. Eventually, she realized it was a far more sane method of expressing anger than hurting her children. She was a verbal woman who also did a lot of screaming at the same time she was hitting the pillow. She would yell, "I'm so damn mad I'm going to hit this god damn pillow! I'm not going to hit you kids but I sure as hell am going to knock the god damn stuffings out of this god damn pillow!" The neighbors were probably horrified at the language she used in front of the children, but it worked. She had more to learn before she began to understand how her own hidden, unmet needs were sabotaging her life and feeding her anger, but at least she was no longer directing her verbal or physical assaults directly at her children. Another plus was that her kids were learning there are other things you can do when you get angry besides hit and yell at people. This mother later told about a time her five-year-old daughter got angry at her four-year-old brother. The girl ran into the bedroom, and started whacking her pillow all the while shouting, "I'm so damn mad but I'm not going to hit you! I'm going to hit this god damn pillow!"

Working with anger at this level is only a beginning, but the important point is that this family was starting to learn some workable methods of coping with anger. In the context of the former physical and verbal violence in this particular family, swearing was a minor problem.

Anger is much less likely to arise if you can act immediately to carry out the correction the first time you see the misbehavior taking place. By having a plan, and by acting immediately, you will take control of the situation thereby avoiding the downward spiral of frustration, anger, and punishment. As a general rule, it is best not to get carried away with any intense feeling during disciplinary times. Intense feelings give too much attention and power to the misbehavior. As much as possible (and it is asking a lot) save your emotional energy for the neutral and positive times. *Emotional energy is what children want and need from you. Try not to give it to them when they are misbehaving.* It will only encourage the misbehavior.

Children are learning an incredible amount these first years of their lives. Behavior is just another thing they have to learn. Keep in mind what you want the children to learn and which methods you are going to use to help them learn. Try not to become emotionally distraught when children make behavioral mistakes. We all make mistakes. It is an integral and necessary part of learning. That does not make us bad parents or teachers. It is how we learn. The same is true for the child; *the fact that the child makes mistakes does not mean he or she is a bad child.*

The second major way we sabotage our own discipline is through TALKING AND TALKING about it. A disciplinary action should be carried out, finished, and forgotten. You need to be firm about carrying out the correction the first time the misbehavior occurs and then *do not mention it again.* As Rudolf Dreikurs so beautifully phrased it, "Act, don't talk." Both A and C adults have problems sabotaging themselves with this one.

EXAMPLE A:

Dad sends Shelley from the dinner table because she is
messing with the food, making loud burping noises, and
generally causing everyone else at the table to lose their
appetite. Dad tells Shelley to go to her room without any
more to eat. Shelley goes off to her room complaining all
the way that Dad is mean. On the way down the hall she
whines that she is hungry, and finally, just before she goes
into her bedroom, she loudly promises not to do it anymore
if she can come back to the table. Dad sticks to his decision
and refuses to give in. So far, so good. But now Dad
proceeds to sabotage himself. When dinner is finished, Dad
goes into the bedroom where Shelley is sobbing, her face
buried in a pillow. Dad is a C type parent, a loving father
who does not like being what he thinks of as the "bad guy."
Dad tries to explain to his daughter why he did what he
did. He sits down on the edge of the bed and pats her on
the back. "Look, Shelley. This wasn't any fun for me
either. Do you think I can enjoy my dinner when you can't
have yours? Next time, think about that when you start
acting like a goof ball at the table, Okay? Okay? Come on.
Let's see a big smile. That's Daddy's girl." Dad is
exasperated, and amazed, when a week later at Grandma
and Grandpa's Shelley repeats the performance. Shelley
has learned she can get lots of special, emotional attention
from her father by misbehaving.

EXAMPLE B:

Or take the A type parent, also a loving father, who
grounds his son from riding his bike for two days because
his son left the bicycle out in the driveway right behind the
car where Dad nearly backed over it. This A type father
does not think of himself as the "bad guy" because he has
to discipline his child. He is quite comfortable in the
parental leadership role, but still he sabotages himself.

When the two days grounding are over and Dad gives his son the bicycle back, he launches into a lecture. "Okay, Ralphie. Remember this next time you park your bike in the driveway. What if I hadn't seen it? It would have been run over. Then you wouldn't have any bike at all to ride. I can't afford to buy you a new bike every time you wreck one. I wouldn't do that even if I could afford to because you've got to learn to be more responsible. I was all ready to leave for work and I had to get out of the car and waste my time because you were irresponsible. This isn't the first time either. Now I hope this helps you to remember." A week later, Ralphie leaves his bike out behind Dad's car again.

Both of these fathers used corrections with their children's misbehavior which should have been effective. Instead, both children continued to misbehave. The problem with both fathers' approach was that they sabotaged themselves with all their talking, which in these two instances took the form of cajoling, advising, pleading, warning, reminding, reassuring and scolding. Like many adults, these two fathers believe they can teach children positive behaviors only by talking at them about it.

As strange as it seems, *talking undermines effective discipline,* even if the talking takes the form of good, reasonable advice. Talking gives a tremendous amount of attention to the child for misbehaving. Misbehavior is encouraged when you give the child this kind of social reinforcement. The attention you give your child at the time of a correction should be as brief and nonverbal as possible. Pretend you have put a piece of duct tape over your own mouth. Bite your lip. Count to ten. Advising, lecturing, moralizing, or verbally trying to teach in any way when either the adult or child is seething with negative emotions will turn off the child's ability to listen. Children have an inner door they can lock tight against any adult if they choose. The child can simply refuse to accept what the adult is saying, even when both child and adult know full well that everything the adult says is true. Children are exactly like adults in this matter. Think of a time someone gave you advice you did not want to hear. What was your response?

A classic example is the man who comes home from work after a day of extreme tension and anxieties about his job. He comes storming in the door, slams it behind him and starts complaining about his no good, stupid, power hungry boss. His wife has herself just come home from work. If she responded with a lot of self-sabotage talking she would say something like this, "Now Honey. You know your boss is having a hard time of his own right now, going through a divorce and everything. And remember, when you took the job, Carl warned you that your boss was difficult even in the best of times to get along with. You knew from the beginning he was an S.O.B. Why don't you just go take a nice bath. Things will seem better in the morning. How about a big smile, honey?" Or, if she is feeling discouraged about her own job, she might say, "Well, I've had a hard day, too. My job isn't all that easy you know." Imagine this husband's reaction. The fact is, we usually do not talk this way to other adults, but we often talk this way to children.

The normal human response when we are forced to listen to unwanted advice is resentment and anger. The advice may be good advice, it may be reasonable and well intentioned, but if we do not want to hear it, we will not hear it. Not only will we refuse to heed the good advice, we will blame the person who is forcing us to listen.

Some children sit quietly with downcast eyes while their parent or teacher advises, reminds, or scolds. They have learned to keep their resentment hidden. Other children very early begin to find flaws in the adult's logic and learn to argue endlessly as to the fine points of the case. "No one told me I had to do it by today," or "Why can't Susan do it? Why do I always have to do every thing?" or "I *was* going to do it, right after dinner." Any adult who tries to respond reasonably to these arguments ends up in an endless debate in which the child always has the last word or gesture. The parent or teacher ends up frustrated and angry, while the child feels demeaned, his or her sense of integrity threatened by having to sit and listen to all this talking. The resentment which arises from being forced to listen to things children do not want to hear triggers a powerful negative response, "They can force me to listen, but they can't force me to do what they say." This is a crucial point: *In order to maintain a sense of integrity and self-respect, the child very often feels compelled to do exactly the opposite of what the adult is warning against.* The self-sabotage of talking about the misbehavior has created a power struggle between adult and child.

Power struggles are especially destructive to the adult's efforts to instill a sense of responsibility in the child. When the parent or teacher lectures, advises, warns, scolds, even by so subtle and nonverbal a method as arching an eyebrow or using a tone of voice which implies, "Now you've done it, after all the times I warned you," it becomes easy for the child, out of resentment, to blame the adult, to feel that the child, not the adult, is the injured party. In the eyes of the child, the adult becomes the cause of the child's misbehavior. "It's not *my* fault. If they weren't always picking on me. I'll show them they can't push me around." Children caught in these power struggles grow up making decisions based on whatever the adult does not want them to do. If Mom says do it, Natalie will *not* do it. If Mom says do not do it, Natalie will try to do it at least once. Children like this often grow into adulthood blaming everyone else for their own poor decisions.

I am not suggesting that adults stop talking with their children about their values or their philosophy of life. The sabotage problem arises when adults try to verbally teach their values during negative, emotional, high-stress times. Talking, when both you and the child are in a confrontation situation, only results in increased resistance and tension between you and the child. Of course you want to talk with children about your deeply held beliefs, about the importance of manners, about all varieties of values and opinions. But the time to teach children these things is when you and they are in neutral or positive situations, for example, when you are planning the day's schoolwork together, working on the car, walking across the schoolyard, or raking leaves in the yard.

The third way we sabotage our discipline is FORGETTING TO PAY ATTENTION TO OUR CHILDREN FOR POSITIVE AND NEUTRAL BEHAVIORS. We sabotage ourselves when we focus only on the child's negative behaviors. I cannot overemphasize how important this is. *The ratio needed to bring about desired behavior and attitude changes is to give the child at least four positive attentions for every one negative attention.* This means that every time you give one negative attention to a child, you need to concentrate on giving four positive attentions to the child as soon as you see him or her in a neutral or positive behavior. The four-to-one ratio might seem impossible to you if you and the child are presently stuck in an extreme negative behavior pattern. How can any adult be positive with a kid who is constantly misbehaving? Do not get discouraged. Things will get better. Meanwhile, try to catch the child at neutral times with as much positive attention as you can muster. Use lots of nonverbal attention if you cannot think of anything positive to say. Give frequent friendly eye contact to the child during group conversation times if you cannot think of anything else to do. Most adults can carry this kind of attentive behavior off successfully even if they are not feeling particularly loving towards the child at the moment.

Marcella and her teenage son were locked in a power struggle which she was unable to break. One day she was taking him to a soccer game. They were driving along in the car, her son seated in the passenger seat beside her, sullen and withdrawn as usual. She thought about what she had learned in her parenting class, to try to pay nonverbal attention at neutral times. Even though she was afraid of being rejected, as she had been so many times before, she summoned up her courage and reached out to touch his hand. To her surprise, he squeezed her hand in return and looked over at her with a big, affectionate smile on his face. "Things have been better since then," she told the group. As Marcella discovered, nonverbal attention is often even more powerful than verbal attention.

Finally, we come to the fourth sabotage, NEGATIVE SCRIPTING. Children begin their lives believing that parents and teachers are all-knowing. Children believe that what the adults who take care of them think about life and about them must be true. As children grow older and their brains function at a more abstract level they will begin to question adults' value systems, but not until the adult belief systems have sunk deeply into the very core of their beings.

Imagine then, the impact on a child overhearing his mother talk on the telephone to her best friend about him, "William is just impossible to be with. He drives me crazy sometimes. Sometimes I think every parent should be able to throw away the oldest kid and start in all over again." Mother does not really mean this. She is just venting some frustrations and even trying to make a half-hearted joke. But consider how William must feel. Or take Lupe, who is in the third grade, whose teacher says to the principal in front of her, "Lupe just can't be trusted. She is a born liar." Consider what kind of decisions Lupe is beginning to make about the kind of a person she is.

Below is a list of negative scripts which are commonly used, either spoken directly to the child, or within the child's hearing. As you read them, pretend that you are the child and that you believe the person saying these things is all-knowing, and all-wise:

1. "She is so clumsy. She's been this way since she started to walk. Honestly, every family needs a klutz and I guess Mary Sue is ours!" (Spoken to a friend at a baby shower over the head of a four-year-old girl who, in passing the nut dish, dropped half of them on the floor.)

2. "She complains from morning till night. Even as a baby she was always whining." (Spoken to a friend within the child's hearing.)

3. "If you don't shape up, you're going to end up in jail just like Uncle Ed. The police will come and take you away just like they did with him."

4. "Sure you can take her out of the class. Keep her forever as far as I'm concerned. She's driving us all nuts." (Said in a clearly audible whisper by the classroom teacher to the school counselor who has come into the classroom to take Mia to her office for a visit.)

5. "What a bad boy you are. Bad, bad boy."

6. "Prue has an awful hard time in school. But school is so easy for Sid. He never seems to have any problems. He got all A's and B's last term." (Spoken to Grandma within Prue's hearing.)

7. "Come here, Dummy!" (One parent told her group that as a very young child she thought her name was Stupid because that is what her parents always called her.)

8. "I give up on him. He never listens. Things just go in one ear and out the other." (Spoken to a friend within the child's hearing.)

9. "Shame ...Shame on you!"

10. "My God! Sometimes I wish I'd never had any kids. They are driving me crazy." (Spoken on the telephone to a friend within the children's hearing.)

Using a harsh, scornful, or disparaging tone of voice is often part of negative scripting. Even if we speak to the child in a foreign language when we say these things, if we use a harsh, scornful, or even flippant tone of voice, the child will clearly hear the negative message. The child will hear from your voice and see from your body language the message that, "You are not a competent and respected person." At its deepest and most extreme level, children can interpret the message of the negative script to mean they should never have been born.

These few examples give you some idea of how common and how destructive negative scripting is. If we talked to, or about, our friends and acquaintances like this, we would soon be without friends. In fact, most of us would never talk this way in the presence of an adult with whom we felt irritated, yet we often, unthinking, say these things to a child. This is ironic, because it is the child who will actually believe what we say. Children have not yet acquired the conceptual ability and the world experience which allow them to be critical of your opinions. They believe that you know everything. They believe that what parents or teachers say about them must be true.

"They say I am bad. She wishes she could throw me away. The teacher and all the kids wish I were not in the class. I am an outsider. People don't like a person like me. I am going to end up in jail. I am clumsy. I am a dummy. I'll never be as smart as my brother. Mother wishes I'd never been born. I'm a bad person. I am the reason Daddy's life is so unhappy."

Not only does the child make intellectual decisions about himself or herself based on the negative scripts given by beloved adults, the child is also being deprived of the emotional needs described in Maslow's staircase of needs. Remember the needs for security, belonging, Being-Love, and competency/respect? The staircase of needs is chipped away and undercut each time a negative script is repeated to the child by an important adult.

Fortunately, adults can also write positive scripts for the child. Every time you give positive verbal attention to the child, think of it as an opportunity for positive scripting. Imagine how children begin to think of their roles in life if they overhear statements like these:

1. "Rufus was a big help to me today. He set the table and got me diapers for the baby." (Mother says this to Dad when he arrives home. She ignores the fact that Rufus whined a good deal about going down for his nap.)

2. "Kayla played quietly with her legos when the baby was taking a nap today. It was a big help to me because I needed a rest too." (To a neighbor within Kayla's hearing.)

3. "Daniel must have been working hard on his math this grading period because his math grade went up a whole point. I knew you'd be proud of him. " (To Grandma over the telephone.)

4. "Kimberly spoke up today and defended her friend against some kids who were teasing her." (Teacher to Kimberly's father who has come to take Kimberly to a dentist's appointment.)

5. "Ask Teddie to show you the art work he did. He worked all period on it." (Teacher to school counselor in audible whisper.)

6. "I noticed you helped Richard carry all those books. I bet he appreciated that." (Teacher to child.)

7. "Carla worked on her social studies map for a whole hour this afternoon. She sure stuck to it and didn't give up." (One teacher to another in Carla's hearing.)

8. "This morning when I woke up I thought to myself, 'I'm so happy the kids were born!' " (Father to mother within the children's hearing.)

9. "I am so grateful to have kids who will pitch in and help with the housework like they did this morning." (To Grandpa within the children's hearing.)

10. "Jennifer spent a whole hour helping Chris practice catching and hitting. I hope she enjoyed it as much as he seemed too." (Spoken to a friend over the phone within Jennifer's hearing.)

What a difference in children's perceptions of themselves to hear this kind of positive scripting. Just as before, the child believes the adult is all-knowing. But this time, the child makes the decision that he or she is an okay person. The emotional needs for security, belonging, unconditional love, and competency are met. Children who are given these kinds of messages are free to grow and learn from their mistakes instead of staying stuck in the negative role of the bad guy, or the stupid guy, or the clumsy guy, or the child who should never have been born.

Once you become aware of them, the four sabotages are fairly easy to deal with. They at least have the virtue of lying at the surface, where we can see them, talk about them, and try to change them. The deepest sabotage of all is so hidden, that it cannot be classified with the other four. The vast underlying base of all the other sabotages is our own hidden, unmet needs. We may be parents and teachers, all-wise and all-powerful to the still developing minds of our children and students, but you and I know we are fallible human beings, like our kids, who have needs of our own, who *had* needs of our own which may not have been met when we were children. The mass of these unmet needs lies hidden, even from ourselves. Like the underwater bulk of an iceberg, they lie waiting to sink our best efforts at relationships with other people, and especially with our own children. This base of the iceberg, our unfulfilled needs, is the source of much of the puzzling anger and resentment we so often hurl blindly at the very people we love the most.

So the father who was physically and emotionally abused as a child is likely to abuse his own children and his spouse. But he denies that he himself was abused as a child. Over the years he has tried to avoid the hurt he endured as a child. "Sure I used to get the belt, but it was good for me. I had it coming." He is not in touch with the humiliation and the pain he suffered as a child. He is not in touch with his own low self-esteem which is the result of his long childhood experience of never having enough sense of security, Being-Love, belonging, competency. Instead, he hides from his own inner pain. But now he is powerful enough to protect that small child within him against his tormenters, maybe even to at last extract some revenge. Unfortunately, he now sees his tormenters as his wife and children. "Why do they irritate me like this? Why do I always have to tell them? Why do they get me so angry? It's their fault I have to hurt them." His bewilderment is real since his unmet needs are hidden even from himself.

Or, consider the mother who was taught she should always take care of other people's needs before her own. She is the good little girl who, as an adult, feels guilty at the very thought of directly asking for what she wants. After all, as a child she was belittled and shamed whenever she asked anything for herself. "You should wait to be asked. You should take the smallest piece. You should go last through the door. You should speak only when spoke to." As an adult, she is closed off from the burial grounds of her own unmet needs. But the bones still lie there and, in some hidden place, she still remembers. So she finds quiet ways to protect the small child within her. She is continually disappointed in her children and her husband. "I always did what *I* was told. Why can't my children be more considerate. Why don't they come to see me more often? Why am I so unhappy?" She spreads the guilt around unceasingly. In her quiet way, she self-sabotages on as grand a scale as the punitive father. John Bradshaw calls these hidden unmet needs a "gaping hole," somewhere deep inside, that yearns to be filled. But children cannot fill that gaping hole left over from our own childhoods. If we expect that they will, we will always be disappointed and angry at them.

If you often feel angry or resentful at the children in your care, it would be helpful to spend some time trying to discover the source of that anger. As in the two incidents given above, the anger may be coming from long ago, unresolved emotions from your own early childhood experiences. As children, we are often taught that anger is a "bad" emotion and that we are "bad" if we express or feel anger. But anger is not "good" or "bad." It exists. It is a part of reality. There is nothing wrong with anger unless we use its energy to hurt ourselves or someone else. Unfortunately, when the basic feelings which give rise to the anger are not dealt with openly, the anger builds and builds until it blindly takes control of all facets of our lives.

For example, one father told the members of his parenting class that he frequently erupts with rage at other people, including his children. As he talked about the experiences of his childhood, of being moved from foster home to foster home, of never belonging anywhere or to anyone, of being scolded for talking to the neighbors because "they don't want to be bothered by the likes of you," the other members of the group helped him identify his primary emotions of rejection, humiliation, loneliness, and shame. A constant and terrible rage arose out of those primary feelings. The anger was necessary, even helpful, to him during his childhood. Without the anger, he might have given up totally. The anger gave him the energy to survive the suffering of his bitter childhood.

Unfortunately, like this father, many of us use our anger to hurt ourselves or other people. It is how we *use* our anger energy that can be harmful, not the anger itself. We need to explore, to share and to talk about those early primary feelings and the situations which gave rise to them before we can let go the anger. (More about this in Chapter Nine, the section on feelings.)

Another hidden, unmet need which gives rise to anger is when we are not having any fun right here and now. When our life gets to be a drudgery, when we have no time to take care of ourselves, no time to play and laugh and relax, we start feeling resentful. Eventually the resentment erupts in anger which often ends up hurting those we love the most. Recently, Rita was so busy and feeling so harassed that she asked her husband if he would do all of the housework jobs for a couple of months. Since his life was calm at that time, and since he is a loving person, he agreed. A few weeks later, Rita told us she was looking through the cupboards for a plastic container to store some leftover chili and could not find the lid. The damn lid was not where it was supposed to be! She felt frustration and then rage at her husband for putting the lid in some stupid place instead of where it should be. Luckily, the feelings lasted only for an instant before Rita noticed what was happening. She said, "I think the anger erupted because I was feeling sorry for myself. I was working all my waking hours. I wasn't having any fun. I realized it was time to do something nice for *me,* even if it was only to take a long hot shower." Rita recognized that her husband had nothing to do with her anger. In the same way, our children often have nothing to do with the anger which sabotages our discipline and relationships with them.

Chapter Nine, the chapter on feelings, will discuss anger in more depth. If you suspect that anger is presently your major self-sabotage problem, you might want to skip ahead and read Chapter Nine right now.

If, after you work your way through this book and things still are not markedly better in your relationships with your kids, it may be time to look for clues in your own childhood for the roots of how you are sabotaging your relationship with your kids. Find a good therapist or support group for adult children of dysfunctional families to help you uncover the hidden pain of your own early unmet needs and of those feelings you were never able to express openly. The purpose of a counselor or a support group is to help you heal those old, festering wounds. It may be that this is the root cause of problems in the adult/child relationships within your family or classroom, and that only with this kind of healing will you be able to stop sabotaging your discipline and your relationship with your children. Dennis Wholey's book, *Becoming Your Own Parent,* is one good place to begin looking for an understanding of how childhood experiences of shame and rejection can affect your adult/child relationships today.

EXERCISE:

This week, concentrate on learning to identify the four sabotages when you see them. Use the following "The Four Sabotages" chart to observe yourself or other adults interacting with children. Watch for any of the four kinds of sabotages: (1) Procrastination; (2) Talking and talking about the misbehavior; (3) Forgetting to pay attention at positive and neutral times; and (4) Negative scripting. If you see any self-sabotage going on, write a brief description of the incident in the appropriate box so you can share it with your group at the next meeting. As you did last time, either give yourself a twenty-minute time segment each weekday to observe, or if you prefer, you can watch less intensively throughout the entire day. Remember, do not chart your spouse or partner. It is very important that you *do not observe and analyze your spouse.*

THE SELF-SABOTAGES

PROCRASTINATION

NOT GIVING POSITIVE ATTENTION AT NEUTRAL AND POSITIVE TIMES

TALKING AND TALKING ABOUT THE MISBEHAVIOR

NEGATIVE SCRIPTING

HIDDEN SABOTAGE: The unmet needs of the adult.

DISCUSSION IDEAS: CHAPTER 3: SELF-SABOTAGE

1. Share this week's charting of the self-sabotages you observed.

2. Are you involved in a power struggle right now with any of your children? Talk about what happens.

3. When you were a child, did your parents sabotage their discipline in any way?

4. Do you sabotage yourself in any way in the process of disciplining your children?

5. Everyone write down five things they remember their parents saying to them when they were children. Do this very quickly. Do not take more than a couple of minutes. Take turns sharing your list with the other members of the group.

6. Are you aware of any scripts you are giving your children?

7. Make a two column list of (a) ways to express anger which will *not hurt* either you or the people around you, and (b) ways to express anger which are *hurtful* to yourself and the people around you. Make a similar two column list for ways in which children express anger. Are the adult/children lists different in any way?

8. Ask if anyone in the group wants to talk about any of their own unmet needs, past or present, which are getting in the way of their relationships with their children? Go ahead and share if you want to, but do not pressure anyone to do this.

9. If anyone is interested in joining a support group for adults who were once children in a dysfunctional family, call your local mental health association or Al Anon chapter for information. Some suggested readings are, *Codependent No More* by Melody Beattie, *The Family* by John Bradshaw, and *Becoming Your Own Parent* by Dennis Wholey.

4 Identifying the Four Misbehaviors

Not-minding, Self-indulgence, Routine-not-minding, and Aggression

So far, we have lumped all misbehaviors into one category called "negative behaviors." We are now going to separate these negative behaviors into four specific types. It is important for you to learn to identify these four basic types of misbehaviors because each of these misbehaviors requires a different corrective response from you. Four misbehaviors: Four different corrections. We will examine how to interpret the patterns of the misbehaviors you see happening so that you can make an intelligent decision about how to prevent them in the first place, and how to respond to them at crisis times when you cannot prevent them from happening.

Finding patterns in human behavior is not so different from finding patterns in any other sphere of human activity. For example, human beings have, from the beginning, tried to define their relationship with the Earth. In the process, people have invented certain patterns. One example of a pattern is the way we have learned to measure the earth with a grid system of parallel and meridian lines. The meridian lines stretch from pole to pole. The parallel lines measure the distances in ever decreasing circles parallel to the equator. We find our way around on the surface of the earth by locating ourselves relative to the intersections of these parallel and meridian lines. It sounds simplistic, but it works. The earth goes on as before, complex and mysterious, but we are able to navigate our way around it. Even on a small sailboat, over great oceans, we can find our way without getting lost because of the patterns we have created.

In the same way, you can learn to recognize the pattern of your children's misbehaviors, and how to apply appropriate corrections. Learning the patterns of children's misbehaviors and the appropriate corrections for those misbehaviors will enable you to begin to find your way around in the complex web of discipline interactions between you and your children. As in the case of the parallel and meridian lines which measure the earth, the human behavior patterns you will learn are a human invention, a kind of tool or grid. The patterns are not human behavior itself. The basic source of human behavior will remain unchanged, just as the great Earth continues to move beneath our feet, as it did long before there were any human beings around to impose patterns on it.

The specific human behavior patterns you will be learning in Chapters Four through Eight involve four misbehaviors and four corrections. Corrections are not punishments. Punishments humiliate and degrade the other person. Punishments erode the staircase of human needs. The needs of security, belonging, Being-Love, competency and respect are worn away by punishment. Corrections, on the other hand, are a teaching method which, if carried out without self-sabotage, will keep the child's staircase of needs intact and strong at the same time you are teaching desired behaviors.

As a first step in this process, you need to become skillful at recognizing and categorizing the four misbehaviors as you notice them occurring in your children. Once you learn to recognize which of the four kinds of misbehaviors is occurring, you will be able to apply the appropriate correction for that misbehavior. As you read through the explanation of each type of misbehavior, can you pick out the category most typical of the child with whom you are most frustrated?

1. NOT-MINDING

   Children who are misbehaving by not-minding do not follow reasonable directions the first time they are asked. Not-minding behaviors are often associated with the very young child who is in the process of learning what is expected. Not-minding often involves situations in which children would not have known they were supposed to do something until an adult asked them to do it; for example, "It's time to go home now." They may fuss and complain while they avoid doing what they have been asked to do, or they may give every indication that they did not even hear you as they proceed to go quietly about their business. They have to be told again and again. Eventually they may do it, but only after great effort on your part.

2. SELF-INDULGENT

   Children who are being self-indulgent behave in aggravating ways which bring them lots of attention. They may whine, argue, intimidate with accusations as, "You like her better than me," or "Why do I always have to do all the work?" or "I hate you!" They may refuse to speak when they should be talking, or they go on and on about what a bad, mean person they are, or they constantly ask questions to which they already know the answers, hide from you, are bossy with adults as well as children, or make a fuss when they do not get their way. Fighting is often a self-indulgent behavior.

3. ROUTINE-NOT-MINDING

   Routine-not-minding behavior happens when children do not carry out tasks which they know in advance must be done on a regular basis. This misbehavior is similar to not-minding but is more associated with the older child and routine tasks which you should not have to keep reminding the child to do; for example, cleaning a room on Saturday, brushing teeth before bedtime, going to bed at 8:00 p.m., getting off to school by 7:30, doing school work on time, not touching off-limit items in the school or home, not going to off-limit places, and observing school rules. If there is a problem, it becomes increasingly apparent as children head into the teenage years. By now, they know what is expected of them. Adults feel they should not have to be constantly telling the child what to do. As in not-minding behavior, the child may eventually do what needs to be done, but seldom takes the initiative to go ahead and do it without continual reminding by an adult. Parents and teachers usually feel they are working harder at these routine tasks than the child.

4. AGGRESSIVE

Aggressive behaviors are those actions which deliberately hurt people, either physically or emotionally, in an attempt to get even. In aggressive behavior, children behave in ways which use situations to their own advantage in a deliberate attempt to hurt others. Occasionally, the child loses all self-control and starts to destroy property and physically hurt people (sometimes including himself) in a kind of blind rage. This severe loss of self-control needs to be dealt with as an aggressive behavior.

It is sometimes difficult to distinguish between self-indulgent and aggressive behaviors. Fighting between children, as was mentioned earlier, is often a self-indulgent behavior designed to get the attention of adults, but if a child is really intent on getting revenge and seriously hurting another child, you need to regard it as an aggressive behavior.

If children turn their aggression inward and hurt themselves, for example, if they bite themselves on the arm hard enough to actually draw blood, bang their head against a wall, pull out their own hair, or abuse drugs or threaten suicide, you will need more help than this book can give you. These inward turning aggressive behaviors require that you contact someone who can give you personal counseling assistance.

Most of the behaviors parents and teachers would like to eliminate are contained somewhere in these four broad categories of misbehaviors. You can no doubt add many specific examples of your own to each of the four categories. After reading through the four misbehavior descriptions, can you choose the category which is most typical of your child, or of the child in your classroom who gives you the most concern? For the moment, do not worry about what to do about these misbehaviors, just focus on trying to figure out which kind of misbehavior is occurring at the time it occurs.

Learning to distinguish between the four basic types of misbehaviors takes practice. Human behavior cannot be squeezed into a mold, but you can recognize and work with the patterns it forms. If you are not certain in which category a specific misbehavior belongs, make your best guess. You do not have to be right 100 percent of the time. At the end of a week's charting, you should have a pretty good working knowledge of which kind of misbehavior is happening.

NOT ALL NEGATIVE BEHAVIORS ARE MISBEHAVIORS: THREE PROBLEM-SOLVING AREAS.

Sometimes what seems to be a misbehavior on the part of the child, is really an attempt to solve a real life problem. As you begin to learn to recognize the differences between the four basic types of misbehaviors, you also need to stop and ask yourself whether the child is actually misbehaving or whether instead the child's negative behavior indicates he or she needs some help from you in solving a problem. There are three major problem-solving areas for the child in which the concerned adult can help:

A. ADJUSTING THE ENVIRONMENT

Sometimes the child is not developmentally able to perform up to the adult's expectations. When adults have unrealistically high expectations of a child, which the child cannot fulfill even if he tries, adults usually assume the child is misbehaving by not doing what he or she is "supposed to." An obvious example of unrealistic expectations are the parents of a fifteen-month-old baby who expect their baby to be potty trained by fifteen months. While it is possible that a rare fifteen-month-old can learn to control his or her muscles of elimination, the vast majority cannot, and so efforts to push the child to achieve sphincter control are doomed to failure. The parents can help the child by adjusting the environment so that the problem disappears. By providing diapers as long as needed, and being calm and matter-of-fact about matters of wetting and messing, the adult can turn an apparent misbehavior into a normal, age appropriate, neutral behavior.

A basic rule to remember is that *babies and toddlers never misbehave*. When babies and toddlers behave in ways that seem negative to you, it means they need their environment changed. Negative behaviors on the part of babies and toddlers means they are hungry, tired, curious, have a tummy-ache, ear-ache or are teething. They need to be picked up, changed, held, fed, comforted, removed from certain situations, and cuddled. As Fitzhugh Dobson says, don't worry about spoiling babies and toddlers. "Babies don't spoil. Only fruit spoils."

More examples. Parents of two-and-a-half-year-old twins complained that their twins were constantly out of their car seats and bugging their eight-year-old sister whenever the family went for a ride. Rather than treat this as a misbehavior, other parents in the parenting class began to think of ways to adjust the environment. How about putting one of the kids in the front seat with one of the adults sitting in the back seat between two of the children? What kind of a car seat was it? Someone suggested bringing the car seats to class next time so we could figure out a way to buckle them up so they could not undo the buckles. Another example of adjusting the environment to meet developmental needs: Preschool teachers know that if preschoolers are given juice in styrofoam glasses, they will constantly spill their juice, not because they are misbehaving, but because at this age they do not have the coordination to use a light-weight glass without tipping it over.

Every age has its own developmental rate beyond which children should not be pushed. Children need to be allowed to grow up at their own inner pace. Many young parents talk with their friends about each others' children. They compare notes, "Clyde started walking at ten months." "Lilly was speaking in whole sentences at fifteen months." In this way, parents sometimes get very competitive about developmental rates and, without even being aware of it, push their children along faster than is good for any child. If this is happening to you, try to stop, and take comfort in knowing that once your kids are all grown, you can laugh to think you ever cared how young they were when they started walking or talking or learning to read. What matters is that you accept them as they are and that you take joy in their day-to-day progress. In this way, you are building their self-esteem staircases as they grow toward adulthood.

One of the values of working through this material with a group of people is that you can compare your expectations for the child with theirs. Ask yourself the questions: Am I expecting too much of my children? Could I change the environment for now and just wait awhile for them to grow a bit more?

Every parent who has an attention-deficit child, and every teacher who works with attention-deficit children, needs to consider how to adjust the environment so this child can experience success. The attention-deficit child is not capable of sitting and listening in the same way other children can. All children need space to move and use their muscles: No child should be expected to always sit quietly and never run and yell. But the attention-deficit child has an even more difficult time with sitting and listening. Sometimes medication seems to be all that can help. Many parents and teachers tell of complete behavior turnarounds after the child begins medication with Ritalin. An adult who had used Ritalin all through her childhood recently said she believed that even though Ritalin gets most of the credit for getting her through those early years with her self-esteem staircase intact, she also blesses the training program she took which taught techniques for focusing. For example, she was taught to doodle as she listened to a talk or a story. To this day, she still pulls out her pen and pad to doodle at church or other meetings. "As an adult I can get along without the Ritalin, but I still find it hard to concentrate and the doodling still helps." This woman was lucky that the environment could be adjusted for her in two ways: One, she was able to use Ritalin without ill effects, and two, she was allowed by her teachers to use coping skills like doodling.

A word of caution: Even though medication is sometimes necessary to help the attention-deficit child cope with the world, please explore every other avenue before you medicate a child. Regrettably, some doctors prescribe medication too freely. *Find a doctor who will prescribe medication only after everything else, including diet changes, has been tried.*

B. HELPING CHILDREN SOLVE DISAGREEMENTS BY TEACHING ASSERTIVENESS AND NEGOTIATION

Fighting often happens not for revenge, or to get attention, but because children have a real life issue which needs to be solved. Fighting which is an attempt to solve a problem between children is not a misbehavior because, in these situations, children are trying to solve a problem by trying to get what they think they have a right to have. They do not want revenge (aggression.) They do not want the attention of adults (self-indulgent.) Their primary goal is to protect their own interests and get what they want. Infringing on another person's rights by hurting that person is secondary. Hence this kind of fighting cannot really be classified as a misbehavior. In these situations, children often do not need to have a correction applied by an adult. What they need is help from an adult to learn other ways of solving the problem.

Children, especially very young ones, usually do not know how to go about solving problems without hitting and yelling. This is not surprising since human beings have an instinctive reflex to lash out and protect themselves whenever they feel threatened. In this culture, children also see hitting and yelling glorified on television. Further, hitting and yelling are widely used by adults to punish young people. The double standard is obvious. Adults are allowed to hit children but not other adults. Children are not supposed to hit either adults or other children. In this way, children learn that hitting and yelling are quasi acceptable problem-solving techniques.

Occasionally, adults find themselves tacitly recognizing that fighting is sometimes the only viable solution they can find to a problem, by advising a child to fight back against a bully. Maybe you have had this experience yourself. Here's an example told by a high school teacher:

Jerry was a huge, quiet, good natured, high school junior. Tim was a small boy, the same age as Jerry, who had trouble making friends or gaining any positive recognition for himself. In an effort to win the admiration of his peers, and secure in the knowledge that Jerry was a nonaggressive person, Tim began to ridicule Jerry, making fun of him, accusing him of being dumb, an ape, and a coward. Since Jerry was aware of his own superior strength, he patiently tried to ignore Tim's taunts. Unfortunately, Tim gained tremendous amounts of negative attention from the other students who kept telling him to leave Jerry alone. Jerry continued trying to ignore for several weeks, but the more he ignored Tim, the more satisfaction Tim seemed to take in the whole affair, escalating the teasing until he began to actually push and punch Jerry. Tim was starved for attention. Negative attention from the other kids was better than none at all. This went on for weeks with Tim making Jerry's life more miserable every day. Finally, the teacher advised

Jerry, "First try warning Tim. Tell him, 'Leave me alone or I'll punch you out.' If that doesn't work, then *hit* him a good one. " You can guess the result. One day, a much subdued Tim appeared, with a swollen lip. There was no more harassment from Tim. And gentle Jerry went back to being gentle Jerry. In Jerry's case, this kind of fighting was not self-indulgent, nor was it aggressive in the sense that he was using another person in an uncaring way. This was clearly a case of trying to solve a problem.

In spite of how much we may sympathize with the occasional seemingly justified solution of "punching someone out," it is clearly a desperation measure. Children often initiate fights with another child because they simply do not know how to handle the situation any other way. Yet there are other ways to resolve disputes which children can be taught from a very early age. Whenever you see a fight between children, first consider whether or not it is a problem-solving situation. Do not try to categorize it as self-indulgent or aggressive until you have first worked on helping the kids to solve their problem. Here is an example of a fight between two children which began as an attempt to solve a problem:

> Six-year-old Josh wants to take a turn on the swing during school recess time but six-year-old Linda will not get off the swing when he asks for a turn. Finally, Josh grabs at the swing and stops it. Linda yells and kicks at Josh who, in turn, yells and hits at Linda.

Linda and Josh have a real life problem; how to share the swing. They are not fighting for attention from the teacher (self-indulgence) or from being uncaring and using the other person for their own ends (aggressive.) They have a problem and do not know how else to solve it, they are fighting to get what they think they have a right to have. They need an adult to intercede and help them learn some beginning rudiments of problem-solving. Here are five steps the adult can use to help:

1. *Do not place blame or innocence on either child.* Innocence or blame has nothing to do with problem-solving. Both children have rights which must be protected. Keep yourself focused instead on how to help them solve the problem. *Describe the situation* by saying, "I see two people who want a turn on the swing," or "Gosh. Here are two upset people." Stay away from blaming statements like, "Okay. Who started this anyhow?" or "Can't you two ever get along?" Common blaming words are, "bad," "wrong," "always," "never," "stupid." Stay away from any word or phrase that implies the child intended to misbehave.

2. *Reduce the stress level in both children so they will be able to listen.* Go over to the children and put one arm around Linda and the other around Josh. First comfort the one who appears to have gotten the worst of it, and then comfort the other one.

   "I am sorry you are hurt, Linda." Then turn to the other child, "And you seem awfully upset, Josh." Be calm and friendly with both children.

3. *Prompt each child to use words to state the problem.*

   To Linda say: "Tell Josh what you didn't like." If Linda does not do this, pretend to be Linda and say firmly, "Say, 'I don't like it when you stop my swing. And I don't like it when you hit me.'" When Linda says anything even approximating this, paraphrase it, nod your head in approval and say, "Good for you for using words to tell Josh what you didn't like."

   To Josh say: "Tell Linda what you didn't like." If Josh does not do this, pretend to be Josh and say firmly, "Say, 'I don't like it when you won't let me take a turn. And I don't like it when you hit me.' " When Josh says anything even close to this, paraphrase it, nod your head in approval and say, "Good for you for using words to tell Linda what you didn't like."

Now repeat the above sequence, this time using the word pattern, "Tell Josh what you want," and "Tell Linda what you want." Again, you may have to speak for a child if he or she cannot verbalize his or her own needs: for example, "Tell her, 'I want a turn on the swing, too.'" Stand beside the child you are speaking for, as though you *are* that child. If you do this for one child, be sure to do it at some point for the second child, too, so the second child does not get the impression you are favoring one child over the other.

4. *Help them figure out some kind of solution to try.*

Say to them both: "Do you have any ideas for making it go better next time?" If they can't think of anything, make some suggestions, "I could look at my watch and tell you when three minutes was up. Then you could both have a three minute turn. What do you think of that idea?"

They may like this idea, or Linda may very well say, "Well, he can have a turn and I'll go play on the merry-go-round." Remember it is not up to you to find a solution for their problem. Then give each one of them a friendly look or hug and leave the scene.

5. *They do not have to find a solution.*

Strange as it may sound, the children do not have to come up with a solution. If they cannot agree, you can shake your head and say, "Well, maybe later on you will get an idea. Will you come let me know if you think of something?" If there is an object, like a favorite toy, they are fighting about, you can put it away until they figure something out. Do not do this in a punishing way. Just be matter of fact, "I'll just put this up until you get a plan."

The advantages to this approach to problem-solving fights is obvious. Both children feel heard and respected. They are consequently able to hear what you and the other child have to say. There is no placing of blame or innocence. There will be little, if any, residue of resentment left over to stain any future relationships with either you or the other child. The need for revenge will not develop. You have left the responsibility for choosing a solution up to them. In this way, they are gradually learning the art of assertiveness and compromise. You are empowering them to effectively take charge of their own lives. The example given involved very young children, but the basic ideas behind these five steps can apply to any age group.

Notice that you do not ask the children to say they were sorry. If they are sorry they will probably say so. If they are not sorry, do not chip away at their inner integrity by pressuring them to lie about something as important as their own feelings, and to burden them with guilt or resentment because they do not feel sorry. Also, do not ask the children to share their feelings of humiliation or sadness or anger about what just happened. Turning the discussion into an exploration of feelings would detract from the task at hand. The task at hand is to teach problem-solving skills in a way that reaffirms both children.

The pattern given above is helpful to use with small groups of children during a crisis time. Later, in Chapter Eleven, we will discuss how the family and classroom meeting can be used to help children solve problems on a more regular basis.

C. HELPING CHILDREN DEAL WITH THEIR OWN TROUBLING INNER FEELINGS: LISTENING TO THE CHILD'S INNER-REALITY

Sometimes when a child complains, the child is not seeking attention (self-indulgent behavior) but is deeply bothered about something. For example, the child who comes home from school and throws a spelling test down on the table yelling, "I'm stupid. I never get things right," might really be feeling miserable about difficult schoolwork. In that case, this is not a self-indulgent behavior, but a problem which you can help with by listening to the child's painful inner-reality feelings. The concept of listening to inner-reality feelings is too broad to be covered here. It will be dealt with in depth in Chapter Nine. If you want more information right now on how to listen to a child's inner-reality feelings, go ahead and skip to Chapter Nine.

EXERCISE:

Try to identify the negative behaviors you see this week. On the following page, you will find the "Negative Behaviors" chart which is designed to help you learn to recognize each of the four different misbehaviors (Not-minding, Self-Indulgent, Routine-not-minding, and Aggressive) as you observe them. You can focus your observations intensely for a twenty-minute period each weekday or be a casual observer all day long. Notice the top section is for recording the four misbehaviors, with a separate section at the bottom of the page for you to write about possible problem-solving situations. (Does the child's negative behavior indicate a need to adjust the environment, help solve conflicts, or deal with feelings?)

When you chart the misbehaviors you see happening this week, write down more than just a word or two. Describe the situation in enough detail so that you will remember what happened when you share the story with the rest of the group next week.

Keep in mind that many negative behaviors can be placed in several different categories, depending on the context of the situation. We have already discussed how fighting can be classified as self-indulgent, aggressive, or problem-solving, depending on the situation. There are many other behaviors which can also be placed in several misbehavior categories. It all depends on the specific situation. Furthermore, maybe the negative behavior is not a misbehavior at all. Maybe it is a problem-solving behavior. Whenever you see a negative behavior this week, have a little fun with trying to decide which, or how many, of the misbehavior or problem-solving categories it could fit into.

You can choose just one of your children to observe, or you can observe an entire class or family. Do not write a specific child's name on the chart. You are not trying to change anyone's behavior right now. You are only an observer. Keeping a record of the misbehaviors for a week will not only sharpen your ability to distinguish between the four different misbehaviors and the problem-solving situations, it will also help you zero in on which misbehaviors you want to work on changing first. As before, if the children ask about the new chart just tell them, "I am learning some new things about being a parent (or a teacher.) You do not need to explain more than that.

NEGATIVE BEHAVIORS:
The Four Misbehaviors
(and 3 Problem-Solving Situations)

NOT-MINDING

SELF-INDULGENT (Attention-Getting)

ROUTINE-NOT-MINDING (Will not do routine tasks)

AGGRESSIVE (Deliberately Hurting)

Negative Behaviors Requiring Problem-Solving Which Do Not Fit Above:

1. Adjust Environment   2. Solve Conflicts   3. Listen to Feelings

DISCUSSION IDEAS: CHAPTER 4: IDENTIFYING THE FOUR MISBEHAVIORS

1. Share this week's "Negative Behaviors" chart. Do you see how the same misbehavior can often be placed in several different categories depending on the specific situation?

2. Which of the four misbehaviors bothers you the most when you see it in your children?

3. Are you aware of any negative behaviors in your children which might fit into one of the problem-solving areas? (Remember that babies and toddlers never misbehave. They always fit into one of the problem-solving areas.)

   Problem solving areas: a. Child struggles in an unrealistic environment; or b. Child attempts to get what he or she wants which causes conflicts with others; or c. Child feels inner pain from some difficult real life situation.

4. Share with each other some examples of times, when as a concerned adult, you had to go behind the scenes and adjust a child's environment without the child even being aware of it.

5. Work as a group. Make a list of the negative behaviors you would like to eliminate in your children. Using the observation charts you have worked with during the week, try putting each of the negative behaviors into the appropriate misbehavior or problem-solving categories. Be creative and have some fun with this. Spend some time discussing the differences in each specific situation. You will see that fighting is only one example of a misbehavior which can be placed in two or three different categories. How many others can you find?

6. If your group feels ready, try role-playing a situation in which two children are having a fight in an attempt to solve a problem. You can choose the situation given in this chapter of the two children who both want the swing, or choose any other

situation you want. Be sure it is a true problem-solving situation before you begin. When you play the part of a child, choose to be a child you know well. Try to get into the feeling of how you think that child would behave and feel in a similar situation.

You will need two "children" and one "adult." Let other people in the group be observers who can offer their ideas after the role-play is over. The person playing the adult will try to help the "children" solve the problem as suggested in this chapter. Use the following review sheet as a guide. After each role-play is finished, have the "adult" ask the children how they felt during the adult's efforts to help them solve their problem.

When you play the part of the "adult," remember, role-playing is a wonderful opportunity to make lots of mistakes. Making mistakes and getting feedback from your pretend "children" is how you will learn to help your real kids. Relax and have fun with the role-play. Try not to be perfect.

REVIEW: *Helping Children Solve Disagreements* **by Teaching Assertiveness and Negotiation**

1. ***Do not place blame*** *or innocence on either child.* Focus on the fact that there is a problem both children need to solve. Be calm and friendly with both children.

2. **Reduce the stress level** *in both children so that they will be able to listen.* First, comfort the one who appears to have gotten the worst of it, then comfort the other one. Example:

   "I am sorry you are hurt, Annie." Then turn to the other child: "And you seem awfully upset, Roger." Put your arm around each child, if that seems appropriate for their age.

3. *Briefly **describe** the situation.* "I see two upset people," or "Here are two people who want a turn."

4. *Prompt each child to **use words** to state the problem.*

   To Annie say: "Tell Roger what you didn't like." If Annie does not do this, model her part and say firmly, "I don't like it when you stop my swing. And I don't like it when you hit me!"

   Then turn to Roger and repeat the process: "Tell Annie what you didn't like." Again, model for him if he cannot find the words.

5. *Prompt each child to **use words** to tell the other child what they want.* To Annie say, "Tell Roger what you want," and to Roger, "Tell Annie what you want."

6. *Help them figure out some kind of **solution to try.***

   Say to them both: "Do you have any ideas for making it go better next time?" If they cannot think of anything, you can make a suggestion, but remember, *they are the ones who must solve the problem.*

7. *It is **okay if a solution cannot be found.***

5 The Correction for Not Minding

Physical Assist & Broken Record

The next four chapters will outline for you how to carry out the appropriate correction for each of the four misbehaviors. Corrections are not punishments. They are part of a step-by-step process of teaching the child to see the sense in behaving in certain ways. You are probably already using these corrections in one form or another. The key point about using the corrections is to learn *when* to use them, plus remembering not to sabotage yourself.

Some of the corrections will be emotionally difficult for the A parent and teacher to carry out. The A adult often has difficulty in allowing the child to make independent decisions. The A parent and teacher sometimes also find it hard to accept the concept that corrections should not be punitive.

Other corrections will be hard emotionally for the C parent and teacher. The C adult often finds it hard to carry out a correction because of the fear that if the adult is too controlling the child will not grow up to be an inner-directed adult, able to make independent decisions. The C adult also tends to worry that the child will not love the person who demands certain standards of behavior. Both A and C adults have strengths in different areas: We can learn from one another. A adults can reassure C adults that kids will love you even when you insist on certain rules. C adults can help A adults see that corrections need not be punitive, and that children can be trusted to control certain areas of their own lives.

THE PHYSICAL ASSIST and the BROKEN RECORD are the corrections for NOT-MINDING. The physical assist and broken record are ways to help children learn to follow reasonable commands. Young children especially, because they are learning so many new behaviors in their brand-new world, need this type of guidance more often than the older child. The older children get, the more they understand beforehand what is expected of them. When the new behavior has been learned so that children can integrate it into their belief systems, it becomes routine, something children "know in their bones" they are expected to do. For this reason, the physical assist and the broken record are used most often with with younger children. The not-minding misbehaviors of older children usually fall into the routine-not-minding category, and call for a different correction which you will learn in Chapter Seven.

HOW TO GIVE A COMMAND: Not-minding behavior happens when the adult gives a reasonable command which the child refuses to carry out. One of the most important things to learn about the correction for not-minding is how to give a command in the first place. Here are some basic guidelines for giving a command:

1. *Give a choice if at all possible.*

No matter what our age, each of us wants to be in control of our own life. By saying to the child, "You can choose to do either this or that," you empower the child and give him or her a sense of control. Human beings will resist you if they feel you are trying to take control of their lives.

However, both choices must be choices which you can live with. For example, a grandmother told about the time her three-year-old granddaughter, Sally, was visiting. When the girl's mother told her it was bedtime, the child started whining and complaining. The girl's father said, "Sally, you can go to bed right now, or Grandma can read you a story and then you can go to bed." Sally immediately chose to hear the story, stopped fussing and went happily off to bed with Grandma (who had intended to read her a story anyhow.)

Other examples of choice-commands are: "We can leave right now or we can go in ten more minutes." "You can finish your schoolwork at the work table or at the back desk." "You can finish playing your guitars in the garage or in the basement." "You can play with the kick ball on the playing court or on the back field." "You can play without pushing or you can sit out part of the game."

You can see that the choices are limited only to those choices you can live with. Never give a choice when there is no choice. Do not ask children if they *want* to do it. For example, "Do you want to go to bed now?" or "Let's go to bed now. Okay? Okay?" By asking children if they *want* to, or if it is *okay,* you have given them the option of *not* going to bed. It is not fair to expect a child to mind when you have not given a clear choice or command. Rather than offer a choice you did not really intend to give, it is better not to give a choice at all and simply say, "Now it's time to go to bed."

An important point: If children refuse to act on either choice, *you must make the choice for them.* If the choice you gave was, "You can finish your schoolwork at the work table or at the back desk," and the child refuses to move, then you must choose for him. If the child still will not move, you can then step in to use the physical assist or the broken record.

2. *If you cannot give a choice, describe what needs to be done in a positive way.*

Examples are, "It is time to go home," or "The table is not for sitting on," "Please put the candy bar back on the shelf," or "That clock is not for playing with. Please leave it alone." Human beings are more apt to cooperate if they are told to do something in a positive way. If you cannot think of a matter-of-fact way to describe what needs to be done, concentrate on using a positive tone of voice. A positive tone of voice lets children know you respect them. Commands which are delivered in a harsh tone of voice, such as "Stop that right now!" and "You kids get in the car this minute!" invite a personal power struggle.

3. *The fewer words the better.*

Be as brief as possible. Give only one, or at most two, commands at a time. Giving many commands at once is confusing. "Gary, go upstairs and bring me a diaper for the baby, and on your way, turn off those bathroom lights, and when you're done with that, you can choose to either take the letters on the hallway table out to the mailbox before we watch Sesame Street or before lunch." A command like that is too complex. It is too hard to remember, even if your child is a good auditory learner. The shorter the better. A one-word command is sometimes the best of all.

4. *Give lead time, if possible.*

Give some advance notice that you are going to want something to happen soon, for example, "In five minutes I want you to start picking up the blocks," or "In ten minutes we all need to be ready to leave for Grandma's." Giving lead time is a way of showing respect for the child's activities and is much more likely to result in cooperation when you actually give the command.

5. *Be reasonable in the type and number of choices or commands you give.*

You will have to be the judge of how many commands a day are reasonable, but remember, the fewer commands you give, the more likely the child will take notice when you do give a command. As the child grows towards the puberty years, you should need to give fewer and fewer commands. The older the child, the more areas of life should be in his or her own area of control. We do not own children. Any command which orders children around just because the adult wants to wield power over them is not reasonable.

Any command which tries to force a bodily function on the child is unreasonable. "Eat that food," or "Stop wetting your bed," or "You have a bowel movement before you leave that bathroom," or "I want you to go to sleep before I come in here again," or "You stop that crying right now," are all unreasonable commands in that they attempt to control another human being's interior bodily functioning. Even "I don't want to hear one word out of you while we are in the store," is unreasonable.

If behaviors which relate to the child's body functioning are a problem to you after the age of three, like pants messing for example, go for professional help. Your doctor or school counselor should be able to refer you to someone experienced in this area. But never try to physically assist or use the broken record regarding a child's bodily functions. All body functions belong solely to the person who lives in the body, of whatever age.

6. *Be sure you can follow through with the correction, otherwise do not give the choice or command.*

If you cannot carry out the correction, or follow through on the choices, do not give the command. If you are in a public place, like the grocery store, or at the school play, and you know you will be too embarrassed to carry out the correction, do not give the command. You must be consistent in carrying out the correction the first time the child does not mind. It is better not to give the command than not to follow through.

7. *Do not respond to self-indulgent behavior.* (The next chapter will tell you about the correction for self-indulgent behavior.)

Concentrate on dealing with the not-minding behavior. Do not let the child's accusations, complaints, whining, name calling, or scolding deflect you from carrying out the correction for not-minding. You will sabotage yourself if you get hooked into responding in any way to the self-indulgent behavior. You are the latest in a million-year-old line of teachers and parents. Adults have an obligation to pass along cultural expectations to their children. You have the authority of all society and all nature behind you. Do not sabotage yourself and all those thousands of ancestors by turning this into a personal power struggle.

HOW TO CARRY OUT THE PHYSICAL ASSIST:

When the child does not mind the first time you give a choice or command, you physically lead him or her through the task. Leading the child through a task is called the PHYSICAL ASSIST. The physical assist is done in this manner: When the child has disobeyed, say "No." Then restate the command as you *physically lead the child through the task.* There are a wide variety of ways to physically assist a child; from walking over to stand very close to the child, to touching the child lightly on the shoulder, to actually picking up the child and removing him or her. The main idea is to use your own body in a nonverbal way to help the child do what you have asked the child to do. Use as little physical force as you possibly can. Very often, just the knowledge that the adult is right there, only a few feet away and ready to step in, is enough to convince the child it is time to carry out the command.

Do not restate the command more than once. Say nothing else throughout the physical assist procedure. Think of yourself as a force of nature, like a river, or a steady breeze. You are carrying out the necessary teachings of human society which all adults have an obligation to pass on to their children. Try not to get too emotionally involved. Remember, this is not a punishment: It is a teaching method.

EXAMPLE A:

Mother and her two-year-old daughter, Reanna, are at Grandma's house. Reanna starts playing with Grandma's precious objects on the coffee table. Mother would prefer to adjust the environment by removing the objects to higher ground, but she knows Grandma does not approve of that, even for two-year-olds. So Mother says, "Reanna, the things on the coffee table are not for playing with. You can play with this." Mother gives Renna a two-year-old kind of choice by offering her a toy to play with. Reanna continues with what she is doing. There is no sign that Reanna even heard what Mother said.

Mother, again with a pleasant but firm tone of voice: "No. Those things are not for playing with." As Mother restates her command, she walks over to Reanna, picks her up and removes her to a different part of the house where she gives her the toy to play with.

The younger the child, the more easily she can be distracted with something else. For a two-year-old, being distracted by a toy is a form of giving her a choice. In cases where young children like Reanna cannot be distracted by another choice, you need to continue to carry them away from the place they are not supposed to be.

EXAMPLE B:

> Third-grader Kelly is pushing and shoving to break into the
> front of the line which is forming outside the school door
> as the children prepare to come in from recess. The teacher
> is too busy to stop and help problem-solve. Her mind goes
> blank. She cannot think how to give a choice, so she
> simply says, in a firm but calm voice, "Kelly, you need to
> go to the back of the line." Kelly stands in his new spot at
> the front of the line, avoiding the teacher's eyes, with a
> pout on his face, and refuses to budge.
>
> In the same pleasant but firm voice, teacher says, "Back of
> the line," as she puts her hand on Kelly's shoulder and
> walks him to the end of the line.

You may have noticed that when the command is restated in the
two examples above, you do not use the child's name. This is
because a person's name is one of the sweetest sounds in the world
to that person. Using a name at negative times is giving too much
social reinforcement. Your goal is to not give any more attention
than absolutely necessary during the physical assist.

EXAMPLE C:

> Sometimes the physical assist can be used without even
> touching the child. A diminutive resource room teacher
> told this story. She had a fifth grade student who towered
> over her. Walking down the hall together they looked like
> Mutt and Jeff. The boy had been having a hard week. He
> had refused to finish his class work. "Cliff," she finally
> told him, "you will have to stay after school and finish
> your work before you can go home today." The teacher
> cleared this plan ahead of time with Cliff's mother who
> promised to come pick him up later in the day when his
> work was done. Immediately after school, Cliff tried to
> escape by taking his regular bus ride home. The teacher

called Cliff's mother and asked her to bring her son back to school, but the mother said she had already tried and could not make him get in the car. The determined teacher marched out the school door, drove her car over to Cliff's house, knocked on the door, and commanded, "Get in the car." The astonished boy got in the car without protest. She did not have to touch him; her determined body language, and the waiting car, told him all he needed to know.

EXAMPLE D:

A three-year-old girl and her mother were visiting Grandma. It was time to leave. The mother started getting the baby ready to leave while Grandma began picking up the toys left lying around the living room. "Help Grandma pick up the toys, Nettie," the mother said. Nettie ignored her. Mother put the baby down, walked over to Nettie and using a matter-of-fact, calm voice said, "No. I said the toys." Mother stood at Nettie's side and reached over to hold Nettie's hands. In this four-handed way, Mother "helped" Nettie pick up the toys. "Thank you, Nettie," the mother said as she went back to the baby. Both Grandma and Mother continued to talk and visit happily with both Nettie and the baby. Nettie grumbled a bit during the procedure but as no one self-sabotaged by mentioning the incident again, she was soon chatting merrily away with the rest of the group. It is worth noting that this child is a very powerful little personality, yet no power struggle emerged because her mother was able to be a quiet force of nature and did not sabotage herself.

Never use more force than absolutely necessary. You can be firm without hurting the child either physically or emotionally. There should be no nonverbal message to the child of, "I'll teach you to disobey me, you little S.O.B." The nonverbal message to the child should rather be an inexorable, Mother Nature, matter-of-fact statement that, "This must be done. This is the way things are."

The physical assist is not a punishment. It is part of a teaching method which will temporarily stop the misbehavior and put you in charge of the situation. When the physical assist is finished, go back to whatever you were doing. *Do not mention anything about what just happened.* As soon as the child engages in neutral or positive behavior, pay attention in positive ways with friendly eye contact, a touch, a smile, or just carry on with the conversation which was interrupted by the not-minding behavior.

Talking about the misbehavior is one of the surest ways to sabotage yourself. Talking about the misbehavior is perceived by children as demeaning, a way of "rubbing their face in it." *Talking about the misbehavior in any way will set up a power struggle in which children will attempt to protect their inner integrity by disobeying you again.* When the incident is over, let it be over. Take up where you left off. As soon as children exhibit the slightest neutral or positive behavior, immediately reinforce the new behavior with friendly eye contact or touch or word. This treatment may be confusing, at first, when children have been accustomed to receiving negative feedback from adults for extended periods of time after misbehavior occurs. Their confusion will soon clear, however, and your nonverbal, matter-of-fact type of physical assist correction will quickly convince them that it was their behavior you did not like, not them as individuals. The minute their behavior changes, why shouldn't you be friendly? After all, they are dear people and you care about them. Their misbehavior was just a natural part of their learning and growing.

HOW TO CARRY OUT THE BROKEN RECORD: The broken record is an assertiveness technique in which you simply state what you need to have happen, again and again, in the same even, calm tone of voice. *Notice that this is just the opposite of the physical assist, in which you give a command only once. So be clear in your mind, before you start, which correction you plan to use.*

Consider the example of Carlos, a student of mine when I was a high school teacher. Carlos was a withdrawn, sullen young man with many personal problems. He never gave me any trouble, but also never allowed me to get to know him. One day he came to class angry and upset. He started interrupting and making insulting remarks. I tried to ignore him but finally decided I had to give him a choice, "You can stop what you are doing, or you can leave the room." Carlos was quiet for a while, but soon was back interrupting and insulting. I said, "I guess you choose to leave." Carlos started arguing. I closed my eyes, shook my head slowly back and forth and said, "No. Leave." More arguing from Carlos. I looked not at Carlos but at the door. "You will have to leave." I waited. The other students were absolutely silent. I tried to keep my voice low and even and said again, "No. You have to leave." Finally, after repeating myself seven or eight times, Carlos slouched out of the room. The rest of us went back to what we were doing without comment. When Carlos showed up the next day, I greeted him with a smile and did not mention the incident. He did not exactly smile back but did give a grudging low, "Hello." Carlos never did anything like that in my class again. And I never found out what painful thing had happened in his life to trigger that event.

1. *Avoid turning this into a personal power struggle.*

Avoid commands like, "I said you get down to the basement this minute." or "You better get out of this living room right now if you know what's good for you." Instead, put the whole inexorable force of nature and society behind your initial command, "It is time...," "You need to...," "You will have to...," Do not respond to self-indulgent arguments or accusations. Do not respond to anger. Be as firm and calm as you can. Concentrate on keeping your voice even. Let your nonverbal body language convey the message that you, too, have rights and that you are in this for the long haul. Plant your body in one spot and stay there. Remember you have a million-year-long-line of teachers and parents behind you. Try to be a force of nature which must be obeyed, like a wide river, the ocean, or a steady wind.

Limit eye contact during the broken record correction. Eye contact gives powerful emotional attention to the child during the misbehavior. It will fuel a power struggle. Rather than look at the child, look in the direction you want the child to go, or toward the objects you want removed. In the example just given, I concentrated on looking at the door and not at Carlos. Sometimes it helps to close your eyes and slowly shake your head from side to side as you quietly restate the command.

As with all the other corrections, remember not to sabotage by talking about it when children finally do what they have been told. Simply say, "Thank you," and go back to what you were doing before the incident started. Do not sabotage yourself by indicating in any way that you think you are the winner and they are losers. Next time you see them, pay attention to their neutral and positive behaviors. Try not to sabotage yourself by holding on to your resentment that they did not obey you the first time. Let the incident go.

2. *Tell the child what you want to have happen.*

Give the command as many times as necessary in a calm, firm voice. Be a BROKEN RECORD. Tell the child what you want to have happen. If the child does not respond, be quiet for a moment, then repeat it again. If the child does not respond after another silence, repeat it again. Alternate repeating the command with a silence for as many times as necessary. For example, here is a situation where the choice-command was, "I'm afraid it's too loud for me when you play your guitars in the living room. You and Carol can play in the garage or in the basement." If, after waiting and giving the two children a chance to finish the piece they are playing, and still nothing happens, or if they start to argue with you, you must make the choice for them. Describe what you want to have happen. "You will have to leave." After the initial command, use only one or two words. The fewer words the better. You may have to repeat yourself many times. Remember to wait quietly for a moment after each time you repeat the command, "No. Leave."

EXAMPLE A:

Here is an example involving a five-year-old child. Dad is getting ready to set the table for dinner. His daughter Melissa is playing a game on the table. In a friendly way Dad says, "Melissa, it's time to pick up the game and clear the table." (Hopefully, Dad has earlier remembered to give Melissa some lead time so that she could plan ahead.) Melissa starts to wail, "I'm not done yet!"

Dad says, "No. I said it is time to pick up the game." Dad walks into the dining room, plants himself firmly beside his daughter and waits. Again he says, "The game." Melissa screams, "But I'm not done. You're mean!" Dad ignores this self- indulgent behavior. "The game," he says again. Finally, Melissa, grumbling under her breath, clears the table. Dad ignores the grumbling, says, "thank you," walks back into the kitchen and says nothing more about it.

EXAMPLE B:

One teacher tried the broken record technique while substituting in an inner-city middle school. Two ninth grade boys started a fight on the ramp leading to the school door where she was standing at recess time. "Get off the ramp," she said. The boys looked over at her but kept on pushing and swearing at each other. She moved a step closer to them. "Get off the ramp." They stopped and looked at her, each shouting that the other one had done or said something to start the fight. She moved another step closer and in the same, even tone of voice she repeated, "The ramp." They turned away and left the ramp. To her amazement, they also stopped fighting. This teacher's eyes sparkled as she held her hand high above her head, "And they were *this* much taller than I was."

EXAMPLE C:

Karen was growing increasingly concerned about the belligerent behavior of her fifteen-year-old son. He consistently defied her and refused even her most reasonable requests. He had even begun leaving butcher knives around the house in prominent places, which she took as a deliberate attempt on his part to intimidate her. One behavior in particular which made her life miserable was his habit of playing hard rock music, which he knew she detested, at maximum decibel levels. Besides feeling assaulted by the noise, Karen felt she had lost ownership of her own home.

In spite of her growing fear of her own son, Karen decided to try the broken record. That night, as soon as the stereo was turned up full blast, she walked into her son's room and said, "The stereo is too loud. Will you please turn it down." Her son barely glanced at her. "Get lost," he said. She moved a step closer and tried to visually imagine herself as a huge, immovable boulder. "Turn it down, please." Her son reached over and turned it up as far as it would go. Karen closed her eyes and shook her head slowly back and forth. She waited. Her son ignored her. Karen looked at the stereo. "Turn it down," she repeated. The noise was so deafening, she knew he couldn't hear her but at least he could see her lips move. She kept looking at the stereo and continued to imagine herself as a huge, immovable rock. Every so often she said, "Turn it down." She was amazed when finally, her son reached over and turned the stereo to a bearable level. "Thank you," she said and left the room. No more was said by either of them about the incident but Karen felt that somehow their relationship had moved to an improved position of increased mutual respect.

EXAMPLE D:

A mother who was having endless troubles getting her three children, (ages five, eight, and ten) to stay in bed at night had just started reading an early draft version of this book and had come upon the concept of the broken record. She decided to try it. She went through the regular bedtime routine, read them stories, gave them drinks of water, and kissed them all goodnight. Then she came out to the living room, sat down with the book in her lap to await the onslaught. Soon they started calling for her. "I have to go to the bathroom. Whitney is bugging me. Can I have a drink of water?" She ignored all that. Finally, as usual, they came trooping down the hall continuing their complaints and requests for water. She kept looking at the manuscript in her lap. "Bed," she said in what she hoped was a firm, calm voice. They kept on complaining and whining. "Bed," she said. After she said, "Bed," about five times, the kids retreated down the hall. Mother could hear them in one of the bedrooms talking it over. "What's Mom doing anyhow?" Then they came out and tried complaining again. "Bed," she said, concentrating on keeping her voice even, still looking at the book. More complaints. "Bed," she said. That did it. They went back down the hall in silence and climbed in bed. The next night the kids tried it again, but with less intensity, and after the third night, mother went through the usual bedtime routine of stories, kisses, and tucking them in with real pleasure, because after that they actually stayed in bed.

When children, of any age, *do* mind you, do not take it for granted. Let them know you appreciate it. Give them lots of immediate positive attention. In the bedtime situation above, "immediate" means the following morning. The next morning, mother does not have to mention how happy she was that they finally stayed in bed last night. It would be sabotage to talk about last night, but she can give lots of hugs and good morning smiles and even offer a super good breakfast. The rule of giving the child four positive attentions for every one negative attention you give still applies, and is absolutely necessary for changing the child's behavior over the long-term. The PHYSICAL ASSIST and the BROKEN RECORD corrections primarily stop the misbehavior and put you in control. Positive attention, given at neutral and positive times, is what will help to bring about long-term behavior change.

EXERCISE:

Keep identifying the negative behaviors as you see them this week. Do not rush in to try the new corrections until you feel pretty confident you know where to begin. Before you begin to administer any of the corrections, you need to become proficient at identifying which of the four misbehaviors is occurring, and whether or not the negative behavior is actually an attempt to solve a problem. Using the corrections before you have some idea of *when* to use them will result in confusion for both you and the child.

Continue for the rest of this week to carry out your regular discipline methods. Continue to write down your observations and experiences of the four misbehaviors and problem-solving behaviors during the coming week. Use the "Negative Behaviors" chart on the following page.

NEGATIVE BEHAVIORS:
The Four Misbehaviors
(and 3 Problem-Solving Situations)

NOT-MINDING

SELF-INDULGENT (Attention-Getting)

ROUTINE-NOT-MINDING (Will not do routine tasks)

AGGRESSIVE (Deliberately Hurting)

Negative Behaviors Requiring Problem-Solving Which Do Not Fit Above:

1. Adjust Environment   2. Solve Conflicts   3. Listen to Feelings

**DISCUSSION IDEAS: CHAPTER 5: PHYSICAL ASSIST
AND BROKEN RECORD**

1. Share this week's "Negative Behaviors" chart.

2. What percentage of the time do you expect children to obey
    you? Eighty percent? Sixty percent? One hundred percent?
    Talk together about what kinds of commands are reasonable. If
    you expect one-hundred-percent obedience, or perfection in
    any form from either the child or yourself, you will be
    disappointed in both yourself and the child. Do you expect
    perfection of your own behavior as a parent or teacher? Try to
    give yourself and the children the right not to be perfect. It is
    okay to be human. Making mistakes is how everyone learns.

3. Each person in the group needs to learn how to give the basic
    physical assist and the broken record correction since they are
    sometimes necessary for carrying out other corrections.
    Hopefully, two members of the group will volunteer to act out
    a not-minding situation using the physical assist and the
    broken record. Let each person who is willing have a chance to
    play an adult role so they will have some experience when
    they go home or back to the classroom to try it out with their
    children.

4. Role-play a situation in which the "adult" gives the broken
    record correction. The best way to experience how children
    will feel and how they will react to the broken record is to be a
    "child" yourself. When it is your turn to be the "adult," feel
    free to make lots of mistakes. Making mistakes is how you
    learn.

REVIEW: Correction for *Not-Minding* Behaviors

1. **Give a choice** instead of a command if at all possible. If the child refuses to act on either choice, you must make the choice for him.

2. If you cannot give a choice, **describe** what needs to be done in a **positive** way.

3. **The fewer words the better.** One word is often the best of all.

4. Give **lead time** if at all possible.

5. Be **reasonable** in the type and number of commands you give.

6. Be sure you can **follow through** with the correction. Otherwise, do not give the choice or command.

7. **Do not respond to self-indulgent behavior.** Do not get emotionally hooked by responding to arguments or accusations.

8. **Avoid turning this into a personal power struggle.** Give as little emotional attention as possible. Especially **avoid eye contact** with the child.

PHYSICAL ASSIST

1. State the choice or command only *once.*

2. If the child does not mind the first time, *physically lead him or her through the task.* Do not use more force than necessary.

BROKEN RECORD

1. *Tell the child what you want to have happen.* Give the command as many times as necessary in a calm, firm voice. Alternate commands with silence.

2. *Use as few words as possible.* One word is often best of all.

REMEMBER NOT TO SELF-SABOTAGE

6 The Correction for Self-Indulgent Behavior

Ignoring and the Either-Or Choice

Self-indulgent behavior is guaranteed to irritate even the most long-suffering teacher or parent. You can recognize self-indulgent behavior when children whine, argue, throw themselves on the floor and scream, accuse the adult of not loving them, threaten not to love the adult, clam up when they are spoken to, interrupt, pout, criticize ("Stop singing, that hurts my ears!") bicker with other kids, cry even when there seems to be no real reason for it, tattle, constantly demand that adults do things for them, and on and on. More than any of the other misbehaviors, the goal of self-indulgent behavior is to control the situation by being the center of your attention.

There are two parts of the correction for self-indulgent behavior. The first part of the correction, given when the child is just being irritating, is to IGNORE THE BEHAVIOR. The second part of the correction is to be used when the child is not only being irritating, but also infringing on your rights. It involves setting up a situation in which you can again ignore the behavior by giving the child an EITHER-OR CHOICE. When self-indulgent behavior is ignored, there is no reason for the child to continue the behavior. Attention is what the child is trying to get from you. Behavior you pay attention to will continue, especially self-indulgent behavior.

Behavior which is ignored will drop away, if you remember not to sabotage yourself.

Ignoring is not an easy correction to use. It may seem like a passive, even cowardly, response, especially to all you A type parents and teachers. But ignoring is not a passive correction. It is one of the most difficult of the corrections to administer effectively because it requires that you give the child no attention at all. This means no eye contact, no facial response, in fact, no body language response at all, and especially *no talking*. Remembering to do all this at a time when you probably feel like giving the child a whack on the bottom is not an easy thing to do. Ignoring means to treat children as though they are invisible, as if they are not even in the room with you. Some adults cannot believe what a powerful correction ignoring can be until they role-play a situation in which they act out the part of a self-indulgent child. During the first role-play, when they are paid attention to by much scolding or cajoling and pleading from the "adult" these "children" find they have a wonderful time screaming and yelling and fighting. They break out into big smiles or gales of laughter to experience how much fun it is to get an adult's emotional attention focused totally on them. During the next role-play, in which they have a chance to experience what it feels like to have the same behavior ignored, they scream and cry and complain while no one pays any attention to them. Gradually, as the other adults in the room continue to ignore the self-indulgent behavior, sometimes by taking refuge in the bathroom, the adults playing the part of the self-indulgent child feel their energy draining away, and the light of understanding dawns. As one mother put it, "I felt like a punctured balloon."

Ignoring self-indulgent behavior in a public place is one of the hardest of all corrections to pull off successfully because the adult usually is keenly aware of all those strangers eyeing the situation disapprovingly, waiting for the adult to *do something about that child.* As you can imagine, teachers have difficulty with this one.

Hard as it is, you must resist the temptation to treat the child as you think other people expect you to. Stick to your own program.

EXAMPLE A:

A parent goes to the grocery store with her four-year-old daughter. The child picks up a candy bar. Mother says, "No, Melina. You can't have any more candy today." Melina protests loudly. Mother says, "No, Melina. I mean it!" Melina promptly flings herself on the floor, screaming and kicking. Mother is embarrassed. She pulls Melina to her feet. Mother is angry but she tries to keep the peace, "Oh, all right. Just this once. But no more." Melina immediately quits crying and smiles happily. She has gotten the candy bar she wanted, plus Mother's undivided attention. Melina is in control of the situation, not Mother.

To use the ignoring correction, Mother needs to say, "No, Melina. You can't have any more candy today." Then go on her way down the aisle and say no more about it. When Melina whines, yells, and throws herself on the floor in a fit, Mother should pay no attention to her and continue on down the aisle with the shopping cart. You have probably heard stories of children holding their breath until they pass out during a tantrum. Rest assured that the instant a person passes out, the body will again resume the process of breathing. Breathing is controlled by the autonomic nervous system and it will not stop just because your child holds her breath. Have you ever heard of a single child, or adult for that matter, who killed himself by holding his breath? If you have any doubts, set your mind at ease by consulting your pediatrician.

If the incident happens right beside the check stand where Mother cannot move away from Melina, she will have to grit her teeth and ignore, in spite of the the fact that ten people behind her in line are looking at her disapprovingly.

EXAMPLE B:

Another example of ignoring, this time in the classroom, was told by a resource room teacher. The teacher had a third grade student named Karrie assigned to her room. Karrie came into the room looking sullen and angry. The teacher ignored Karrie's cross looks and did everything she could think of to help the child feel she was welcome and that she belonged. Finally the teacher put a math work sheet in front of her new student and explained it to her. Karrie sat back in her seat, folded her arms across her chest and said, "I'm not going to do it!"

The teacher, who has a very expressive face, arched an eyebrow and stopped to think for a moment. Which category of misbehavior was this? Should she treat this as a not-minding behavior, a routine-not-minding behavior, or a self-indulgent behavior? She decided to treat the situation as self-indulgent behavior by ignoring it. She reminded herself that she was the latest of a million-year-old-line of teachers. She put on her best nothing-can-be-done-to-change-the-way-things-are-look and ignored the refusal by saying matter-of-factly, "We do three of these papers every day." Then she moved away to help the next child. She told us she was prepared to come back later and be a BROKEN RECORD if the first approach did not work. A little later she glanced over at Karrie who had begun working on her math sheet. No more was said about the incident and needless to say, the teacher gave her new student plenty of positive attention for working on her math assignment. This teacher laughed as she reenacted the scene for us. "I am so tough. I demand they do their very best, and they all seem to love me anyway. I think it's because now I know how to keep each of their emotional needs staircases strong."

If you are at home when the self-indulgent behavior occurs, and you cannot stand to ignore the commotion a minute longer, leave the room. Go play the piano to drown out the noise, or go outside to pull a few weeds. If your child follows you, you can always go into the bathroom and lock the door. Your child may pound on the bathroom door or try to force the door knob. Continue to ignore it. If the child bangs on the door with something sharp and therefore is actually damaging the door, then you will have to give an either-or choice. But usually that isn't necessary. Turn on the water, take a shower, pretend not to hear the ruckus.

EXAMPLE C:

A common self-indulgent behavior the classroom teacher must contend with is the unknown child who starts belching just when the class has settled down to a quiet study time. Most children, of whatever age, will first quickly glance at the teacher to check out her response, before they decide whether to join in the belching or the laughter. To carry out this correction, the teacher ignores. But if the ignoring does not work and the belching and laughter begins to escalate, she can glance up briefly, catching some of the other children's eyes and convey a look of, "How childish. This kind of behavior is not worth noticing," and go back to her own work again. Hopefully, the teacher will not sabotage herself by giving the belching child the satisfaction of seeing that this is really bugging the teacher. If this does not work, the teacher can always fall back on the either-or choice, which we will discuss later (if she has by this time figured out *who* is doing the belching.)

EXAMPLE D:

Another common example of self-indulgent behavior is the child who yells or whines or uses some other inappropriate tone of voice with parents or teachers. Say *only once* to the child, "I don't talk to people who yell at me," (or whine or boss or whatever voice the child is using with you.) After you have stated your position, then ignore. After your one-time explanation, *do not respond until the child uses a normal, acceptable tone of voice.*

One first grade teacher said she had a boy in her class who argued about everything. Since he also happened to be a good reader, she decided to make up some identical slips of paper, all of which said, "I am not going to argue with you." Whenever he started arguing with her, she gave him one of the slips and turned away from him. After a few times of this, she had only to make a move towards her desk to get one of the slips of paper and he stopped arguing.

A mother had a three-year-old boy, Kit, who constantly whined and complained. The mother decided to ignore her son whenever he whined. The first day he whined for three whole hours. The mother was nearly at the end of her rope. At one point, Kit demanded, "Do you mean you're just going to stand there and ignore me?" The mother said, "Yes." From that day on the whining stopped. It has not resumed.

At first, when you try ignoring self-indulgent behaviors, children will often *increase* their misbehaviors. They will not believe you are really going to ignore them. After all, you have always before (or nearly always) given in and given them what they wanted, your undivided, intensely emotional attention. Do not get discouraged. The increase in misbehaviors is only temporary while they check out your new response. You will be doing them a favor by being firm and not giving in. If you let children whine and scold for two hours and then finally give in, they will have learned that if they whine and scold for two hours next time they want something, they will get what they want. The self-indulgent behavior will have become even more firmly entrenched. Ignoring can be an agonizing correction to carry out, but hang in there. If you ignore every time the self-indulgent behavior happens, you will have to go through a big scene only once or twice.

EXAMPLE E:

Another example of a self-indulgent behavior is the child who constantly interrupts and monopolizes adult conversation. Will was an eight-year-old boy who continually interrupted whenever his aunts and uncles got together. Will was a bright and outgoing boy who was unfortunately becoming the most disliked person in the family. The adults tried to ignore his efforts to control the conversation but would eventually give in and pay attention to him, either negatively, "Will you please stop interrupting," or positively, "Well, what is it you want to say?" Since they were mostly C type adults, they tried being polite to him even though they often felt like throwing him out the door.

Will's counselor tried to change Will's behavior by suggesting to the family that they use a combination of ignoring Will (correction) whenever he interrupted and then immediately attend to him with smiles and warm eye contact when he was quietly listening to someone else (4-1 positive social reinforcement.) It helped. From then on Will was much more likely to listen and take his turn talking. One of his aunts commented, "Have you noticed that Will is not so bratty lately? He must be growing out of it."

Notice that the family used more than just the correction of ignoring: They also gave Will many kinds of positive nonverbal attentions for the behaviors they liked. *If they had only ignored him and not given him lots of attention at neutral and positive times, Will's behavior would have gotten worse, not better.* This is also an effective technique for using with a child who constantly tries to dominate the conversation in a classroom situation.

FIGHTING AND BICKERING AS
SELF-INDULGENT BEHAVIORS

We have already discussed how to deal with fighting when you suspect it is primarily a problem-solving behavior. Now consider what to do if you suspect the kids are bickering and fighting mostly just to get your sympathy and attention. Strange as it may at first appear, children often fight and argue to gain the sympathy and attention of their parents and teachers. Since the basic correction for self-indulgent behavior is to ignore it, adults often recoil in horror from the suggestion to ignore self-indulgent fighting. "Won't the big child hurt the little one?" If you do not dare leave two children alone, because the stronger one will seriously hurt the weaker one, then the fighting is not self-indulgent. It is aggressive. We will deal with the correction for aggression in Chapter Eight.

Self-indulgent fighting or bickering is often started by the younger or weaker of the children. When the older or stronger child retaliates, sometimes after having tried to ignore the teasing and goading for a while, the adult will often come to the rescue of the younger child.

Take a typical brother and sister self-indulgent fight. Melanie is five and Brian is eight. Brian has brought his friend Todd home with him to play. The two boys are playing with Brian's legos in the bedroom. Melanie wants to be included in the boys' game but they do not want to play with her. This has been a problem in the past which mother has earlier tried to help them solve. Today Melanie is again feeling lonely and left out. She ignores the ideas for making things go better for herself which have been suggested during other problem-solving fight situations and decides to make the boys miserable instead. She starts to call them names: "Brian is a big dumbbell. Stupid, stupid dumbbell!" Brian and Todd try to ignore her. Finally, Melanie runs into the bedroom and kicks over their elaborate lego structure, strewing legos all over the room. This is too much for Brian. He chases her from the bedroom, yells at her and hits her from behind as she runs down the hall screaming for protection from Mother.

Melanie: "Mother! Brian is hitting me. Make him stop. I never did anything to him."

Brian: "She did too. She started it. She wrecked our legos."

Melanie: (Crying pitifully.) "They won't be nice to me. He hurt me."

Brian: "She's a brat!" (Tries to hit her again.)

Mother: (Decides that her earlier efforts at helping them problem-solve have not worked. She grabs Brian's arm.) "Brian, you stop this hitting right now! I know little sisters can be aggravating but can't you be more patient with her? After all, you're older than she is. Melanie, you tell Brian you are sorry. Brian, you tell Melanie you are sorry. Now go back and play nicely. If I hear any more fighting Todd will have to go home and you two will have to stay in your rooms until dinner time."

In the above example, even though Mother is trying to be fair to both parties, Brian feels unfairly punished. After all, he was minding his own business until Melanie started bugging him. And why should Todd have to go home? That's just what would make Melanie happy. Brian may infer from incidents like this one that Mother loves Melanie better than she loves him. Otherwise why would she always stick up for Melanie? Teachers, too, will recognize this kind of squabble. Teachers are often expected to get to the root of every child disagreement. And, like parents, they often fall into the trap of expecting themselves to have the wisdom of Solomon.

As has already been pointed out, the younger sibling, or the weaker child in the school relationship, is often the one who starts the fight, even though it is the weaker child who apparently gets the worst of it. It is safe for the younger child to start the fight if

Mother or Dad or Teacher can be counted on to intervene. In this way, the younger child not only becomes the center of the adult's attention, he or she is also protected from experiencing the natural consequences of the behavior. Even when the parent or the teacher tries to be fair by sending both children to separate rooms or opposite corners of the school yard, the older child still feels unfairly punished since, as he sees it, he was minding his own business until the other child came along and bothered him. If this happens regularly, a cycle of resentment and anger builds within the older child until he is no longer fighting for attention or immediate self-defense but really wants to hurt the younger sibling or school mate.

In the above example, Mother can extricate herself from the no-win referee position by treating Melanie's and Brian's fighting as self-indulgent behavior. She can wait until both children are in a neutral or positive situation, when they are watching television, driving in the car, or working with her in the kitchen, for example. She can then explain her new approach to their fights:

Mother: (In a friendly tone of voice.) "You know, I have been thinking about that argument you had yesterday. I never know who actually starts it. You two are big enough now to do your own problem-solving and settle your own arguments. From now on, I'll keep out of it."

Mother can also lay down some ground rules at this time. If the children have been hitting each other with objects or throwing hard things at one another, for example, she can say:

"There's just one important rule about your arguments. There can be no hitting with hard things like bats or rocks. If you use hard things for hitting I will have to give that person a time-out." (Time-out will be explained in Chapter Eight.)

The basic idea you need to convey is that it is the responsibility of the children to solve their problems with one another. You can, of course, help problem-solve, if they ask for your help, but do not offer unless they both want you to help. If you believe that these arguments are self-indulgent on the part of at least one of the children, stay out of it. The main idea is to covey the message that this is *their* problem, not yours. If asked, the adult is always available to help find solutions, but basically things are up to them.

Next time they fight, one or the other, probably the youngest, will come running to Mother. Mother can then carry out the correction of ignoring by saying, "I'm sure you two can talk this over and figure out a solution," and next proceed to emotionally withdraw from their arguments, and, if possible, to also withdraw physically. If Mother is alone with them in the house, she can withdraw to the bathroom and lock the door. It is a good idea to leave some magazines in the bathroom for something to do during such incidents. The kids may stand outside the door screaming and crying and pounding on the door, but she should continue to ignore them. This kind of behavior is closely related to a tantrum and should be treated as such. If one child hits another with a hard object, the fight has become aggressive and you can intervene with a time-out. (We'll discuss the time-out correction for aggressive behavior in Chapter Eight.)

Do not assume, just because the youngest one cries "Brian hit me!" that this is an aggressive situation. As we have seen, Melanie may very well have done something to provoke the hitting. Brian's hitting may be his attempt to find a solution to the problem of his sister's self-indulgent behavior. Hitting may stop Melanie's self-indulgent behavior faster than any problem-solving a parent or teacher can do. If, after you stay out of the fights for several weeks and Brian seems to be escalating the fighting with his sister, then it is time to assume his behavior is aggressive and stop using the ignoring correction. If the older child is so angry at the younger child that he is seeking to hurt her out of a need for revenge, it is time to protect the younger child. It is also time to try to figure out what is causing so much anger in the older child.

In the school setting, teachers do not have the option of treating hitting as a self-indulgent behavior. *Physical fighting cannot be ignored at school because there are too many children to monitor.* In the interests of creating a safe environment for all kids, no type of physical fighting can be ignored. All hitting must be treated as either a problem-solving or an aggressive behavior. Bickering between children at school, however, is a self-indulgent behavior and can be dealt with as such.

GIVING THE EITHER-OR CHOICE

Now the second part of this correction. Every parent and teacher knows it is not always possible to ignore. Sometimes the child will engage in self-indulgent behavior in a way which interferes with your or with other people's rights. It is impossible in a classroom with twenty six other children to let one child make a lot of noise and disrupt the entire classroom atmosphere. If you are a parent at home alone with your child, you can leave the room, go to the bathroom or outside. But you cannot very well leave a classroom of twenty six children unattended. In the home environment, if the children jump on your furniture, for example, or argue and yell when you are trying to talk on the phone or when you have visitors in the house, or when you and your spouse are trying to watch a favorite television program, you need to stick up for your own rights by giving an EITHER-OR CHOICE. In these situations you use the second step of the ignoring correction because *when children infringe on your rights, you can no longer ignore the behavior.*

EXAMPLE A:

If Melina, the child in the earlier grocery store situation, escalates her self-indulgent behavior and infringes on your rights or the rights of others, by pulling groceries off the shelves or banging the cart into you or other people, one possible either-or choice could be, "You can either stop all this fussing or we will have to go home." If Melina continues, say, "I see you choose to go home." If she refuses to go, use the physical assist. Leave your groceries where they are, pick Melina up, carry her out to the car and drive home. Do not lecture and scold her about the inconvenience this has caused you. Do not let her argue you out of it. Let your nonverbal message be that you are in this for the long haul. Be a force of nature with the whole power of the patient ocean behind you. This may be aggravating for you, but it is how she will learn. Try not to take it as a personal insult. Melina is not winning and you are not losing, nor is it the other way around. You are teaching her a new way to behave. Teaching behaviors takes time and patience. Most children like to go to the store. Going home early means Melina has missed the treat you usually buy her. Please do not sabotage yourself by mentioning that to her. Children are smart. Melina will know and remember.

EXAMPLE B:

A family goes to a pizza parlor for dinner. Eleven-year-old Sharon complains that she does not like pizza, all they ever do is go to pizza or hamburger places, the other kids get to go for Chinese food, this food is no good, and this is a dumb family. Mom and Dad try to ignore all this but finally come to the conclusion that Sharon is infringing on their rights. After all, they are paying hard earned money for this meal and they have a right to eat it in peace. Instead of trying to scold or reason with her or persuade her that her accusations are not true (which gives her enormous amounts of attention and is likely to increase her self-indulgent behavior) they can set up a situation in which they are free to ignore her again. If it is a small town and they can see the car from their booth, they can say, "You can stay here and quit complaining or you can go out to the car with your pizza and stay there until you are ready to come back without complaining." Or, if the car would not be a safe place for her to be, Mom and Dad can say, "You can quit complaining or we will move to a different booth. You can join us when you decide to quit complaining." Then when Sharon continues to complain, Mom and Dad and the rest of the family can pick up and move to a different booth to finish their meal. If Sharon decides to join her family and does not complain any more, they should accept her back into the group *without comment* in a friendly way, as though nothing had happened. After she returns to the group, Sharon immediately needs lots of positive attentions from her parents when they notice neutral or positive behaviors. If Sharon starts complaining again, they can point to the other booth and say, "I see you choose to finish your meal alone." After that, assume she has made her choice and do not let her return to the new table.

Keep in mind that either-or choices are not intended to be punitive. *You are simply setting up a situation in which you are free to ignore the self-indulgent behavior.* The fact of the matter is that this time, your dinner out will probably not be much fun. You might have to pretend to be having a good time with the other members of the family. Only by convincing Sharon that she cannot control the rest of the family with her self-indulgent behavior will you teach her not to act this way. You are involved in a teaching process. Teaching new behaviors takes time. If you can carry out this correction consistently, and remember not to sabotage yourself, Sharon's behavior will change. The day will come when you can have fun when you go out to dinner together. But you must be willing to invest time and energy in the effort to change her self-indulgent behavior.

The either-or choice is different from the choice as part of a command. In the last chapter, when we talked about the correction for not-minding, the goal of giving a choice as part of a command was to get children to do what they are told to do. The goal of the either-or choice is to set up a situation in which you can ignore the child's self-indulgent behavior. *The main requirement for the either-or choice correction is for the child to go somewhere else so you can continue to ignore the self-indulgent behavior.* "You can either choose to ...(stop the self-indulgent behavior) or ..."You can go... (be self-indulgent somewhere else.)"

EXAMPLE C:

Jana and Paul, who were brother and sister, somehow got into an argument during a card game which soon escalated to hitting and yelling. Their father was satisfied that he had earlier given them plenty of practice in problem-solving, so he decided to give them an either-or choice. "You two can either stop fighting or you can go outside and settle things out there." They ignored him and continued to yell and throw cards at each other. Dad said, "No. I said the argument must be settled outside." He took their arms firmly and walked them over through the door, and shut it behind them. (Notice the physical assist.) Jana yelled through the door at him that it wasn't her fault, that she certainly didn't start the fight. Paul yelled that it was too her fault. Dad ignored the yelling and went back to reading his newspaper. He was prepared to put Jana and Paul back outside if they came in still arguing and complaining. Eventually, things quieted down outside. Soon Jana and Paul came in the door and went back to the card game. Dad said nothing but he gave them some positive attention by giving them a warm smile and friendly eye contact as if to say, "I knew you two could handle it yourselves."

EXAMPLE D:

As a substitute teacher, I was confronted with a boy and a girl in a seventh grade classroom who were suddenly involved in a wrestling match, right in the middle of a quiet study period. They pushed and shoved, each of them loudly complaining that the comb belonged to them. I used my best matter-of-fact Mother-Nature voice, "You two can either stay here and take your seats, or you can go out in the hall to decide who owns the comb." The boy immediately blushed a fiery red and handed the comb back to the girl. He sat back down in his seat. "I guess it's hers," he said.

EXAMPLE E:

The student who constantly disrupts by talking, teasing, scraping his chair and desk across the floor, and throwing wads of paper at his neighbors is infringing on the rights of other students in the classroom in a way that cannot be ignored. This child is especially difficult to deal with in the elementary classroom in which the teacher has organized the desks in clusters so that the students are seated very close together. Ignoring on the teacher's part often will not help because the attention this child is getting is coming mostly from fellow students who either are tempted to join in the fun, or who scold and blame the misbehaving student. This situation calls for a creative either-or choice. Remember, the choice should be as nonpunitive as possible. You only need to set up a situation where the self-indulgent behavior can be ignored. Following are some either-or ideas for this situation which have been used successfully by teachers. The situations given in this section take place in a school setting, but the quiet corner idea works equally well in the home.

Ask the custodian for one or two extra desks. In the farthest corner of the room, set up a "quiet corner." When children disrupt, they have the either-or choice of being quiet where they are or taking their work to finish in the quiet corner. When the work is finished, they may return to their own seats and try again. Quiet corners are not punitive places. The Lewiston, Idaho Head Start class calls their quiet corner, "Henry's Chair." Henry is a rascally little critter in the "Little Critter" series by Mercer Mayer. Each year, the children are told the story of Henry, who is a loveable soul, but who keeps getting into trouble. Whenever a child begins to infringe on other people's rights, the teacher says, "You had better use Henry's chair for awhile." Children often go sit in the chair without anyone even telling them. "I think I better go sit in Henry's chair for awhile." One little boy once pulled a chair next to Henry's chair and sat there. When the teacher asked what he was doing, he said, "I'm keeping Henry company." At Fanno Creek Children's Center in Portland, Oregon they used a rocking chair. Another preschool classroom used bookcases to make a fenced off area with big pillows and books available.

If children continue to disrupt to the extent they cannot be ignored in the quiet corner, they can be given the either-or choice of staying where they are and working quietly, or going to another room and finishing the work there. If you use another room, try to find a place other than the principal's office or the hallway. The principal's office and the hallway are too interesting; there are too many people coming and going there who will either sabotage you by scolding or reminding or by expressing interest in why the child is there. An upper grade classroom makes a good quiet corner backup. The older children need to be forewarned by their teacher that occasionally a younger child will come in to use a quiet corner. They should be asked not to give the younger child any attention, just pretend he or she is not even there. As soon as the child's work is finished, he or she is free to return to the original classroom.

Whenever possible, move the child to a higher grade level. This will avoid the pitfall of making the choice seem punitive. There is no doubt that sending a child to study with the younger kids would be perceived by most children as a demeaning and punitive choice. If the child is already in the highest grade level in the school, look for a neutral zone. A classroom on his own grade level sometimes works, or maybe the health room area would do. Look around your school and see what might be suitable.

Everyone involved must remember not to sabotage. You want to convey the message that this either-or choice is a part of the natural order of things. This is not a personal, punitive move on your part. It is the way things are. Nothing can be done about it. The whole force of society is behind you. You are the latest in a million-year line of parents and teachers. The minute the child returns to his or her place, give immediate warm eye contact. Act as though nothing has happened. Give recognition for the finished work. Welcome the child back into the group with no mention of the self- indulgent behavior which caused him or her to leave in the first place.

Do not remove children to an isolated spot for longer than it takes to finish their immediate assignment. Immediately give them a chance to come back into the group and try again. Do not isolate them from their classmates for days, weeks, or months at a time. Long-term isolation, which places disruptive children off to one corner of the room all by themselves, tears down their staircase of emotional needs. Isolated children lose their sense of belonging to the group. They no longer believe they are respected and liked by you and their classmates. Over the long-term, the behavior of the isolated child will deteriorate, not improve.

When you use the either-or choice for a self-indulgent situation in which the child is infringing on someone else's rights, remember that the basic idea is to set up a situation where the child can choose to *leave your presence*. In this way, you can again ignore the child's behavior. If children are not infringing on anyone else's rights, they are even free to scream and yell. At home, children are free to scream if they go into their bedroom, or outside. This is not an infringement on other people's rights (as it would be if children make the same kind of noise at the dinner table) and so you are free to ignore them once more. Let your whole attitude convey the idea that people, of any age, have a perfect right to be angry and frustrated. It is okay with you if they let out their feelings by yelling and screaming. But, on the other hand, you have the right, as a parent, a teacher, and as a human being, to expect that children will respect your need for quiet during a special television show, or when you are visiting with a friend, or when you are explaining a lesson in the classroom.

EXAMPLE F:

An example of this lack of respect for others rights is when the child whines, complains, and generally spoils the mealtime for the rest of the family. Like the situation in the restaurant, this kind of behavior is an infringement on other people's rights. You have the right to a peaceful meal time. Use the either-or command, *"You can choose to be quiet or you can leave the table,"* (go to your room, outside, or whatever.) If the child continues to complain, say, "I see you choose to leave the table." If the child refuses to go, use the physical assist. Take the child's arm and walk him or her off to wherever the choice indicated. Concentrate on the idea that you are merely setting up a situation where you can again ignore the behavior. *If the child shouts and yells in his or her room, pretend you cannot hear it.* Remember, this is not a punishment, this is a teaching method. Ignore as many self-indulgent behaviors as you can when the behaviors are merely irritating. Only when the behaviors pass the boundary of interfering with your rights should you step in with the either-or choice.

If children begin to break things in their room, you can treat this new misbehavior as either routine-not-minding or aggressive, depending on how extreme it is. We will talk about these corrections in the next two chapters.

On rare occasions there might be an instance when children get so carried away with self-indulgent behavior that they could be a danger to themselves. For example, if Julie starts flinging herself blindly around on a subway platform, you will have to take her firmly by the hand, or in some way physically restrain her, so she does not accidentally fall onto the tracks. Whenever the child is in physical danger, of course she must be physically protected.

You probably noticed in the examples given earlier that when the either-or choice was given, not-minding behavior often occurred along with the self-indulgent behavior; the child refused to take either choice. As in the examples above, you may have to physically assist the child to leave the table, or use the broken record until he or she leaves the room. This is often the case, so be alert. *Switch from the ignore correction to the not-minding correction when the child disobeys.*

As with all corrections, try to carry out this one as though you were the patient wind, or any other force of nature. Try not to get emotionally involved in the child's self-indulgence. Try to take the attitude of the young mother who had just told her three-year-boy it was time to go home. He wanted to stay at Grandma's house a little longer, but Mother said, "No. We have to go now." He shouted at her, "I hate you!" His mother looked down at him calmly and said, "Well. I guess I can live with that," and she continued to walk towards the door. He followed along behind her pouting and scolding which she ignored. Both Mother and Grandma continued to cheerfully visit with one another as they walked down the front steps. By the time they reached the car, the boy was smiling and waving goodbye at his grandmother. I have never forgotten that mother's words, and her quiet shrug, "Well. I guess I can live with that." Yes, we *can* live with that because the truth is that our children will not hate us if we expect reasonable rules to be obeyed. On the contrary, they will love us all the more because we gave them the security of firm and reasonable guidelines.

EXERCISE:

As in previous weeks, continue to use the "Negative Behaviors" chart to write briefly about the four misbehaviors and the problem-solving behaviors as you observe them. You will find a new chart on the following page. If you attempt to carry out any of the corrections, write about these, too. Also, continue to watch for those self-sabotages.

NEGATIVE BEHAVIORS:
The Four Misbehaviors
(and 3 Problem-Solving Situations)

NOT-MINDING

SELF-INDULGENT (Attention-Getting)

ROUTINE-NOT-MINDING (Will not do routine tasks)

AGGRESSIVE (Deliberately Hurting)

Negative Behaviors Requiring Problem-Solving Which Do Not Fit Above:

1. Adjust Environment   **2. Solve Conflicts**   **3. Listen to Feelings**

DISCUSSION IDEAS: CHAPTER 6: IGNORING AND THE EITHER-OR CHOICE

1. Share the past week's "Negative Behaviors" chart. Which of these behaviors bothers you the most when you see it in your children?

2. Did you sabotage yourself in any way this week?

3. Did anyone try the physical assist or broken record correction this week? Were you able to carry it through without sabotaging yourself? How did it feel to be in this Mother-Nature, nothing-can-be-done- about-it role? If any person has a hard time being this firm with a child, listen to him or her talk about why being firm is so difficult to do. Go easy on giving your opinions or advice. The rest of the group can help by just listening so that the other person can "think out loud" about it.

4. Each individual take five minutes to fill out the chart on the following page. Share your lists with one another. Do you have similar tolerance levels for self-indulgent behaviors, or are you quite far apart as to the irritating behaviors you can endure without resorting to the either-or choice?

5. Check back with the guidelines for conducting these weekly discussions which are given at the beginning of the book. Is your group having difficulty with any of the guidelines?

AN EXERCISE TO HELP YOU FIGURE OUT WHEN TO IGNORE AND WHEN TO USE THE EITHER-OR CHOICE:

IGNORE	EITHER-OR CHOICE
Examples of self-indulgent behaviors which strongly irritate you:	Examples of self-indulgent behaviors which not only irritate you, but are infringing on your or someone else's rights:

REVIEW: Correction for *Self-Indulgent* behavior

1. *Ignore* if the behavior is merely irritating. Remember to ignore both verbally and nonverbally.

or

2. If the behavior is infringing on your rights, give the ***either-or choice:***

    "You can either choose to..." *(stop the self-indulgent behavior)* or

    "You can go..." *(be self-indulgent somewhere else.)*

3. You may have to use the *broken record or physical assist* if the child switches to a not-minding behavior. Remember to keep ignoring the child's self-indulgent behavior as you carry out the broken record or physical assist correction.

4. As soon as the child makes the choice to stop the self-indulgent behavior, be pleasant and cheerful with him. *Do not mention it again.*

REMEMBER NOT TO SELF-SABOTAGE

7 The Correction for Routine-Not-Minding Behavior

Making choices and living with the consequences

Children who avoid or refuse to do the daily chores of their lives are engaging in routine-not-minding behavior. Not finishing school work, not cleaning their room, continually leaving the bicycle out in the rain, leaving their snack mess in the kitchen, not following basic playground rules, not being responsible for feeding the pet, not taking out the garbage, "sneaky" behaviors like getting into off-limit items and stealing are common examples. The child knows the behaviors that are expected, knows certain behaviors are to be done on a regular basis, knows he or she will encounter strong negative attention from adults if the jobs do not get done, yet does not follow the rules or do the tasks until pushed. This kind of misbehavior causes parents and teachers to shake their heads and wonder, "Why on earth is that kid so irresponsible?"

By not doing the ordinary tasks of life, the child gets incredible amounts of negative attention from caring adults. The child's routine-not-minding behaviors make him or her the focus of vast numbers of social interactions, both verbal and nonverbal. The adults try to gain control of the situation by reminding, scolding, reasoning, threatening, and punishing. The child tries to gain control of the situation by not doing what the adults want done. In order to keep his or her sense of independence and integrity intact, the child refuses to be "bossed around." The adults, in turn, give the child a constant barrage of negative attention. Children caught in this dilemma believe that if they finally give in and do what the adults want, they will lose their inner integrity and independence. These children begin to feel justified about their irresponsible behavior. Some children even come to believe it is the fault of the adults and blame them for all the problems. They sometimes convince themselves that if adults would just leave them alone, things would turn out okay. The irresponsible child is like a glacier adults have to push through life. The adults are exhausted and angered by their efforts. The child is sullen, uncooperative, and angry at the adults. It is a downward spiral from which the child cannot extricate himself without help from you.

We have already talked about offering a choice as part of giving a command, and giving an either-or choice as part of the correction for self-indulgent behavior. For the logical consequence correction, however, choices become not just a part of the correction, but its central core.

THE CORRECTION FOR ROUTINE-NOT-MINDING BEHAVIOR IS TO SET UP A SITUATION WHICH GIVES THE CHILD AN OPPORTUNITY TO EXPERIENCE THE NATURAL OR LOGICAL CONSEQUENCES OF HIS OR HER CHOICES.

Practice in making choices and living with the consequence of choices is the foundation of developing responsible behavior patterns. Once children learn what "yes" and "no" mean, what "this one" and "that one" mean, they have begun the process of decision making. Teaching children responsible decision making is a long term effort. Choice by choice, consequence by consequence, like water dripping on a stone, like building a self-esteem staircase brick by brick, children learn responsibility for their own behaviors. In the process, children are empowered and strengthened from the real life experience of living with the consequences of their choices.

One morning our preschool class got a new student. Jeanette was a beautiful, delicate looking three-year-old. Every morning she would break into the most heart rending wailing when her mother left her to go to work. The mother was guilt ridden about leaving her daughter. Each morning she apologized to the child and to the teachers for having to go to work. The entire staff tried to reassure the mother there was nothing to feel guilty about and that the best approach was to be matter-of-fact and cheerful as she went out the door. The mother tried her best, but each morning we had to practically push this teary-eyed mother out the door, leaving her little girl wailing behind her. Despite our attempts to comfort and reassure her each morning, Jeanette would continue to sob pitifully for thirty to forty minutes. After that she settled in to being a perfectly happy, self-assured child.

After observing all of this and satisfying herself that the little girl was more upset by her mother's expectations than at actually being left behind, the head teacher suggested, "Tell Jeanette she can choose to sit in the rocking chair to cry or she can choose to work at the paint easel. If she keeps crying say, 'I see you choose to cry.' Be very friendly, pick her up, sit her in the rocking chair, put a cuddly bear in her arms and say, 'Tell me when you are ready to choose something else to do.' Then go off and pay no more attention to her."

Desperate, we decided to try the new idea. The first day Jeanette cried for her full thirty minutes or so, rocking in the chair, hugging the bear and watching the activities at the nearby water table and paint easels. When she finally stopped crying and left her rocking chair for the water play table one of the adults immediately smiled at her and said, in a friendly and interested tone of voice, "I see you choose to work at the water table now." No more was said to her about it.

The second day, Jeanette stayed in the rocking chair only a few minutes before she went over to the paint easel. One of the adults said as before, "I see you choose to work at the paint easel now." Again, no more was said about it.

The third day, when Jeanette started to wail as her mother disappeared out the door, a teacher asked, "Do you choose to sit in the rocking chair and cry this morning or do you choose to do something else?" Jeanette opened her mouth to cry, then stopped almost in mid wail and said, "I choose the paint easel." Jeanette never fussed again when she was left at the preschool and her relieved mother was finally able to be cheerful and matter of fact when she waved goodbye.

Notice that no one tried to argue Jeanette out of her feelings. No one tried to interfere with her body functioning by telling her to stop that crying. She was given reasonable choices and allowed to experience the consequences of each choice. Everyone involved, Jeanette, her mother, and the school staff, learned a valuable lesson. Each of us has the power to choose our own behaviors.

In learning how to use the logical consequence correction, it is important to understand the difference between "natural" and "logical" consequences. When the natural consequence occurs, life itself provides the consequence without anyone having to plan it ahead of time. For example, if a child goes out without a coat and it starts to rain, the child will get wet. If teenagers drink and drive, they are likely to have an accident, or will perhaps get arrested and lose their license. If a child does not do schoolwork, the natural outcome will be failing grades. If teenagers are sexually active without taking proper precautions, they are apt to become teenage parents, or even worse, contract AIDS. If children eat too much candy, they are likely to get a stomach ache. If you stay up to watch the late movie on television, you will be tired when you get up next morning to go to work.

Natural consequences are the basic experiences of life from which all thinking creatures have for millions and millions of years learned how to survive in the world. In all these "natural" situations, no one has to plan a real life experience for the person involved. The consequence followed naturally from the choices the person made. Natural consequences arise naturally, either out of Nature herself, or from the culture in which the person lives. The major problem with natural consequences is that they are often delayed until the consequences are extremely severe and, sometimes, even life threatening. A consequence is natural, but too severe, for example, if children are allowed to fail at schoolwork until they fall so far behind they have to repeat a grade. No parent or teacher wants a child to be dealt with in as harsh a way as the natural consequence often provides.

Logical consequences, on the other hand, are real life situations which an adult plans for ahead of time. The situation needs to be as natural as possible, yet with consequences that are not really harmful or life threatening to the child. Even though the logical consequence causes discomfort to the child, it is not as severe as the natural consequence could be. The logical consequence is also different from a natural consequence in that it always provides a way out for the child. The child can always improve the situation by making a different choice. As in the situation above with the tearful three-year-old, at any time she had the option of choosing a different behavior which would result in a different situation for her.

Logical consequences need to be perceived by the child as reasonable and fair, as part of the natural order of things. The inherent logic of the situation, the life experiences themselves, will do the teaching. If you sabotage yourself, especially by talking about the misbehavior, the consequence can easily be perceived by the child as punishment or personal revenge on your part. *If you sabotage yourself by talking about the misbehavior, children will see the consequence as a punishment personally given by you instead of a natural result of their own choices.* Remember, you have all the parents and teachers who have ever lived on this earth behind you. You are the growing tip of a branching tree of humanity whose roots reach down a million years. Your task, like our ancestors, is to teach children about the outer-reality of the world and still keep their spirits strong and independent. You have the authority of society and the generations behind you. Do not sabotage your own authority by scolding, lecturing, and otherwise personally venting your emotions at the child.

THE BASIC PREVENTION PLAN: GIVING CHILDREN DAILY OPPORTUNITIES TO MAKE, AND TO LIVE WITH, THEIR CHOICES.

1. *Give your child practice in making fun choices.*

Even a two-year-old can choose between, "Do you choose orange juice or apple juice for lunch?" or "Which of these two books do you choose for me to read to you?" As children grow older, you should increasingly provide more and more areas of life for them to exercise control. This is hard for some A adults because they often automatically assume adults should make most decisions for children. Children will often not choose what adults would choose; children are developing their own view of the world. One mother said she allowed her preschoolers to choose which of two outfits to wear for the day. It helped speed up the dressing process each morning. As they got older, they chose clothes all by themselves. "They didn't always match, but they were so proud."

2. *Never give a choice if there is no choice.*

Sometimes it is not possible to give children a choice. If that is the case, do not confuse them by giving them a choice when there really is no choice. "Do you want to go home now?" or "Let's go home now, okay?" Okay? implies that you are giving a choice between staying where you are or going home. Use the word "choose" instead of "want" or "okay?" It will help you keep the difference between choosing and wanting clear in your own mind as well as teaching children that they are actively "choosing" instead of passively "wanting."

A grandmother was changing her two-year-old grandson Nate's diapers. It was time for his nap. Grandma was chatting with a friend while she changed her grandson's diapers and casually said, "It's time for a his nap now." Nate heard this but seemed to accept the situation as he continued to smile up at his grandmother. Then Grandma said to him, "Let's go to bed for a nap now. *Okay? Okay?*" Nate immediately stiffened his body and started to scream. You can see that when she acted as though the nap was inevitable, Nate accepted it, but when she gave him a choice, (okay?) he chose not to go down for a nap.

If there is no choice, simply describe the facts of the matter. "Now it is time to go home." The sun goes up and the sun goes down. Nothing can be done about it. In the same way, "Now it is time to go home." If an adult initially offers, "Want to go to bed now?" and the child says, "No," the adult is left in the uncomfortable position of having to switch tactics, either cajoling or forcing the child into going to bed. If the adult insists on going to bed as a personal and emotional issue, "I said you are going to bed right now!" it invites rebellion and a power struggle. If instead, from the very beginning, the adult uses the inexorable, unemotional needs of nature and society as the reason for going to bed, "Now it is time to go to bed," the personal power struggle can often be avoided. No one, not even Mother and Dad, or Teacher, can argue with the natural order of things.

3. *Keep the choices limited and appropriate to the child's age.*

"Do you choose chicken noodle soup or Spaghetti O's today?" is enough choice for a three-year-old. "What do you want for lunch?" is not an appropriate choice. It is hard enough for *adults* to decide what they want for lunch. A three-year-old will not be able to choose among so many possibilities and will probably end up changing his or her mind. The three-year-old who is given too many choices will likely end up frustrated and crying at whatever you finally do serve for lunch. As a child grows older, you can expand the concept of choices, for example, it would be appropriate for a ten-year-old to help decide *when* the weekly chores should be done, or to help choose *which* of three different vacation options the family could take that year.

4. *Once the child makes the choice, even at this early preventative stage, let the child live with the consequences of the choice.*

Some pre-schoolers will, at first, apparently get a bit drunk on their new decision making powers and continually change their minds. They are just testing to see how far their power goes. For example, when you give the choice between apple and orange juice the three-year-old may choose orange juice and then abruptly push away the orange juice and say, "No. I want apple juice." It is important for you to treat this refusal as a self-indulgent behavior. Say only one time, "No. You chose orange juice," and then pay no more attention to the demands for apple juice. If the child tantrums at this point, for example, if he or she throws the orange juice on the floor, assume the choice has been made for no juice at all. Remember not to sabotage yourself by scolding as you clean up the mess. (Or, as many an A parent has told a C parent, you can give the child a rag to clean up the spills himself.)

Some C adults have trouble being firm on this one. They think, "Well, this child is only three years old, and, after all, I am an adult who shouldn't act as petty as a little kid." It is not petty to teach children they must live by their choices. If you allow them the opportunity to experience the consequences of their small choices, you will be saving them from suffering the serious and long lasting consequences they are capable of precipitating in their teen years. If you insist that children experience the short-term consequences of their behaviors now, they will gain the experience needed to avoid long-term and calamitous natural consequences in later life.

C adults are prone to let the child have "one more chance," especially if the child is properly contrite and promises, "I won't do it any more." Allowing children to evade consequences because they are cute or because they say, "I'm sorry," in a sincere tone of voice only teaches them that if they learn to be charming enough they can always do pretty much as they please. This is a sure-fire formula for raising irresponsible adults. *Allowing children to do whatever they want, as long as they apologize sweetly afterwards, teaches them to cultivate charm instead of responsible behavior.* A charming but irresponsible adult has not learned basic survival skills for living cooperatively within the human family. We have all met adults like this. No one likes living with them, because they continually blame everybody else for the consequences of their own poor choices.

EXAMPLE A:

Sometimes, unknown to you, children will make an unwise choice and then at the last minute expect you to save them. Your fourteen-year-old daughter, Elsa, may come to you at dinner time and plead, "I need to go to the library tonight to do a report for English class. It's due first thing in the morning. Will you take me to the library tonight? Please!?" Of course it is okay to help your daughter if it is no problem for you and you want to go to the library anyhow, but, if your daughter has made a habit of this kind of thing and if you have a prior engagement, or if, in any way, taking her to the library means you will wind up feeling resentful, it is better to say no. It is fine to show sympathy for her plight, just as you would do with any other friend, but do not place yourself in the position of suffering the consequences of her shortsighted choices. You can say, "Gosh, I'm sorry, but I have choir practice tonight," (if that is the case) or "I am just too tired tonight. I'd planned to clean up this kitchen and then go straight to bed." If your daughter chose to watch television or go visit her friends earlier in the week rather than do her schoolwork, she needs to experience the consequences of her choices. If she continues to wail and plead, treat it as a self-indulgent behavior and ignore it.

The only exception to allowing children to live with the consequences of their own behavior is if their choices have produced a situation which is in some way life threatening, or at least has the potential for damaging their future. If the consequences of the choice are especially severe and long lasting, of course you should not say, "Well, I feel really badly about it but you made your own bed and now you will have to lie in it." An example of this is if Elsa got pregnant. If that happens, like any loving parent you need to step in and move heaven and earth to help Elsa do what needs to be done. We all make mistakes. If children make a really big one, they deserve all the help they can get from caring adults.

Perhaps the hardest part of letting a child live with his or her choices is remembering not to scold, lecture, remind, or in any way let the tone of your voice say, "I told you so." It is absolutely crucial for the success of teaching children to "own" the consequences of their choices, that *they perceive the logical consequence as a fact of life, as a part of the natural order of things.* If they see the consequence as a punishment which you are personally dishing out to them to get even with them, it will set up a destructive power struggle between the children and you. If you want children to become independent, responsible persons, you need to learn to side-step the power struggle and, as someone put it, "Take your sails out of their wind." Hence the advice which, at the risk of boring you, is repeated: *Do not mention it again.*

THE BASIC CORRECTION OF SETTING UP A LOGICAL CONSEQUENCE EXPERIENCE FOR THE CHILD:

The choices and consequences described above form a basic prevention plan for keeping a child from ever developing extreme irresponsible behaviors in the first place. But what if the child has already established a specific routine-not-minding behavior? If the basic prevention plan is not enough to change an old behavior pattern, here are some guidelines showing you how to use logical consequences as a correction:

1. *Decide which routine not-minding-behavior you want to change.*

You cannot change everything at once. Choose the one routine-not-minding misbehavior which troubles you the most. It may be that the child is never ready for school on time, or perhaps never finishes schoolwork on time even though the school has done testing and found him or her to be capable of doing the work, or maybe the child will not give the dog food and water on a regular basis. Focus on only one routine-not-minding behavior at a time.

2. *Look at the situation you want to change. Sit down with another adult, if possible, and make a plan.*

Planning a logical consequence requires flexibility, creativity, and, sometimes, a sense of humor. The possibilities for designing logical consequence plans are endless and depend somewhat on your own personality, the child's personality, and whatever seems comfortable to you. It is important to brainstorm ahead of time with your spouse, another teacher, or a friend to decide on what your specific plan will be. If you are not sure what you are going to do ahead of time, the consequence may turn out to be more punishing than logical. Sometimes, of course, the consequence may occur to you on the spur of the moment and you will not be able to resist "just doing it."

One mother expected her son to do a few morning chores before he left for school, among which was to set the table for breakfast. One morning he sat down as usual, not having set the table, and started reading a book. His mother took the pancakes off the griddle, saw there were no plates on the table, and on impulse, without saying a word to him she flipped the pancakes onto the bare table. Then she went back to the stove and started the next batch of pancakes at the same time as she continued to talk to her husband about something else. The boy sat staring at the pancakes for a second, then got up, and went to the cupboard for the plates. Next day, he put dishes on the table without being asked. His mother resisted the temptation to laugh although she said it was all she could do to keep a straight face. This kind of spur-of-the moment consequence is fine, especially if you are the kind of person who feels comfortable just winging it, but most situations require some preplanning.

Sometimes you will need support from another person for the plan to work. For example, if you feel a particular misbehavior is important enough, you can ask a friend to help backup your plan. Take, for example, the case of three-year-old Mimi, who tantrumed nearly every time her father took her to the grocery store. The father finally asked a friend to help out. The next time he took his daughter to the grocery store and she began her tantrum, he left his groceries in the aisle, picked Mimi up, carried her to the pay phone and called his friend, who was waiting by the telephone at her nearby home. "Will you come get Mimi? She doesn't know how to act here at the store." The friend promptly came to get the child and matter-of-factly took her home, being careful not to give her too much attention. The father finished his shopping. When the father got home, he pretended he had forgotten all about the incident, but he brought no treat home for his daughter. (She usually got a treat when she went to the store with her father.) Both the father and his friend were careful not to self-sabotage by laughing or talking about it in front of Mimi. *All logical consequences must be carried out as though they are nothing special, as though they are natural events like eating and sleeping,* and certainly not a cause for humor. If the father and his friend continue to be successful in not sabotaging themselves, Mimi will learn that if she wants to go shopping, she must change her behavior.

Even though you may have spent considerable time and effort planning a logical consequence, it is okay if the consequence comes as a surprise to the child. After all, life's natural consequences usually come as a surprise. An example of a logical consequence which was totally unexpected by their children was told by a couple whose children used abominable table manners nearly every evening. Dinner time was a miserable experience. The parents were constantly reminding, scolding, and punishing. One evening they decided on a bold surprise consequence. They said nothing to their kids about their plan; everyone sat down at the table and things went from bad to worse. As usual, the kids yelled at each other, chewed loudly with their mouths open, reached across the person next to them, and spilled food. Finally, Dad stood up and said, "I don't like to eat at the table with you kids when you act like this. It makes me lose my appetite. I'm going to take my food and eat in the bedroom. Want to come with me?" he asked his wife. "I sure do!" she said, and off they went, taking their food with them. There was a stunned silence at the table. The parents finished their meal on a card table in the bedroom where they carried on a lively conversation about what had happened that day at work. The kids silently finished their meal in the dining room. After that, table manners were noticeably improved. The parents remembered not to sabotage themselves by talking and laughing about it in front of their children, although they had a wonderful time relating the incident to their parenting class.

You can see there are elements of the either-or choice correction in the above examples. It is true that the parents in both situations could have given their children a firm either-or choice ("Either you stop fussing or you can go home," and "Either you stop that behavior or we are going to eat in the bedroom,") but it would then not have had the element of surprise and naturalness which these did. Parents and teachers are often delighted and amazed when they find out how much fun these consequences can be. Parents often start laughing when they talk about the logical consequence plans they have been trying at home. And this from parents who were in tears a week or so earlier. The laughter probably comes from a sense of relief at having discovered that logical consequences are so much simpler and so much easier on the adult than the old way of pushing the child ahead of you through life.

3. *The logical consequence situation should ensure that the child, not the adult, will have to deal with the problem.*

If children can begin to experience the discomfort of having a problem because of a choice they made, their misbehavior will have been magically moved from a behavior that gave the adult a problem, to a situation in which the child is having a problem. If you will look at the "Taking Charge Overview" chart on page 247, you can see that the negative behavior listed in the misbehavior box as "Routine-not-minding" can, with the help of a planned logical consequence situation, be shifted down to the box entitled "Child Has A Problem." Once the negative behavior becomes the child's problem, he or she may sometimes need help from you in sorting out his or her feelings about the matter, but mostly the child will have to deal with the problem by making some different choices. In other words, if you have set up a true logical consequence situation, the child, not you, should be the one feeling unhappy about the situation. It is now the child who has the problem, not the adult. It is the child who will have to start thinking about how to make some different choices so the situation can improve for the child.

In the case of the mother who flipped the pancakes on the table, she no longer had the problem. Her son did. Or, in the case of the parents who went to their bedroom to eat, the children left to eat alone at the dining room table had the problem. The parents were having a good time in the bedroom. Remember the three-year-old girl who cried every morning? We gave the problem to her by going about our own business and letting her be the one to choose what to do about crying or not crying. Think back to the example of the girl who expected her mother to drop everything at a moments notice to take her to the library; her mother finally gave the problem back to her daughter by saying, "Gosh, I just can't do that tonight."

Here is a logical consequence plan told by a bus driver who has learned to turn the problem of noisy, out of their seat kids over to the kids themselves. Early in the fall, the first time the noise gets to the discomfort level for him, he pulls off the road and just sits there. He does not say anything to the kids. He pulls out a magazine and pretends to read it. Eventually someone asks when they are going to leave. He says, "It isn't safe to drive with all this commotion. I'm not going until things settle down." Before long, the bus grapevine has passed the word along and things begin to quiet down. Nobody wants to just sit in a school bus. When things are quiet again, the bus driver pulls back into traffic. He never mentions it again and he continues to be pleasant to the kids. He has to do this only a couple of times a year. He has one of the quietest bus loads of kids in the school district. Parents have also successfully tried this tactic with their children. One father and mother parked the car and went to sit on a grassy knoll to read their books while they waited for the kids to quiet down.

Here is a different logical consequence used by a mother with two teenage sons, ages thirteen and fifteen. Several times a week Deborah took Barry and Brian in her car to various sporting and school events, returning to pick them up when the event was over. Lately, they were becoming more and more rowdy in the car, telling dirty jokes in off-stage whispers amid uproarious laughter, swearing, and leaning out the window to yell insults at passersby. Deborah asked them many times to stop, telling them it was embarrassing to her. They ignored her and continued the behavior. After talking to a friend about it, she came up with a logical consequence plan.

The next Saturday afternoon, as she was taking them to a school event, Barry and Brian began to sing an off-color song in loud voices, rolled down the window at an intersection where their mother had to pause for a red light, and stuck their heads out the window in order to serenade numerous pedestrians with the bawdy lyrics. "Okay," Deborah thought to herself. "This is it." Without saying anything to her sons, she drove to the nearest park-and-ride bus terminal. (She had scouted out the closest bus terminal the day before.) She pulled into a parking spot in the park-and-ride lot and said, "You boys will have to get out and take the bus. I don't want to drive you anymore when you behave like this. Here's some money for your fare."

Barry and Brian just laughed. "Hah! You can't make us. Don't be such a prude. Get with it, Mother."

Deborah left the money on the seat, and got out of the car taking the keys with her. She sat down on a bench at the bus stop. Barry and Bryan sat in the car, confident they could outwait her. To their surprise, ten minutes later their mother boarded a bus and went home. Several hours later, a subdued Brian and Barry also showed up at home. Deborah had to ask a friend to drive her to the bus terminal to pick up her car later that evening. The relationship between mother and sons improved after that experience. Although Deborah was prepared to do it again if need be, her sons never gave her the opportunity. She never mentioned it again, and neither did they.

4. *As you draw up a plan, keep asking yourself whether the child will perceive the consequence as part of the natural or social order.*

The consequence should follow logically and naturally from the misbehavior situation itself. Every logical consequence situation should give the child the gift of experiencing what it is like to live in the real world. Consequences which do not follow logically from the social or natural order of the situation will be perceived as punishment.

A mother, when she first began learning to give the logical consequence correction, told this story. Her nine-year-old-daughter, Maggie, was invariably late getting up, late getting dressed, and often late for the bus. The mother always took her daughter to school after scolding and lecturing her on the trouble this was causing the mother. On Halloween, which fell the night before our regular meeting, the mother came up with a consequence. On Halloween morning she told her daughter, "If you miss the bus today, there will be no trick or treating for you tonight." At our meeting the next day, the mother told us, "Maggie got up yesterday and made it to school on time, but today I couldn't get her out of bed again." There was a round of sympathetic laughter and one parent asked, "Yes, what *are* you going to do for the other 364 days of the year?"

The consequence of not being allowed to trick or treat because the child missed the bus had nothing to do with the natural or logical order of things. Whether or not a child is allowed to go trick or treating one night out of the year has nothing to do with being on time at the bus stop every school day. *Taking away a privilege which is unrelated to the misbehavior will fuel the power struggle because the child will perceive it as a punishment.* On the other hand, here are three examples of logical consequences, all having to do with getting to school on time, which arise naturally and logically out of the situation:

EXAMPLE A:

> One mother felt it was like fighting a war to get her first-grader ready for school. She was under tremendous pressure to get to work on time. She had been warned about being late twice by her boss, but the more she pushed and urged her son to get dressed and out to the bus stop, the slower he went. She formulated a plan with a neighbor who was always up and at home each morning. After the plan was ready, the mother told her son, "From now on my boss says I have to leave for my job at 7:30. I will set the

timer so you know that it is almost time to go." (She set the timer to give him a ten-minute lead time.) Next morning, the timer rang and her son continued to play with his trucks. Ten minutes later she said, "Gosh, time for me to go." Trying to be cheerful and matter-of-fact, she picked up her son, who was still in his pajamas, gathered up his lunch and school clothes and deposited them all on the front porch, locking the door behind her. (Notice the use of the physical assist.) "Mrs. Riley said you could finish getting dressed at her house if you want to." Hoping she was still being cheerful and matter-of-fact, Mother drove off waving to her son as she went. The neighbor watched out her kitchen window as the boy frantically gathered up his clothes, hid behind a bush while he changed, and scurried off to the bus stop. From that day on, he got dressed on time without any nagging from mother. The neighbor and Mother both remembered not to self-sabotage by telling the story in front of the boy or to anyone else who might repeat the story or laugh about it within his hearing.

EXAMPLE B:

Another mother, who did not work outside the home, was continually nagging her daughter, Crystal, to get ready in time to catch the school bus, but in spite of scoldings and an occasional spanking, she usually ended up taking her daughter to school in her car. She asked for the teacher's help in carrying out her plan. She asked the teacher not to pay much attention to Crystal if she was late to class. She did not ask the teacher to be punitive, just to be busy, too busy to have much time to orient the girl to what had happened during the first part of the morning. This mother was determined to try to withdraw emotionally from feeling more responsible than Crystal was over whether or not she was late for school. Knowing that the teacher approved of the plan helped set her mind at ease. The first time Crystal missed the bus, Mother said in a friendly voice, "Oh, gosh, did you miss the bus? That's too bad. Well, I can't take you right now but as soon as I finish doing my morning chores I am going to the grocery store and I could drop you on my way." Notice that Mother was sympathetic about her daughter's problem. It is perfectly alright to be sympathetic with children when they have gotten themselves into an uncomfortable situation. In this way, you let them know that you care about them, but it is still *their* choice and *their* problem. In spite of Crystal's crying and carrying on about being late, Mother took her time about getting her chores done. The girl arrived an hour and a half late to find the class already involved in a project, with a teacher too busy to give her any personal attention. Neither teacher or parent ever mentioned it to her again. When the mother told this story, she laughed and said, "It *worked* and it was so *easy.*"

EXAMPLE C:

In this example, a mother was afraid to let her daughter, Rosie, go to the bus stop alone because there had been a report in the neighborhood of a man stopping along the road and trying to entice small children into his car. As in all the other examples, Rosie did not get ready in time without continual reminding and scolding from her mother. The two of them always made it to the bus stop in time but not until Mother was exhausted and angry. The plan she formulated for this situation was for her to say, "I will be ready to go to the bus stop in five minutes." Then in five minutes, Mother was to put on her coat, say cheerfully, "see you at the bus stop," and leave the house. The first time Mother put this plan into operation, Rosie was out of the house just a few minutes behind her and from then on was ready when her mother was. Mother was a very talkative woman, but she managed not to mention it to Rosie again, and the problem evaporated.

Each of the examples given above not only takes the problem away from the adult and gives it to the child, but each situation also arises naturally and logically from individual circumstances. Each example also involves the element of the unexpected and contains, at least from the adult point of view, a touch of humor. Discipline does not have to be grimly serious. It can be creative, even fun. But never forget *you must not laugh or talk about the situation in front of children so that they will overhear you telling someone else what happened. Also, do not repeat the story to anyone who will repeat it back to the children.* Assume the role of a force of nature which does what needs to be done and then forgets; otherwise children will feel their integrity threatened, and you will have begun a needless and painful power struggle.

None of the children in the situations above had a self-indulgent tantrum in response to these logical consequences. If you are concerned that your child would "go to pieces" if you tried anything this unexpected, continue to concentrate first on changing his or her self-indulgent behaviors before you move on to correcting the routine-not-minding behaviors. Unless there are some very unusual background circumstances, like a recent death, divorce, or other severe loss in the family, "going to pieces" is almost always just another self-indulgent behavior. If you are convinced that going to pieces is not a self-indulgent behavior, but a serious terror response, you need to take your child for private counseling.

5. Logical consequences should be short-term.

Losing one turn or one recess, one hour or one day, is enough time for a logical consequence. The teenager can handle two or three days, or one weekend. If you go past this point you will find it hard to carry through, and not carrying through on a logical consequence only convinces the child that, "Dad never means anything he says."

The longer you have to enforce the consequence, the harder it will be to keep from getting upset and sabotaging yourself by talking in some way about the misbehavior. It is impossible to let the incident be in the past when you are in the position of continually having to enforce the consequence. When you sabotage yourself by talking about the misbehavior, a power struggle begins, or, if a power struggle is already present, it will intensify.

A mother at first resisted the idea that grounding her fifteen-year-old son to the house for two days would be more effective than the two weeks grounding she usually gave him. Her son, Charlie, was continually coming in past his curfew time. He would no sooner finish having to stay home for two weeks than he would go right out and come in late again. The power struggle between Charlie and his mother was intense. He constantly argued with her and bombarded her with sullen looks.

Since, in her mind, things could not get much worse anyway, Mother finally decided to try a shorter consequence time. The next time Charlie's two week consequence was over, Mother told him that from now on when he stayed out past his curfew time he could not go out again for two days. His only response was to raise his eyebrows. (Besides shortening the time of the consequence, she also tried to stop reminding her son about what would happen if he stayed out late. Not sabotaging herself by talking about it was now easier for her to do because she knew she only had to enforce the consequence for two days.) The next weekend she heard her son talking to a friend on the phone, "If we can't get back by 8 I'd better not go. It wouldn't be worth having to stay home two nights just for that." At her next parenting class meeting the astonished mother asked, "What happened?" What happened was that the power struggle disappeared, at least in this area of their lives, when the son was presented with what he perceived as a more reasonable consequence, and when the mother was able to stop sabotaging herself by not reminding and arguing with her son about it.

Another problem with using long-term consequences is that long-term consequences prevent a child from immediately trying out and learning new behaviors. A common example of this is the parent who insists that once children decide to participate in some organized activity they must continue all year. Many eight-year-olds are in Little League, soccer, cub scouts, church choir, take piano lessons, and are also expected to do homework each evening. One third-grader in particular was an exceedingly responsible child, but showed every sign of an adult type of depression. He rarely smiled, life seemed to hold no joy. This child did not have one single week night with even a fifteen minute unorganized time to just sit or play. When his teacher shared his concerns with the mother that her son be allowed to drop a few of his activities, she protested, "But he wanted to do all those things. He is the one who decided to take these things. And we have always taught him that once he starts something he has to finish it."

Waiting for the end of the school year is too long for an eight-year-old boy. Luckily, this mother sat down and really listened to her son. When she realized the burden he was carrying, she did him the kindness of adjusting his environment by changing her expectations of him. She told him, "I think you just bit off more than you can chew this year. It is okay with me if you drop one activity now, and then in a couple of weeks, if you are still feeling bogged down, you go ahead and drop another one." The boy chose to drop Cub Scouts, and this alone seemed to be enough. He soon stopped looking so depressed and started smiling again. He felt in control of his life once more. He was no longer trapped for the next six months; he had some choices.

It is certainly fair to insist that your child go to Cub Scouts, for example, for six to eight weeks before quitting. He needs time to find out what it is really like. But more than that is too much. Wait to buy a lot of special equipment or clothing until you are certain the child really enjoys the activity. The pre-puberty years are a time for playful exploration. They should not be a time of grimly signing long-term contracts to play soccer or golf or to be a Girl Scout. There is no good reason for becoming an expert at anything when you are eight or nine years old. Watch children play together. Sometimes they stay at one activity for a long time. Other times they run from one activity to another. This variety is a natural expression of how children explore and learn about their world. Give children the gift of exploring the world at their own pace.

6. *Be cautious about taking away a privilege as part of a logical consequence.*

Losing a privilege, like not being able to leave the yard, or forfeiting an allowance, or not being allowed to go out for recess, is often used as a consequence for routine-not-minding behaviors. The consequence of losing a privilege has the advantage of being easy to think up, but it often becomes exceedingly difficult for the adult to enforce. It also often violates the principal of taking the problem from the adult and giving it to the child. For example, if a teacher tells two children who have had a fight that they may not play together all week during recess, then all week long the teacher must take on the duty of prison guard to see that the children do not play together. This is a lot of work for the teacher and not much of a problem for the kids. Even worse, the teacher can give the job of prison guard to whoever happens to be on recess duty, thus shifting the problem to another adult and leaving the kids free to play a game with the unfortunate person on recess duty called, "Are they playing together or aren't they?"

If, on the other hand, you are convinced that losing a privilege makes sense because it arises directly from the misbehavior, set it up so that *you* act instead of having to force the child to act. You want the consequence to be uncomfortable for the child, not for you. For example, if the child has misbehaved the last time you took him to the grocery store, you can say, "I won't take you to the store with me next time I go." Not taking the child to the store with you next time you go is within your power and easy for you to carry out. But if, instead, you say, "You can't go to the store from now until Saturday," you will cause yourself a lot of aggravation always checking to see that your child has not sneaked out to the corner store. You will have given yourself the extra job of being a prison guard. In the same way, it would not make sense for a parent to tell a sixteen-year-old who already has a driver's license, "You may not drive next weekend," because the teenager may have friends with cars who will let him drive when the parent is not around to see. However, the parent can say, "I will not loan you my car next weekend."

Any consequence you can think up will be most effective if the adult concentrates on what the adult can do without becoming a prison guard for the child. "I will not loan you my car," "I will not take you to the store," are consequences which are logical and relatively easy for the adult to carry out. Remember, *the idea is not to force the child to behave, but to set up a situation which results in enough discomfort for the child to see the sense in behaving in a different way.*

A father tells this story of an effective loss-of-privilege consequence which his mother gave him when he was a child, (notice that the loss of privilege consequence is also a logical outcome of the situation): When he was seven years old his mother told him that she was not his servant and that if he left his clothes lying around the house anymore, he would have to pay her one penny for each item of clothing she put away. His allowance was five cents a week. His mother was not a very verbal person, and he does not remember ever being reminded or scolded about it. That first week he left three items of clothing on the floor and paid her three cents, but he never had to pay her again. That was fifty-five years ago. And he still hangs up his clothes.

Here are some more examples of logical consequences. You can see that the creative possibilities are endless:

EXAMPLE D:

Eight-year-old Mike kept forgetting to feed his dog each evening. The dog dish was in the kitchen. It was easy for Mike's mother to see whether or not the dog had been given food and clean water. Weeks of reminding, scolding, and finally even threatening to get rid of the dog had made no impression on her son. Finally, Mother told him, "From now on you can't have your dinner until the dog has his." For all of this mother's adult life, she had served herself only after the rest of her family was settled at the table. It made sense to her that you do not eat until those you are responsible for get something to eat. That evening at mealtime the dog dish was still empty. Mother said nothing until it was time to serve the meal. (In this family, mother dished up each plate at the stove and each member of the family took their filled plate to the table.) When Mike came to the stove to wait for his food, she shook her head and said, "The dog." She then ignored him while she continued to dish up for the rest of the family. He groaned and complained a bit, which she continued to ignore. He finally went to feed his pet. This happened only a few times before her son began to feed the dog without being constantly reminded.

EXAMPLE E:

First-grader Billy was an only child. He had two doting parents who were totally involved with helping him to do everything. In spite of the fact that he seemed very capable and bright, he often complained the work was too hard. Billy constantly asked for help from his teacher and any other adult who came into the classroom. After several weeks of this, the teacher decided that he was able to do the work himself. She told him, "Billy, you will have to finish the work yourself before you can go out to recess." The rest of the morning she proceeded to ignore his sighs, moans, and complaints. Recess came and all the other children went out to play. He tried to leave too, but she said matter-of-factly, "As soon as your work is done." He sat back down and cried softly. She sat down to work at her desk and tried to ignore his sad sniffles. Soon it was quiet. She eventually got so involved in her own work she was surprised to look up and see him at her desk with the finished paper in his hand. "It's all finished," the teacher said in a pleased tone of voice. She gave him a big hug. He grinned and hugged her back before he ran outdoors. The paper was perfect. He was able to do it. He had learned something important about himself, that he was indeed a competent person.

Taking away a recess is a logical consequence in that we all have to get our work done before we can play, but taking a recess away from an elementary school child on a regular basis can also tear down his or her self-esteem staircase, so be cautious about using this consequence. If you find you are often taking away the child's play period, the consequence is not working. It is time to try something else.

EXAMPLE F:

The following example was told by a middle-school teacher. She had a few students who consistently came to class without pen, pencils, and books. They would ask to be excused to go to their locker and get supplies, then straggle back to class having missed the first ten minutes. She first tried the logical consequence of having them stay in class and just sit there not being able to do their schoolwork. This was ineffective because they were perfectly happy to sit and do nothing. No discomfort for them there. Next she told the class that from now on anyone who forgot their supplies could go back to their locker but she would record the time they left and the time they returned. They would then be expected to stay after class and make up their lost time. The next teachers of the day were not too keen about late arrivals to their classes, so the teacher had to clear this plan at a faculty meeting. Just as in a family, things work better if all the involved adults in the school know what is going on. A logical consequence for late arrivals at the next class was to again have the student stay and make up lost time before leaving.

You can see that this kind of consequence is a potential prison guard situation. How is the teacher going to force students to stay? It happened that at this school, the staff had already set up a Saturday school for students who needed to make up lost time or missing schoolwork assignments. They had people available to round up kids who needed rides or who did not show up as scheduled. The staff had a clear concept that consequences should not be punitive. They had made an effort to make their Saturday school into a warm and welcoming place, even providing snacks for the kids. (The adults were surprised and pleased to find that, for some students, it actually became a popular place to study. Kids were getting the personal help and attention teachers were not able to give them during the week.) Parents, teachers, and administrators all took turns working on Saturday mornings so that no one adult had to spend too much off duty time there. As this teacher told us, "Contributing one Saturday morning every three months is no big deal." In the process, she gained the benefit of having a backup whenever she needed to apply a logical consequence for missing school work and lost time. As it happened, none of her late arrivals refused to stay to make up time. Over the long run, the problem dissolved for her. Perhaps just the fact that all students knew Saturday school existed gave her the backup she needed.

Backup systems in schools are exceedingly important. Just as in a family, every teacher needs to have other adults available to help brainstorm logical consequence plans and to provide backup for the plan. Too often, teachers are expected to handle discipline problems all alone. As in the Saturday school example given above, it is much more effective when administrators, teachers, and parents can work as a family, brainstorming and planning together.

EXERCISE:

Using the "Negative Behaviors" chart on the following page, continue to write down any misbehaviors or negative attempts at solving problems which you observe your children doing this coming week. Also, write down which corrections you are beginning to use. Using the chart each week is helpful for refreshing your memory when you join in the weekly discussions with your group.

If you are interested in some ideas for working with children who habitually do not do schoolwork which they are capable of doing, or children who are involved in stealing, you will find detailed discussion of these routine-not-minding behaviors in Sections A and B located at the end of this chapter.

NEGATIVE BEHAVIORS:
The Four Misbehaviors
(and 3 Problem-Solving Situations)

NOT-MINDING

SELF-INDULGENT (Attention-Getting)

ROUTINE-NOT-MINDING (Will not do routine tasks)

AGGRESSIVE (Deliberately Hurting)

Negative Behaviors Requiring Problem-Solving Which Do Not Fit Above:

1. Adjust Environment   2. Solve Conflicts   3. Listen to Feelings

DISCUSSION IDEAS: CHAPTER 7: MAKING CHOICES AND LIVING WITH THE CONSEQUENCES

1. Share your "Negative Behaviors" chart notations. Are you having any problems recognizing which negative misbehaviors are which? Did any problem-solving situations arise?

2. Did anyone have any particular problems with the ignoring correction? Give some examples of what happened this past week with the either-or choice.

3. Has the anger level dropped for anyone in their relationships with their children? Has anyone experienced a lessening of the power struggle?

4. Talk together about how giving children fun choices and helping them to live with the consequences of their choices fits in with Maslow's staircase of needs.

5. Is everybody clear as to the differences between logical consequences and punishments?

6. Each person think of a routine-not-minding incident and, following the guidelines in this chapter, ask the group to help you plan a logical consequence. When you think up your initial ideas, feel free to brainstorm, be creative, and have fun. Afterward, you can be serious, look at the ideas, toss out the ridiculous ones, and choose a situation you feel comfortable with. Do you need a backup person to help with the plan? Finally, ask yourselves, "What can go wrong?"

7. Regarding Sections A and B at the end of this chapter: Has anyone had a problem with children stealing or not getting schoolwork done? What kinds of corrections or punishments did you try in the past? Are the ideas in Sections A and B similar or different from what you have tried before?

Regarding the list of secondary reinforcers: Discuss whether or not you are comfortable using secondary reinforcers with your children. Can you think of more secondary reinforcers to add to the list?

REVIEW: Correction for *Routine-Not-Minding* Behaviors

PREVENTION PLAN: GIVING CHILDREN DAILY OPPORTUNITIES TO MAKE, AND LIVE WITH, THEIR CHOICES

1. Give the child practice in making **fun** choices.

2. **Never give a choice if there is no choice.**

3. Keep the choices **limited** and **appropriate** to the child's age. "Either this or that . . ." is enough for a preschooler.

4. Let children **live with the logical consequences of their choice.**

BASIC CORRECTION FOR AN ESTABLISHED BEHAVIOR: SETTING UP A LOGICAL CONSEQUENCE EXPERIENCE FOR THE CHILD

1. Work on changing **one behavior at a time.**

2. **Make a plan** for the child. If possible, find another adult to brainstorm with you. Find backup help from another adult if needed.

3. The logical consequence plan should ensure that **the child, not the adult, will experience discomfort from the situation.**

4. Logical consequences **should not be experienced by the child as punishment but as part of the natural or social order.**

5. The consequence should be **short term.**

6. **Be cautious about taking away a privilege** as part of a logical consequence.

REMEMBER NOT TO SELF-SABOTAGE

SECTION A: A LOGICAL CONSEQUENCE PLAN FOR DEALING WITH STEALING:

Parents who catch their children stealing are often devastated. Not to be able to trust one's own child to leave off-limit items alone sends many parents into a panic. Teachers, too, are greatly troubled by the child who steals. Stealing goes against some of the most cherished values of our property oriented culture. As a consequence, parents and teachers often manage to thoroughly sabotage themselves in dealing with stealing misbehaviors. They do lots of spanking, grounding for extreme lengths of time, lecturing, advising, warning, even bursting into tears. When it comes to stealing, the basic rule of carrying out the correction and then not mentioning it again seems almost impossible to do. "How will children learn right from wrong," parents and teachers ask, "If I don't let them know just how terribly wrong it is to steal?"

Children already know that stealing is wrong. You must take this leap of faith and try not to lecture about it. The old way of lecturing, hitting, scolding, crying, shaming, and advising did not work so what have you got to lose? Remember what was said earlier about the ineffectiveness of teaching ethical values and morals during negative behavior times? Children will either close their inner door and let your words slide off or they will actively rebel against the talking you do during these times of stress. Giving energy and attention during times of misbehavior will set up power struggles and make matters worse. As upsetting as stealing is, try treating it essentially as you would any other routine-not-minding behavior. Here are some guidelines to help you through the process:

1. *Check very carefully into the situation before you proceed.*

Stealing often happens when the child attempts to solve a real life problem. Maybe the child was hungry so he stole his neighbor's lunch. Maybe the child could not afford a special trinket currently popular with the other girls, so she took one from someone else.

At a later time if necessary, you can go behind the scenes to ensure that from now on this child has enough food to eat, or to set up an opportunity for this child to occasionally earn a special trinket. But for the present, treat the theft as you would any other misbehavior and deal with it. Whatever the underlying reason for the theft, stealing cannot be allowed.

If you suspect the accusers might be mistaken, give the child a chance to tell his or her side of the story. Do this in a concerned, not an accusing, manner. Really listen. If you have no doubts at all about the matter, as for example, if you yourself find a cache of fishing lures still in their store wrappings stashed under the mattress, or you witness the child taking a toy from another child's desk, then do not discuss it beforehand but proceed directly to the next step.

2. *Be honest and direct with the child.*

Be honest with the child. Describe the facts as you know them. Do not ask questions you already know the answers to. Immediately state what you know or believe to be true, for example, "I just found out from your teacher that you stole Dirk's lunch money."

Many parents and teachers are tempted to put the child on a witness stand and force him or her to tell the truth. For example, "What do you know about Dirk's lunch money?" and "Where were you when it happened?" and "Do you mean to tell me you don't know anything about it?" Do not ask for or expect a confession. Resist the temptation to play detective or lawyer. Do not ask questions designed to trick the child into a confession. Do not say, "It will go easier on you if you tell the truth." This puts children in a situation where they may feel forced to solve the problem by lying to you.

The day I ate a whole plate of cookies my grandmother was saving for dessert is still vivid in my memory. My indignant grandmother confronted me and my older brother with the nearly empty plate. "Who ate these cookies?" she demanded. My innocent brother denied it. I was backed into a corner. If I admitted my guilt, I was certain my grandmother would lose all respect for me. I was the apple of my grandmother's eye. I was not afraid of physical punishment because she never punished us physically. But she did emotionally punish us by withdrawing love and shaming us. I was terrified of losing my grandmother's love and respect. In my eight-year-old mind, telling Grandma the truth could not possibly make things easier for me. I dearly loved my big brother. I did not want to get him in trouble, but, in an instinct of self-preservation, I looked up at her and said, "I don't know." My Grandmother believed me and sent my brother to his room for the rest of the day, after telling him at some length he should be ashamed of himself for being a liar. Even though some years ago I finally apologized to my brother for that incident, to this day, I still feel guilty about that lie. But, I know that given the same circumstances, from my eight-year-old problem-solving point of view, I would probably do it again.

3. *You do not have to prove the child's guilt; it is enough that you are sure beyond a reasonable doubt.*

Children may vigorously deny that they stole something, but if you believe beyond a reasonable doubt that they did steal, go ahead and proceed with the correction. They may deny it, argue, tell you they hate you, accuse you of being unfair, of not loving them, or even threaten to run away. Do not allow yourself to be baited into an argument. Treat these protests as self-indulgent behavior and ignore them. If you are absolutely convinced the child did it, say only once, "If I am mistaken, I am sorry, but I think you stole the money."

If it should happen that you later find out that the child did *not* take the money, immediately apologize to the child, and then do whatever you possibly can to see that the child's innocence is made clear to everyone else involved. Go with the child personally to every person in the situation and tell them you made a mistake. But you do not need to be awash in guilt. You did the best you could with the information you had. Part of the child's learning is that each person's credibility is built brick by brick, over a long period of time. Children need to learn it is a fact of life that when a reputation for stealing or lying is established, it takes time for trust to build again. *If you are matter-of-fact in treating the theft as just another misbehavior, and if you do not sabotage yourself while carrying out this correction,* the child can handle an occasional mistake on your part.

4. *If the child has stolen an object, he or she must return the object or its equivalent to the rightful owner.*

Returning an object to the rightful owner is not a pleasant experience for either parent or child, but it is an absolute requirement for helping your child to stop stealing. Children must experience the consequences of their misbehaviors. It may be embarrassing for you but rest assured you are not alone. Many children try stealing at some point in their lives. Most adults who have raised kids themselves understand this. They know it is the responsible parent who cares enough and is gutsy enough to march a child back into the store or school or neighbor's house to return the stolen object. By so doing, you will earn the respect of every sensible adult. Do not return the object *for* your child, as some C adults are tempted to do. Be sure the child returns the object *in person* with you at his or her side.

Try very hard not to sabotage yourself by spanking, scolding, crying, or worrying out loud about what is to become of the child, will he end up like Uncle Ned in prison or whatever. Go ahead and look as grim as you feel, but be matter-of-fact. It is important not to shame or demean the child. Let your nonverbal attitude give the message that you are a force of nature, like the patient ocean or a steady breeze. Say firmly and matter-of-factly, "I can't let you steal. You will have to return it." Be a force of nature. Let your body language convey the message that there is nothing else that can be done. This is the way things are. Nothing can be done to change it.

If the object is food which has already been eaten, children can use or earn their own money to replace it. If the object has been damaged in any way, choose a valued object of comparable value belonging to them and have them return both the damaged object and their own possession to the person they stole from. If children steal a second time, insist they give up a valued possession of equal value even if the stolen object has not been harmed. If the victimized person does not want the child's possession, ask him to take it and contribute it to someone else who could use it.

Give the child as little attention and social interaction during this process as possible. If you do much talking, you will end up sabotaging yourself. After you return home, begin to go about your usual routines. Do not mention the stealing again. Immediately begin to give positive attention, both verbal and nonverbal. Do your regular bedtime routine of reading in bed together or whatever you usually do at bedtime. Let the incident be in the past. Concentrate on giving those four to one positive attentions. Let your nonverbal behavior convey the message, "All that is over and done with. This is a new day." The experience of returning the object will have been an extremely painful experience for the child. Children need to know you do not think they are "bad." Respond to their neutral and positive behaviors with positive attention so that they clearly understand it was their behavior you disliked, not them.

If you cannot think of anything positive to say, use nonverbal communication: Make friendly eye contact, smile sometimes from across the room, ruffle his or her hair as you pass by, give a loving hug. Stealing is just another misbehavior. The fact that your child stole something is not the end of the world. It does not mean you are a failure as a parent or a teacher. It does not mean he or she is a bad kid. Stealing is only a mistake which many of us make on the way to learning how to behave as responsible persons. Making mistakes is to be expected. It is an integral part of learning. If the child seems withdrawn and depressed the day after the incident, bring the subject up at a positive or neutral time. Say in a kindly way, "You must be feeling badly about what happened. Everyone makes mistakes sometimes. You have done what needed to be done to make it better. Today is a new day. Yesterday is over and done with." Give the child a hug, listen if he or she wants to talk about it. Then let it go.

SECTION B: A CONTRACT PLAN INVOLVING CONSEQUENCES AND SECONDARY REINFORCERS (A SAMPLE SCHOOLWORK PLAN WITH AN ELEMENTARY SCHOOL AGE CHILD)

This schoolwork plan is intended to be used only with the elementary age child who is having severe problems in completing school work and as a result is falling far behind his or her peers in maintaining basic academic skill levels.* It is not recommended for children who are generally doing average work and getting "B" or "C" grades and even an occasional "D." If you are worried that getting "C" grades in school will endanger your child's future, relax. *It is okay if your child is an average student.*

School is a temporary situation, and, in many ways, it is also an artificial environment. Many capable children who do only average work in school because they cannot see its relevancy to their lives, will eventually blossom into "A" and "B" students when they enter college or find what they perceive to be more meaningful work to do in the larger world outside the classroom. The basis of a successful adult life is high self-esteem, the belief that, "I am a competent and respected person," and an ability to live in responsible and loving relationships with other human beings. *Success in adult life has nothing to do with getting A's and B's in high school.*

---

* **Schoolwork is not homework.** Schoolwork is academic work which the child is supposed to complete at school. Homework is extra academic work assigned to the child to be completed at home. This contract example deals only with *schoolwork*.

Especially by the time children enter their junior high school years, as long as they are doing average "C" work and becoming well grounded in basic skills like math, writing, reading and critical thinking, let them manage their own schoolwork. Encourage them, help them to build a strong emotional needs staircase, let them know you are proud and happy for *them* when they do well, let them know you are interested in the joy of learning for its own sake, but let *them* worry (or not worry) about the temporary end product of high grades.

If, however, you have a child who is definitely having problems in maintaining basic skill levels because he or she does not do the assigned school work, not doing the schoolwork has become a direct threat to the child's competency needs, and the child will need your help. In this case, you can try this contract plan. It is described from the point of view of the parent, but teachers, especially if they have the help of a school counselor, can also initiate this kind of contract with a child.

A contract is not easy for adults to carry out. Long-term contracts involving consequences such as secondary reinforcers (like earning stickers or a popcorn party) are the most structured and time-consuming of all the logical consequence approaches. This plan has worked for many children, but it takes commitment and the willingness by the adults involved to stick with it, sometimes for months, so be sure you and the teacher are willing to put forth that kind of effort before you attempt it.

Before you ever begin to work out a schoolwork plan for a child, parents and teachers need to discuss ahead of time whether or not the schoolwork is at the child's ability level. Children cannot be expected to do work which is beyond their ability. Besides that, many extremely bright children have attention deficits or other learning disabilities which make it difficult for them to learn in the usual ways. If you suspect this may be true, you have the right to request that a professional evaluation be given to your child by special school personnel to find out if your child is learning disabled. By federal law, every public school is required to create an Individualized Education Plan for every learning disabled child. Parents and teachers must agree together on this Individualized Education Plan, or IEP, as it is called. If your child is eligible for an Individualized Education Plan, make sure that the homework process is included in the plan.

For example, children with an attention deficit are usually very intelligent, but are learning disabled in that their brains cannot screen out incoming information to allow them to focus on just one thing at a time. As a result, these children seem to be in a continual whirl of motion, jumping from one thing to another. They sometimes cannot concentrate on their written school work for more than a few minutes at a time. Some of these children can cope with only ten minutes of written work a night. These children can sometimes be successful if they are allowed to answer most schoolwork orally, using a tape recorder. Maybe it would be better for them to write out ten math problems instead of thirty, and then get up and move around while they are talking into the tape recorder about the rest of the problems. Or perhaps someone needs to sit beside them while they do the written work. Maybe they need special paper with darker lines and wider spaces. Many of the schoolwork problems of the attention-deficit child can be solved by changing adult expectations and adjusting the child's learning environment.

If your child is tested and found to have some kind of learning disability, DO NOT PANIC. Studies have shown many kids outgrow the problem before their high school years.* But in the meantime, these children need special tutoring help which focuses on keeping their competency needs stairsteps strong.

Albert Einstein, the genius who formulated the theory of relativity, had a learning disability. One of his elementary school teachers advised Einstein's parents not to waste money on sending him to

---

* For example, see "Evidence that Dyslexia May Represent the Lower Tail of a Normal Distribution of Reading Ability," by S.E. Shaywitz, M.D., et. al., in The New England Journal of Medicine, Jan. 16, 1992, pages 145-150.

secondary school because he was not intelligent enough. In fact, just the opposite is true. Learning disabled children are of average, or higher, intelligence. Because learning disabled children are often extremely bright, teachers and parents sometimes jump to the conclusion that since these children are not stupid, they must be lazy. "If Cheri would only work harder, she would get good grades." Learning disabilities come in all varieties, sometimes in very unexpected and individual packages. Even experienced classroom teachers do not always recognize when a student has a learning disability. Make certain before you begin any schoolwork plan that this is not the primary problem for your child.

If you are satisfied that not doing schoolwork is truly a routine-not-minding behavior, and not a lack of ability to do the work, go ahead and begin to draw up a plan. First, you need to visit your child's teacher and share the following ideas. In the vast majority of cases, your child's teacher will be delighted to help you in this effort.

1. *Tell your child, at a neutral or positive time, that you are going to help him or her change old habit patterns.*

Don't give your child a choice in this matter. State the facts in a friendly tone of voice. "I sure don't like it when you don't get your schoolwork done. The teacher doesn't like it, and I know you hate it when everyone nags at you about it. I've got a plan to help you change the old habit." Present your plan as something that will make life happier for both of you.

2. *Provide a secondary reinforcer to reward your child for a positive behavior change.*

Secondary reinforcers are objects like stickers, or fun activities. Until now, you have focused on giving children the primary reinforcer of your personal attention. The secondary reinforcer is something you give in addition to personal attention. You will find a list of suggested secondary reinforcers at the end of this section. Choose a few ideas from the list or create some of your own.

One middle-school substitute teacher brings a small gift, beautifully wrapped, to each new class assignment. Every time a child completes an assignment, the child gets one free guess as to what is in the box. The child who makes the correct guess gets to keep whatever is inside. The prize is always an inexpensive little fun gadget of some kind. Almost every parent has used secondary reinforcers at one time or another, whether it is giving children dessert only after they eat their meat and potatoes, or a dollar for every A or B on their report cards. Giving food as a reinforcer is treading on shaky ground because you do not want children to equate food with attention and love, although some middle-school teachers have been amazed with the results they get from a box of Milk Duds. A simple sticker or a fun activity with Mom or Dad is preferable to money or candy. Whatever you decide, use money or food reinforcers with caution. You eventually want to be able to drop the reinforcer. *Both money and food are difficult to drop once you start them.*

Offer a choice of reinforcers to the child. Say, "I know how hard it is to change old habits so I'd like to do something nice for you each day when you get your schoolwork done. What would you like to earn for every day your teacher sends home a note saying your work is finished?" Get out a pencil and paper and make a list together. Be creative. Let your child offer ideas. Together you can brainstorm some fun things he or she can earn. This is the part of the contract children love.

Some parents resist the use of secondary reinforcers on the grounds they are somehow unethical. "Sounds like bribery to me." It is true that you will eventually want to get rid of the secondary reinforcer. Your ultimate goal, after all, is to help the child internalize the pride and satisfaction of doing a job well. However, the secondary reinforcer does serve an important function in the early phases of the behavior change program because it is so tangible. The child can touch, taste, or play with it. It is immediately apparent. It helps to catch the child's attention and makes the difficult process of habit change into a game. It functions as a kind of exclamation point to the primary reinforcement of paying attention to the child at positive times. It also provides a structured way to remind the adult to give more positive attention to the child.

As adults, we like to give ourselves a treat when we manage to change damaging old habits. Many a woman has bought herself a new dress when she lost twenty pounds, and many a smoker has treated himself to a special night out when he has succeeded in not lighting up a cigarette for two months. Why is it so bad to do the same for children? Children's damaging old habits are hard to break, too. Why not celebrate with children when they are successful? Most children, if given the choice, will choose an activity time with Mom or Dad rather than an object, even if the object is food or money. This is not surprising since loving attention from a parent, or other admired adult, is what children need to grow up their self-esteem staircase toward inner strength and independence.

The secondary reinforcer should be something special, something the child would not ordinarily have the opportunity to own or to do. A troubled five-year-old kindergarten boy, Daniel, was willing to work very hard on improving his behavior with the other children after his teacher hit upon the reinforcer of one marble for each day he did not hurt another child. Daniel loved those marbles and seemed determined to acquire the entire sack full. Five marbles and five days later, Daniel's grandmother bought him a whole sack full of marbles. "I didn't realize he loved marbles so much." she told the teacher. Daniel immediately fell into his old ways and his teacher never found a secondary reinforcer which had the power of those marbles for him.

As the weeks go by, keep checking in with your child about the list of secondary reinforcers, "Is there anything about our plan you would like to change this week?" Secondary reinforcers like stickers become boring fast and need to be varied periodically in order to continue to be of interest to the child. Make a weekly appointment with the child to go over the program and see how it is going. Do this at neutral or positive times. Make it a friendly, problem-solving meeting. Remember not to dwell on the failures, or to lecture. Put the appointment on the calendar for next week to insure you do not postpone things until a crisis comes along. It is difficult to be friendly and oriented towards problem-solving at crisis times.

The most common cause of failure of this type of program happens when adults neglect to carry through their end of the bargain. Parents sometimes forget or postpone carrying out their part of the plan. Teachers and parents often stop a program too soon. This is most likely to happen when the child's behavior begins to improve. Teachers are so busy at the end of each school day they often forget to give the child the promised positive note to take home when the behavior is improving. When things are going along better, we tend to turn our attention to the area of most concern. The squeaky wheel gets the grease. For obvious reasons, the negative message home when things are not going well is easier to remember. Parents and teachers should prepare for this eventuality by planning ahead of time for the parent to call the teacher at home if the child says the teacher forgot. Teachers are human, too, and it is possible that this time, Teacher did forget.

Before you even think about phasing children off the secondary reinforcer program, their behavior should be at the desired level for at least a three-week period. Before you quit or decrease the secondary reinforcer, children should have demonstrated the desired behavior for three weeks in a row. Many children will begin to wean themselves at this point and forget to collect the reinforcer. It is wonderful when a child shows more interest in the social reinforcer than the secondary reinforcer, but until those three weeks are up, always offer it just the same. It is a mistake to assume you can forget about the plan after the child has shown good progress for a week or so. If you quit at the end of one week, the child will usually slip back into the old negative behaviors once again. *An important part of the value of using the secondary reinforcer is that it also provides a structured way to remind you, the adult, to pay more attention to the child at positive and neutral times.* If you stop using the secondary reinforcer too soon, you will not have had enough time to change your own old habit pattern of not giving this particular child enough positive attention.

Another important point to keep in mind is that the secondary reinforcer should be given to the child as close to the desired behavior as possible. The younger the child, the less time should elapse before reinforcing the improved behaviors. A rather extreme example of this need for frequent reinforcement was the first grade boy, Bobby, who could not stay in his seat and attend to his work for more than a few minutes at a time. His teacher bought a digital kitchen timer which could be set to quietly beep every few minutes. The teacher started out by setting the timer for three minute segments during math time. He chose math time because that was the hardest time of the day for Bobby to sit still. The beep reminded the teacher to smile or touch or in some way give positive attention to Bobby whenever the beep occurred at the same time Bobby was in his seat. The teacher gradually lengthened out the time between beeps until the child was sitting and working for nearly the entire math period. This method failed when, after having had a moderate amount of success after the first week, the teacher turned his attention elsewhere. The child then reverted to his old behavior pattern and the discouraged teacher did not want to try the program again.

The temptation for a tired parent or teacher is to postpone giving the reinforcer until tomorrow or the weekend when the adult hopes there will be more time and energy available. Unfortunately, if you do this, the child will lose his enthusiasm for the plan. If the adults keep putting things off, why not the child? Be sure you don't promise a reinforcer that takes too much energy or time. Keep daily reinforcers short and sweet. You are both supposed to have fun with this. Do not promise to play a game of checkers if you hate checkers.

Young children need positive and immediate reinforcers. Some parents and grandparents promise distant reinforcers like a trip to Disneyland next summer. The lure of Disneyland next summer is a useless secondary reinforcer. It does more harm than good. Since it is almost certain that a far off Disneyland trip will fail to get children to do their day to day chores, their families will wind up blaming them for not being able to go on the trip. Or, if the family does go to Disneyland in spite of a child's poor performance, that child will have learned that no one means what they say anyhow so he or she can safely continue to be irresponsible about schoolwork.

Reinforcers should not be expensive. As you will see from the list of ideas at the end of this chapter, cheap can be fun. If you can afford to go to Disneyland next summer, wonderful. Wait until a few weeks before it is time to go and say, "I think we can afford to go to Disneyland this year. We are all such neat people, I think we deserve it," or you can say, "We have all been working so hard and doing such a good job, I think we should treat ourselves to Disneyland." You would no doubt have gone to Disneyland even if they were not doing a good job but there is nothing wrong with emphasizing your pleasure at their efforts. Let them know you notice and appreciate their work. But do not offer it six months ahead of time as a reward contingent on good behavior .

Whichever kind of secondary reinforcer you use, make sure that you give your child loving, enthusiastic attention just before you give the sticker or token. People internalize behavior and attitudes through the primary reinforcer of gaining attention from admired fellow human beings, not from the stickers and tokens per se. The secondary reinforcer is useful for awhile but do not depend on it too much. Its major purpose is to catch your child's interest and cooperation while you work on giving the lasting reinforcer of your loving attention.

Many adults ask if it is okay to take away a reinforcer for negative behaviors, instead of giving a positive reinforcer for positive behaviors. An example of this is the teacher who gives a child ten stickers at the beginning of each school day, and then, throughout the school day, takes one sticker away every time the teacher sees a negative behavior. The problem with this use of reinforcers is two-fold: (1) it gives frequent and powerful attention for negative behaviors and (2) it is usually perceived as punishment by the child which, in turn, helps to tear down the child's self-esteem staircase. For these reasons, it is best to stick with giving positive reinforcers for positive behaviors.

3. *Provide a consistent logical consequence for those times your child exhibits the old irresponsible behavior.*

If you and the child are involved in a plan which provides the child with a fun secondary reinforcer, you cannot change the plan without first consulting with the child. You and the child have made a contract with one another. You have made a promise to the child and you must keep your word. But the child has also made a promise to you. The contract should provide for a logical consequence in the event the child does not keep his or her part of the bargain. *In a contract, all consequences, whether they are positive or negative, must be known and predictable.*

For the teacher, the most difficult part of this contract is to send a note home every single day. It is important for the teacher to send a note home every day, because the first time a note does not come home, you will wonder whether your child actually finished the work. Maybe your child dropped the note in a ditch, or maybe the teacher forgot to send it. Maybe your child is "forgetting" to bring the note home as a way of problem-solving a difficult situation. It works best if you expect a note every single day. You and the teacher can provide your child with a special manila envelope for bringing home notes and unfinished schoolwork. If your child does not have a backpack for carrying books and papers, buy or borrow one.

Sending a note home each day is asking a lot of the teacher because the note needs to be written at the end of the school day which is often a hectic time in the classroom. Expect that sometimes the teacher will forget. Teachers are not, and should not be expected to be, perfect. Forgetting to write the note is one of those things which occasionally happens so make up a second plan to use at these times. Maybe the teacher can give you his or her home number for your child to call for the assignment (it is best if children are responsible for making their own calls) or, if your child cannot get in touch with the teacher, it is sometimes possible for the school to temporarily loan you a second set of school books to keep at home. This way, you can give some reasonable substitute assignment on your own.

You also need to talk with your child about the logical consequences of doing the work at home if the work has not been done at school. Decide together on a regular time for doing unfinished schoolwork. Children need a little time to play right after school, but they should not be allowed to do anything special before their schoolwork is done, for example, no television or going to a friend's house. Remember that you must not sabotage yourself with talking about the unfinished schoolwork. When the child comes in the door with a note saying there is work to be finished tonight, do not talk about it. Do not scold by saying, "Well, *now* you don't get to play checkers with Dad tonight," or whatever fun thing the child was to have done.

Set aside a special spot in your home for your child to do his schoolwork. If the child does not have a desk in his or her room, the kitchen table will work just fine as long as the television is off, and the rest of the family are busy doing their own thing, so the child is free to concentrate on the schoolwork. Your son or daughter will also need a regular time to sit down to work. If the two of you have agreed upon 7:00 p.m. as schoolwork time, you can say, "It's seven o'clock." If your child ignores you or refuses, you can use a loss-of-privilege consequence like no television viewing until the schoolwork is done. You can use the Broken

Record. Or, as one parent did, you can say no more about it and wait until your child is asleep, then wake him or her and say, "I'm so sorry to wake you, honey, but that schoolwork isn't done yet." Ask some other adults to help brainstorm a logical consequence to fit your situation which you can feel comfortable doing. Remember to say as little as possible about the schoolwork. Be a quiet, inexorable force of nature. "Act, don't talk."

Sometimes children need your help with directions or understanding a concept. But if you suspect your child is constantly asking you questions to get your attention and to avoid doing the work, put a limit on the number of questions he or she may ask you during a work session. Perhaps three opportunities to ask questions would be reasonable for your child. Let your child know ahead of time that he or she will be able to ask for your help only a specific number of times. It is up to the child to choose when help is needed. Keep your involvement friendly and sincere but keep it to the minimum required. When your child is finished and brings the work to you, check it over, and unless it is obviously a sloppy job, say, in a pleased tone of voice, "Looks like you are all done." Leave it to the teacher to do the actual, in depth correcting. If the teacher feels it is not good enough to accept, the teacher can send it back again the next day.

Do not offer to do the extra activity with your child which would have been the fun consequence if the work had been completed at school, but once the schoolwork is finished, be pleasant and enjoy your child's company. Doing schoolwork is not a punishment. *Having to do the schoolwork at home is just a logical consequence of not having done the work at school.* Remember how important it is to give children those four-to-one positive attentions the minute you see neutral or positive behaviors. Once the old behavior patterns are broken, and children have developed more independent, responsible behavior patterns, you will not need to pay so much attention to giving them the careful structure of a logical consequence, but they will always need your loving attention.

SUGGESTED SECONDARY REINFORCERS:

A. *Single items:* for example, stickers, pencils, popcorn, warm fuzzie balls, bubble gum.

B. *Items which can be collected as a group:* for example, one marble, one jack, one bead, one of a set of stickers, one card, one piece of a puzzle, one chance on guessing what is in the prize box.

C. *Activities to do with Mom, Dad, or other adult:* (Set a time limit of 15 to 20 minutes or whatever you are comfortable with.)

   1. Play checkers, chutes and ladders, hopscotch, or cards.
   2. Go for a walk.
   3. Color in a coloring book together.
   4. Help cook something for dinner.
   5. Practice playing basketball, or throwing and hitting the softball.
   6. Pop popcorn and watch an extra half hour of television together.
   7. Get a card lesson on a grown-up card game.
   8. Work on or wash the car together.

D. *Activities to do alone: (Set a time limit of 20 or 30 minutes.)*

   1. Work with hammer, nails, and wood scraps.
   2. Stay up an extra half hour past the regular bedtime.
   3. Mix up bubbles with a mixer in the sink.
   4. Water play in the kitchen sink or bathtub.
   5. Make a tent out of a card table and blankets. (Can invite other people in for a visit or snack.)
   6. Use special clay or paints, or a special coloring book.

A word of caution: If you go ahead and decide to try a plan which uses secondary reinforcers, the other children in the family or classroom may feel left out and consequently worsen their behavior unless you somehow include them. You can put the other children on a similar program, but this is often unnecessary and is at least twice as much work. Often the child earning the secondary reinforcer is happy to earn the reinforcer for siblings or classmates also. Include some such arrangement when you first work out the agreement with the child. Ask, "Would you like to earn a chance for you and Carrie to make a tent to eat dinner in?" or "Would you like to earn a chance for the whole class to have a popcorn party?" In this way, all children in the family or classroom benefit from the one child's improved behavior and are apt to be supportive instead of resentful.

Teachers and parents can also reinforce positive behavior for a group of children. An example would be putting a marble in a jar every time the adult sees someone in the group behaving in a helpful way. When the jar has a certain number of marbles in it, the entire group receives a popcorn party or a special video movie or whatever. No one is left out, by the way, not even the kids who did not earn a single marble. Being left out of a popcorn party because he or she did not earn a marble would be perceived by the child as a punishment which would erode the self-esteem staircase. (Unless, of course, the child had actually destroyed the popcorn machine or engaged in some such incident directly related to popcorn parties. In this case, being left out of the popcorn party would be a logical consequence of wrecking the popcorn machine.)

8 The Correction for Aggression and Loss of Self-Control

Aggressive behaviors are actions which deliberately try to hurt, either physically or emotionally. Children are being aggressive, for example, when they destroy objects in a room, bite, spit in people's faces, fling themselves around the room knocking things over and bumping into people, or bang their heads against a wall. It is aggressive behavior when children seem to lose all inner controls by going into a rage and hurting themselves or others. Aggressive behavior can also be carried out in a more controlled way, for example, if the child deliberately tries to humiliate or hurt someone's feelings, or tickles someone for sustained periods of time, or tells a lie in which the goal is to get even and hurt another person.

The basic correction for aggressive behavior is the TIME-OUT. Time-outs are different from the either-or choice which was described earlier as part of the ignoring correction. At first, the either-or choice and the time-out seem similar. If you tell a child, "You can either be quiet during this T.V. program or you can go be noisy in your bedroom," it seems much the same as saying, "Go to your bedroom and take a five-minute time-out." But they are not the same. There are important differences. The child who makes the either-or choice to go to the bedroom rather than stay by the television and be noisy, is free to leave the bedroom whenever he or she chooses. That is, as soon as the child is quiet, he or she is free to come back to the living room. But children may not leave time-out whenever they choose. They must abide by the time frame laid down by the adult for the time-out procedure. That is, they must stay quietly seated for the amount of time determined by the adult.

Time-out is a much more controlling correction than the either-or choice because there is no opportunity for children to have any choice in the amount of time they must stay in time-out. It is the correction most likely to fuel a power struggle if the adult fails to carry it through with a "I am a force of Nature" attitude. For this reason, *try using all the other corrections and preventative measures before you use the time-out.* Think of time-out as a kind of last resort correction. In fact, as you use the other ideas in the book, you will find yourself having to use time-out less and less. A Head Start teacher recently said that after using the ideas in *Taking Charge,* she had to use the time-out correction only three times in a three month period compared to having used it nearly twice a day before she had enrolled in the class.

Like the other three corrections, time-out is not a punishment. Its purpose is to stop the misbehavior, get the adult back in control of the situation, and the child back in control of himself.

THE BASIC TIME-OUT

Here are the guidelines for administering the basic TIME-OUT:

1. *Time-out is not appropriate for the child under two and a half to three years old.*

For the very young child, for example, an eighteen-month-old who is whacking big brother with a shovel, the best tactic is simply to say, "No hurting other people," as you pick the child up and carry him or her to another room of the house, perhaps placing the child in the high chair or a play pen with some toys. (Do not forget to give big brother a hug to help ease the pain and the injustice of being whacked.) If a young child bites you or pulls your hair, say in a strong voice, "No. People are not for biting." If the child does it again, say again, "No." And put the child down. The consequence of being put down is a powerful reminder that if you want to be with people, you cannot hurt them. Or, maybe your toddler is teething and needs something to chew on. Remember that children under two and a half to three years are not yet ready for the time-out which is described here.

2. *Time-out should be short.*

For the preschooler, sitting quietly for three to five minutes is usually enough to stop the behavior and calm things down. For older children, one minute for every year of their age is a reasonable rule. Making the child sit quietly for unreasonable lengths of time is punitive and will escalate a power struggle. Children quickly need another chance to try a different way of behaving. Excessively prolonged time-outs result in increased power struggles which sabotage the learning of responsible behavior.

3. *Act the first time you see the aggressive behavior.*

You learned the value of not procrastinating in the section on self-sabotage. Aggressive behavior especially should be dealt with immediately because every child needs to know that deliberate hurting is not allowed.

4. *Time-out should happen in a place where there is nothing interesting to do.*

A child's bedroom is generally not a good time-out place because it is filled with interesting things to do. The bottom step of a stairway in the front hall is good. Or you can use a chair in some part of the room out of sight of the television, where there are no books or toys. Keep in mind this is *not* a shaming, punishing exercise like sitting in a corner with a dunce cap on your head. The idea is to find an uninteresting place for the child to sit. If you are in a public place, the child can stand by a wall or sit on the floor.

Sending a child to the principal's office is the worst possible place for a time-out because there are always interesting things going on there. The basic idea is that there should be no social interaction and nothing interesting to do. Time-out means just that: To take time out from all other activities.

5. *Use as little talking as possible.*

Say, "Time-out." You might want to reread the section in Chapter Five on how to give a command. Remember the effectiveness of one-or-two-word statements.

6. *As soon as the child is seated quietly, set a timer.*

If you do not already have a timer, buy or borrow one. Set the timer. Put the timer down near the child. Say, "You must sit quietly for five minutes." Then walk away and continue to carry out your normal routine.

7. *If the child fusses or does not stay in the chair use a physical assist.*

If the child argues, complains, or bangs the chair around during the time-out period, go back to where the child is seated, reset the timer and say, "No, I said sit quietly for five minutes." If the child does not stay seated quietly or attempts to run, use a physical assist. Go stand behind the child, with the palm of one hand on his or her shoulder while the palm of the other hand presses down at the base of the child's neck, in this way securely holding the child down in the chair, and say, "No. You must sit quietly." It is important for you to practice this physical assist with another adult before you try it with a child. Pressing down with the open hand just below the child's neck should feel secure and calming to the child. If it does not, you are probably digging in with your fingers or pressing down too hard. Keep experimenting with the other adult until you have taught each other how to do it. Do not use more force than necessary. Do not hurt the child. Release your hold as soon as you feel the child stop the struggle. Try to get into your Nature mode. Be as centered and as calm as you know how to be.

When the child is quiet and stops struggling, restart the timer and walk away. Occasionally, a child will fight the time-out procedure for a long time. Be prepared to stick with this an hour or all evening if necessary. If you do not sabotage yourself, children will generally only try you at such an intense level one or two times. If you are firm and consistent, they will feel safe with you. If they know what the limits are and they know the limits are fair, they will not continue to test them.

One last admonition: Using the physical assist by holding the child in a time-out place can turn into a power struggle if you let yourself become overly emotional about it. Keep in mind that you are using a teaching method, that you are acting as a force of nature like a wide river or a steady breeze. It is not easy, but you can do it. If you find yourself using the time-out correction more and more, instead of less and less, you and the child are caught up in a power struggle. You need to go to another adult who is familiar with these corrections to help you figure out how you are sabotaging yourself.

When I was working as an intern at the Children's Psychiatric Day Treatment Center at the University of Oregon, I had to put an extremely aggressive ten-year-old boy in time-out. As sometimes happens with very angry children, he exploded with rage. The only way I could make him stay in time-out was to wrestle him to the ground and sit with my back against the wall, my legs wrapped around his legs, holding his back against my front. I crossed his arms in front of his chest and held on. He was strong and I had to hold on to him with all the strength I could muster. When he relaxed, I relaxed my hold on him. When he started to struggle, I tightened my grip. We sat there on the floor for over an hour until he finally sat quietly for five minutes. It was one of the longest hours of my life. But from that day on, he was my friend, and he never seriously disobeyed me again. I was astonished at his positive reaction. He did not seem to feel demeaned, probably because, interspersed between our long silences, I also made an attempt to respect and listen to his feelings. "I know this is hard for you. It is hard for me too." (More about listening to feelings in the next chapter.)

Ask another adult to role-play this situation with you in the role of the child. Only then will you understand how safe and secure it feels to be held in this type of physical restraint. No child feels good about losing his or her inner control. Even though it happens only rarely, you will feel more confident if you are prepared for the rare instances you need to help a child regain inner control.

A mother told her parenting class about a time she used this kind of physical restraint with her daughter. The daughter was an attention-deficit child who, for various reasons, had had a long and stressful day. By evening, she had totally lost control of herself, screaming and lashing out at everyone around her. This sensitive mother finally stepped in, and told her daughter, "I am going to hold you until you can be in control of yourself again." The mother took a position on the floor with her struggling daughter similar to the one described above. Almost immediately the child collapsed sobbing in her arms.

A Head Start teacher tells how amazed she was when, as she began holding an out-of-control child in this way, the child immediately began to suck her thumb and curl up in a fetal position.

Priscilla, who worked as a Head Start Family Visitor, told how one day when she was making a home visit, she had to forcibly hold a boy in this same way. The boy, Tommy, had gone into a rage. He was tipping over furniture and smashing things while his mother stood helplessly by. After Priscilla had calmed Tommy by forcibly holding him down on the floor, the boy's mother quite seriously brought up the possibility of placing him in a foster home. Priscilla was amazed when Tommy faced his mother's rejection calmly. He moved to stand beside the person who had so recently held him down on the floor. "That's all right. I'll go live with Priscilla."

Feeling safe is one of the most basic of human needs. Do not hesitate to hold children securely if they explode out of the boundary of self-control. Let children gain the security they need from the strong and matter-of-fact way your body holds them.

(Your own physical size and strength is obviously the limiting factor which will determine the size of child you can hold in this way.)

7. *Once the correction is finished, do not mention the negative behavior again.*

Once the incident is over, try to begin giving positive attention for neutral and positive behaviors. In the same way you would give children a chance to get right back into a canoe if they tip it over, so children need to be given the chance to immediately resume normal behaviors in order to experience success in their interactions with you. As soon as they are exhibiting positive or neutral behaviors, let them know by your positive attentions that you care about them. It was their *behavior* you did not like, not them.

8. *Look for the underlying cause of the aggression.*

If children are frequently acting out in aggressive ways, you can be certain they are responding to some deep hurt which they perceive has been done to them. Children who continually lash out at the world in aggressive ways are acting on an instinctual premise that they must protect their inner core of integrity. They have come to believe that their best defense is a strong offense. It may not be clear to you right now, but inevitably, every child who feels frequently compelled to manipulate or hurt others is doing it from a need to secure himself or herself from further physical or emotional hurt. In order to help the child, you need to know how the child perceives his or her world. *Listen to the child.* The next chapter will give you ideas on how to do that.

Besides listening to the child, talk to other adults who know him or her. Talk about the problem with your spouse or partner. Talk it over with the teacher or members of your family. If you are a teacher, talk it over with the child's parents. Ask each other the question, *"What has hurt Marty so much that she feels the need to hurt and manipulate others?"* If you can discover what it is, you will better know what kinds of specific positive attentions you can give Marty to help her feel safe enough, and loved enough, so she will not have to keep lashing out at other people. If you look deeply enough, every aggressive child in some way feels there is at least one of Maslow's needs which is not being supplied for him or her. The problem is that children cannot verbalize their unmet needs. Often even parents and teachers cannot figure it out without help. The value of going to a good family therapist is the help he or she can give you in finding the answer to that question. If after you have tried everything suggested in this book, and nothing changes, it is time to look for such a person.

It is sometimes hard to figure out whether a misbehavior is self-indulgent or aggressive. Trust your own inner feelings. If your gut reaction is one of shock and hurt because you believe the behavior was meant to really harm or manipulate, or if you sense the child is not just having a temper tantrum but has lost control of himself, use the time-out. If you are experiencing extreme irritation with the behavior, and believe the behavior is primarily a bid for attention, treat it as a self- indulgent behavior.

EXERCISE:

Continue to use the "Negative Behaviors" chart, located on the following page, for recording a sampling of misbehaviors and problem-solving behaviors which you observe in your children. Also, write down how you use any of the corrections during the coming week. (If you are interested in learning more about how to deal with the problem of lying, read Section C at the end of this chapter.)

NEGATIVE BEHAVIORS:
The Four Misbehaviors
(and 3 Problem-Solving Situations)

NOT-MINDING

SELF-INDULGENT (Attention-Getting)

ROUTINE-NOT-MINDING (Will not do routine tasks)

AGGRESSIVE (Deliberately Hurting)

Negative Behaviors Requiring Problem-Solving Which Do Not Fit Above:

1. Adjust Environment   **2. Solve Conflicts**   **3. Listen to Feelings**

DISCUSSION IDEAS: CHAPTER 8: TIME-OUT AND PHYSICAL RESTRAINT

1. Share and discuss your comments on the past week's "Negative Behaviors" chart.

2. Did anyone try offering some fun choices to their children last week? Did anyone try out a logical consequence plan?

3. Practice the time-out procedure: Everyone take a turn being the child and adult in a situation where the adult is holding the child in the chair. Have the "child" struggle while the "adult" practices the physical assist of placing the palm of one hand on the child's shoulder and other at the base of the neck. Do this until you find a position which feels most secure and convincing for the child. The goal is to convey the sense that "I am a force of Nature and this must be done." Use the minimum pressure necessary. Avoid any sense that you are punishing the child.

4. Now, practice the physical restraint procedure: Take turns playing the part of the child. Hold the "child" on the floor in front of you. *Do not hold the child on your lap.* The child needs to feel the firm support of the floor under him while feeling your body giving support by enfolding him in your arms. Remember you will probably have to hold the child's arms by crossing them against his or her chest. Experiment with different ways to hold the child's arms if the child tries to bite you. Be aware of the need to keep your head clear if the child is tall enough to hit your chin with the back of his or her head.

5. Discuss the difference between the either-or choice and the time-out. Is everyone clear as to the difference?

6. Look at "The Four Sabotages" chart again at the end of Chapter Three. Is there one which you feel has been especially powerful in sabotaging your relationships with your children?

7. Regarding Section C at the end of this chapter: If you are interested in the problem of lying, talk about the differences between the three kinds of lying: problem-solving, self-indulgent, and aggressive. Are the differences clear to you?

REVIEW: Correction for *Aggressive* Behaviors

THE TIME-OUT:

1. **A short time-out is best**: 3-5 minutes for preschoolers. One minute for every year of age for older children.

2. The time-out place should have **nothing interesting** for the child to do.

3. Use as **little talking** as possible.

4. **Use a timer**. Reset the timer until the child **sits quietly** for the required amount of time.

5. **Walk away** as soon as the child is sitting quietly.

6. Use the **physical assist** if the child will not stay or sit quietly in the chair. If the child loses all self-control, use the **physical restraint** procedure.

7. **When the time-out is over, be pleasant** with the child. Time-out is not a punishment. It is a way to temporarily help you stop the misbehavior. It is also a way to help the child get back in control of himself or herself.

8. **Look for the underlying cause,** especially if the aggressive behaviors are frequent or severe. "What has hurt the child so much that he or she feels compelled to lash out at others?"

9. The time-out is a **last resort** correction, to be used when everything else has failed.

REMEMBER NOT TO SELF-SABOTAGE

The Four Misbehaviors and Their Corrections

Misbehavior	Correction
Not-Minding	Physical Assist, or Broken Record
Self-Indulgent (attention-getting)	Ignore, or Either-or Choice
Routine-Not-Minding (will not do routine tasks/ irresponsible)	Give children daily opportunities to make, and live with, their choices. Set up a logical consequence situation so children can experience the consequences of their choices.
Aggressive (deliberately hurting self or others)	Time-out and Physical Restraint

Child Has A Problem	Adult Helps The Child By:
1. Child cannot live up to adult expectations, even when he tries. 2. Child has a conflict with someone. 3. Child is troubled.	1. Adjusting the environment 2. Teaching assertiveness and negotiation 3. Listening to inner-reality feelings

SECTION C: WHEN IS LYING AN AGGRESSIVE BEHAVIOR?

One of the most upsetting behaviors for adults to deal with is lying. Seeing a child hit another child is distressing, but hitting another child at least has the virtue of being out in the open. Parents and teachers feel they can at least understand hitting. Lying, on the other hand, seems deliberately premeditated and underhanded. There is an undertone of "sneakiness" about such behaviors which repulses most adults.

Lying, like fighting, generally falls into one of three different categories: Problem-solving, self-indulgent, or aggressive. If lying is done for self-protection, it is a problem-solving behavior, and any correction is of secondary importance. Most important is not to back the child into a corner in the first place. If the child feels cornered, he or she is likely to try to get out of the problem by telling a lie. If this happens, try to help the child figure out a better way to solve the problem.

For a typical **problem-solving lie**, I refer you back to the story about my grandmother and the cookies. Or take the incident of Jonathan, whose father came home and found one of his saw blades snapped in two. It was an accident but Jonathan knew he would be punished both physically and emotionally if his father found out he did it. The father was furious. He promised, "It will go easier for you if you tell the truth." (By this the father means he will not physically hurt Jonathan if his son tells the truth.) "If I find out you are lying, you are *really* going to get it." This is a catch 22 situation. No matter what Jonathan does, he knows he will be punished, if not physically, then emotionally. He decides to lie in the hope his father will believe him and not punish him at all.

Children also learn to tell lies to solve the problem of getting what they want when they see important adults doing it. For example, a child overheard his mother telling his father's employer that her husband could not come to work that day because he was sick. The child knew perfectly well that his father was feeling fine but wanted the day off to go fishing. In this way, the child learned that telling a lie is a quasi acceptable way to get what you want. If Mom or Dad tell lies to get what they want, it must be an okay thing to do.

Sometimes children use a problem-solving lie for deeper reasons. The following incident happened to a grandmother who had taken her grandchildren camping at a state campground. On the next to last day of their outing, her nine-year-old granddaughter, Claire, came to her when Claire's older brother was out of hearing and said, "Mother said you should take us out for breakfast on our last day." (Claire loved eating out and she knew there was a restaurant in the private resort area nearby.)

The grandmother knew the child's mother would never have said such a thing. In fact, Claire's mother felt it was important to teach her children it was rude and selfish to ever ask for things. After her first flash of irritation, the grandmother realized that from her granddaughter's point of view, a child has no right to ask directly. She realized that Claire was trying to problem-solve the situation by using the authority of her mother to let grandmother know what she wanted.

Grandmother tried helping her granddaughter solve the problem in a different way. "Claire, if you want to go out to breakfast, I wish you would just ask me. Say, 'Grandma, can we go out to breakfast?' I would rather you would just ask me what you want rather than tell me things your mother said. If I had enough money, and if your brother wanted to go, we could go." Claire looked at her grandmother with round, serious eyes. She knew she had been found out. Grandma smiled at her granddaughter before she gave her one more piece of information, "After all, what is the worst that can happen? The worst thing that could happen is I might say no." And grandmother shrugged as if to say, this is no big deal.

Later in the day, again when they were alone, Claire directly asked if they could go out to breakfast. The grandmother replied, "Well, let's see if I have enough money left. If we do, we could ask your brother what he thinks." Of course, the brother thought it was a good idea. The next morning, on their way home, they all went out to breakfast. If grandmother had not had enough money, she could have said, "Gosh, Claire. It would be fun to go but I just don't have enough money this time." Claire's self-esteem will not be hurt from being told no. She will not be encouraged to lie again because she was told no.

Claire was afraid to be honest about what she wanted. She was not afraid of being told, "No." She was afraid of being emotionally punished by shaming: "How many times have I told you not to always be asking for things? We certainly will *not* go until you learn not to always be asking for things." It might be confusing at first for Claire to be told by Grandma that it *is* okay to ask for what she wants, when Mother has always told her it is *not* okay. But Claire is smart enough to learn that the relationship between her and her grandmother can operate under different rules: "With Grandma it is okay to ask directly for what you want."

Claire lied to get what she wanted and to escape being shamed. Like everyone else, she wanted something. By lying, she tried to escape the emotional punishment of being told in a scornful tone of voice that she had no right to ask for what she wanted. Claire lied because she could not bear to hear the nonverbal message that she is not an important enough person to ask directly for what she wants.

There is also the **self-indulgent lie**. Here is a typical example: Joe's friend Betsy has just returned from a Disneyland vacation with her family. She immediately runs over to Joe's house to tell Joe and his Dad all about the wonderful things she saw and did in Disneyland. After listening to her for some time, Joe suddenly says, "*I* am going to Disneyland next month." This lie is a self-indulgent behavior. Joe has resorted to lying in order to get some of the attention now being focused exclusively on Betsy. Joe is not being aggressive in the sense that he is trying to get even and hurt Betsy in some way. He just wants some attention. This self-indulgent kind of lying can be best dealt with in the following way: Dad looks at Joe and firmly states the truth. "You *wish* you could go to Disneyland next month." Dad then proceeds to ignore any more references from Joe about the nonexistent trip to Disneyland.

It is important that Dad make the statement about wishing. By stating what is actually the case, Dad is not ignoring Joe's "lie" altogether, but serves as a valuable reality check for him. "You *wish* it was true but it isn't." As soon as Joe shows any sign of neutral or positive behaviors, Dad can immediately attend to him with warm eye contact or an arm around Joe's shoulder.

Remember that young children have a rich fantasy life. It is okay for them to play pretend games, to pretend to have invisible friends, to be a fireman putting out fires, or welcoming a party of Martians who have just landed in the back yard. These fantasy stories are not lies, but part of the normal games of early child-hood.

The following incident is an example of an **aggressive lie** because the child tries to manipulate the situation to deliberately hurt another person: Grandma and Grandpa have come to dinner. Walter and Janice have just brought home their report cards. Walter's report card is much improved over last quarter's report. All the adults are making a happy fuss over him. Janice's report card is also very good but hers is always good and everyone takes it somewhat for granted. A little later, Janice says to Grandma and Grandpa, "Remember that fire engine you gave Walter for his birthday? He said he didn't like it. He said it's too kiddish. He said you never get him good presents." (Janice has just exaggerated a remark Walter made last week about the fact that he is getting too old to play with trucks anymore.)

The correction for this lie is a time-out. One of the parents should carry out the basic five minute time-out procedure, go back to the dinner table and cheerfully continue the conversation with Walter, Grandma, Grandpa, and the other parent. Even if Walter did say what Janice has repeated, Janice should still be given the time-out because repeating such a statement is hurtful both to Walter and to her grandparents. If Grandma and Grandpa want to talk about Janice's accusation in front of the children, say quietly, "Let's not talk about it right now." Explain the strategy of not sabotaging to Grandma and Grandpa, as well as what Walter actually did say, at a later time when the children are out of hearing. When Janice comes back to the table after her time-out has ended, carry on with your normal conversation and do not mention it again. As soon as possible after the time-out, at a neutral or positive time, be sure to tell Janice so Grandma and Grandpa can hear, too, how happy you are for her consistently good grades. It is her hurt feelings that nobody at the dinner table seemed to care about *her* grades which elicited her aggressive behavior in the first place.

9 Listening to Inner-Reality

Young or old, we are all of us moved by powerful emotions. The very young child experiences the same feelings as the adult: joy, sorrow, loneliness, humiliation, fear, anger, embarrassment, contentment. Human beings come fully equipped with the whole wide range of human emotions: As Jean Lawrence says, "Feelings Have No Birthday."* Of course, each individual has unique personal experiences and so interprets each situation differently. For example, a child may feel fear at the noise of an oncoming steam locomotive because the child has never seen one, while you may feel a touch of sadness and nostalgia because you have many prior memories of steam locomotives. At some other time, in a different situation, you may be the one to experience fear while the child feels sadness. The capability of the adult and the child for feeling emotions is the same, even though the experiences and the attitudes that give rise to the emotions may be different.

Yet, adults often find it hard to allow children to express the very same negative feelings which adults commonly experience. If an adult learned as a child that feelings of anger, sadness, jealousy, or resentment are somehow wrong or frightening, it is hard for that adult to witness a young child openly expressing those same forbidden emotions. Complicating the problem is the fact that adults have often been taught it is polite to hide their own negative feelings, whereas the negative emotions of children are right out in the open for everyone to see and hear. The usual response of the adult who has somehow learned to repress his or her own negative

* Title of an unpublished manuscript by Jean Lawrence, founder of Fanno Creek Children's Center of Portland, Oregon.

feelings, is not only to stop the child's open expression of negative emotions, but to convince the child he or she *should not be feeling that way at all*. In other words, with the best of intentions, we often try to convince the child that the child's negative feelings are "wrong."

There are three major reasons why it is so hard for adults to allow emotions like jealousy, anger, and sorrow to be felt and expressed by children. The first is that as loving adults, *we want so much to protect their young lives from emotional pain*. To see our children hurting recalls our own memories of emotional pain and we hurt right along with them. It seems part of our role as parents and teachers that we try to prevent our children from suffering the inner hurts that we ourselves have experienced. The second reason is that because of the raw intensity of some negative emotions, *we are afraid our children might get themselves into trouble or might hurt someone else* if they do not learn how to "control" their feelings. And third, *we sometimes interpret children's expressions of negative emotions as acts of defiance and a personal rejection of us*.

These three reasons, each based in powerful emotional needs of our own, often compel us to try to convince children that they are wrong to be feeling what they are feeling. In so doing, we unintentionally weaken the competency/respect step on their staircase of needs by sending them the nonverbal message, "If you were a competent person, and as smart as *I* am, you would know that what you are feeling is not the *right* way to feel."

Inevitably, the child also begins to assume that if his or her feelings are "wrong," he or she must also be a bad person for feeling that way. In this way, the Being-Love step on the staircase of needs is undermined, as the child asks, "How can I be loveable just for being me when I have such bad feelings inside?" Self-esteem is eroded and all the negative feelings are strengthened.

Children have an inner core of integrity which compels them to be true to themselves. They know that what they feel is true, even when they are not able to verbalize it by giving the feeling a name, and even when other people tell them the feeling is wrong. They know their feelings are real, even though the feelings become increasingly confusing to them when important adults try to convince them they *should not be feeling* that way, or *are not feeling* that way. In order to defend their inner selves and to keep in touch with the feelings they know are firmly rooted in their own INNER-REALITY, children can slam shut an inner door to block any attempt to argue them out of their negative feelings. With the inner door shut, the words of the adult cannot penetrate. A child's ears may hear you, but his or her heart will be closed.

Lois's husband had recently left her and their five year old son. The husband had not called or written the boy for four months. Other than the letter he had left behind, Lois had had no word from her husband. Their son, Phil, cried easily and often erupted in angry outbursts at his mother. Occasionally, Phil tried to verbalize his feelings, "I miss Daddy." Lois continually tried to take away some of his pain by telling him what she believed to be true, "Daddy misses you, too, Phil. He is just upset right now. He has so many things on his mind. I know he loves you very much. You are his own special boy." Phil invariably responded to Lois's attempts to comfort him by yelling, "Shut up! Shut up!" and running from the room. There were many wet eyes in our parenting group as Lois told this story. We realized how painful it must be for her to helplessly watch her child go through the pain of such abandonment.

After learning about the importance of not arguing children out of their inner-reality feelings, Lois, in spite of many reservations, decided to try to stop all her good intentioned reassurances about Daddy. The next time Phil said, "I miss Daddy," Lois was quiet. She went over to sit by her son and put her arm around his shoulder. "I miss him, too, honey." She gave him a hug. He hugged her back and cried a bit. They sat like that for a little while, neither of them saying anything more. Then Phil got up, and started playing with his toy trucks in a perfectly calm manner. "I don't really understand it," Lois told us. "The angry feelings he usually had just melted away."

Here is another paradox: By allowing the child to feel the intensity of his or her inner pain, the child is able to finally let the painful feeling go, whereas, if someone tries to convince the child he or she should stop experiencing the intense inner pain, the child clutches it even more tightly.

Further, children experience a second emotion of anger when people around them try to cajole, or reassure, or argue them out of their first feelings. In Phil's case, for example, his first feelings may have been rejection, feeling unloved, and loneliness. When Phil yelled, "Shut up! Shut up!" and ran from the room, it was the secondary emotion of anger which fueled his behavior. Yelling, "Shut up!" at his mother was not a rejection of her as a person. His expression of anger was a defense which helped give him strength to protect himself against the confusion of being told he was mistaken to feel what he felt, when, deep in his inner-reality core, he knew, that even if mother said his feelings were wrong, *what he felt was real.*

Here is another painful inner-reality situation related by a grandmother: Five-year-old Laura is sitting on the living room floor building a complicated block structure. Her two-and-a-half year-old brother, Roald, is playing with his cars nearby, occasionally helping by handing his sister some blocks. The grandparents are seated in chairs on either side of the children, talking and watching the kids play. Unexpectedly, and without meaning to, Roald bumps into Laura's block structure and the whole edifice comes tumbling down. Laura starts to wail, "Oh, it's wrecked! It was almost done! I was going to use it for the little dolls to live in." Laura begins to sob. The adults recognize these are not crocodile tears. Laura is deeply pained over the loss of her creation.

Both grandparents try to comfort and reassure her by giving what they perceive to be helpful outer-reality information. "Don't cry, Laura. We'll help you rebuild it," and "Never mind, honey. We'll help you make it as good as new." Laura cries even harder at this and begins to stomp her feet and shout, "Why do things *I* make always get wrecked? Why do *I* have to have a little brother?" At this point, Mother comes into the room, immediately realizes and accepts the state of Laura's inner-reality feelings and says, "Oh, you must feel so sad that your block house got wrecked." Laura nods, sniffles, and stops yelling. She gets back down on the floor and says calmly, "Well, I can fix it again." Roald, who has been watching the whole affair with round eyes now says, "I'm sorry," and goes over to hug his sister and tries to help her rebuild the block house. To her grandparents' amazement, Laura even accepts her little brother's apology and inexpert assistance.

The grandmother told us she knew how important it is to let children experience their own painful feelings, but she wanted so much to protect her granddaughter from the pain of losing her block house that she went right ahead and tried to convince her not to feel sad anyway.

Here is the dilemma for all loving adults: How can we convince ourselves that children are strong enough to endure their own inner pain? How can we convince ourselves that children will not necessarily hurt themselves or others when they experience strong negative feelings? And how can we learn to not take it as a personal affront when a child expresses negative emotions like resentment or anger?

Here is a situation in which a second-grader named Scott comes home from school, slams his books on the table and yells, "I'm not going to that dumb school ever again!"

We adults instantly assume that Scott is having a problem at school which *we* must solve. We are upset that he is upset. We try to make him feel happy again. We generally try to convince the child that he should be reasonable and rational. We are reasonable and rational in our advice to him. We ignore his inner-reality feelings and instead try to convince him of the outer-reality situation which we clearly perceive, even if he does not. Here are some typical outer-reality responses adults are likely to give to Scott:

"But look, you *have* to go to school. It's the *law.* I know things are tough some days but it's tough for everyone some days. Going to school is your *job.* I can't quit *my* job just because I have a hard day. You're making too much of this. It's better to try to forget all about it. Let's have a cookie. Tomorrow will be a better day." The adult may even go over to the child, rumple his hair, try to tickle him into giving a laugh. Or, the adult may try to get to the root of the problem by questioning and attempting to place blame: "What happened? Are you sure you didn't do something to cause it?

From the adult point of view, explaining to the child the facts of the situation is a rational and helpful way to approach the problem. This is why it is so puzzling and frustrating to a concerned adult when Scott responds to all the good advice and reassurances by becoming even more upset. At this point, Scott may even angrily run from the room, slamming the door behind him. Some children will stay in the room but will withdraw inwardly. They will answer the adult's questions with a sullen expression and downcast eyes and respond, "I don't know." Like all healthy children, Scott has an inner door he can slam tight against anyone in the outside world who threatens his inner-reality feelings and his honest, inner core of integrity. Bang. He closes the door. When he does, he stops listening to you. He will no longer share his feelings. You can force Scott to sit there, but you cannot force him to agree with you.

Adults, too, have this same inner-reality core, but it is often buried so deep, we sometimes forget it is there. Unlike the young child, who is still very much in touch with his or her inner-reality, we adults sometimes confuse what we *should* feel with what we *do* feel. It is not unusual to find adults who cannot figure out what they want because they so accustomed to wanting what other people have wanted them to want.

At any rate, communication is now closed. If you are the adult in the situation given above, you may be talking but Scott is refusing to hear. He is fending off your words like Wonder Woman fends off bullets with her magic bracelets. Since his feelings are not acceptable to you, he has stopped trying to share them. He may leave, or sit in sullen silence, or he may flip into a kind of self-indulgent behavior by arguing. You can be as rational and reasonable as you like, but Scott can match you point for point. If you are going to act like a judge or a detective, he will be the lawyer for the defense. "Why do you always tell me things I already know?" or, "*You* can change jobs, why can't I change schools?"

What does Scott expect you to say? What does any child want from you when he or she shares a troubling feeling or inner conflict? Like every adult in the same situation, Scott wants someone to confirm that it is a common human experience to feel what he is feeling. Negative emotions and inner conflicts are scary for kids. "If Mom and Dad and Teacher are not blown away by what I'm feeling, I must be okay. If they are not repulsed by me because of these feelings, I must be normal. If they think I can handle it, I must be a strong and capable person."

In a moment of deep negative emotion, Scott opens his inner door to share some of his inner-reality with you. In order for that inner door to stay open, you must give up any sense of being superior to Scott in the matter of emotions. You must give up the role of being the all-wise protector, advisor, problem-solver and judge. You must let Scott take the lead. You must trust that he is strong enough to deal with the power of his own feelings. *You must allow him to feel what he is feeling.*

What can you, as a caring adult, do when Scott comes home deeply unhappy about school and says, "I'm never going to that dumb school again." Whether you keep on doing whatever you are doing, or whether you go sit at the table on which Scott has just thrown his books, you can look and feel sympathetic. You can say something like, "Wow, what a day you had..." or just, "Gosh..." You do not have to say much. Remember how powerful nonverbal attention can be? Quiet listening—intent nonverbal attention—combined with short sympathetic verbal responses is the inner-reality response he craves. Your inner-reality response lets Scott know you respect his right to feel what he feels. You do not have to memorize anything special to say. You do not have to agree with his words and opinions. You do not have to agree with Scott if he says the teacher is stupid or that someone should punch out the principal. Try to accept the feelings which gave rise to those statements. The main thing is to believe *the child has a right to feel what he is feeling.* And believe that *the child is strong enough to endure the pain of what he is feeling,* just as you believe that another adult is strong enough.

Kids sometimes need to blow off steam, the same as adults. You may remember the example of adult steam-blowing given in the chapter on self-sabotage but it is worth repeating here. This time it is the wife who comes home humiliated and discouraged by something that has happened at work that day. She throws down her coat and storms, "I swear to God I'm handing in my resignation tomorrow. We'll eat beans. I'll go on unemployment. I've had it with that S.O.B.!" Imagine this woman's reaction if her spouse gives her a rational, reasonable outer-reality response: "Now honey, you knew when you took that job there would be some bad days. You can't just up and quit. You'd never get a good recommendation for the next job with such short notice, and you know we have to keep up those payments on the new car." The fact is, her husband knows she needs to blow off steam and regain some inner balance by venting her feelings at the events of the day. He knows his wife understands all the outer-reality facts. He does not need to tell her about the car payments and the fact that there are always tough days on every job. She would feel demeaned and patronized if he gave her rational advice or reasonable criticism. Instead he gives her the inner-reality response of a hug and a sympathetic comment, "Oh, what a rotten day you must have had." Children coming home from school feeling discouraged and demeaned also know they cannot quit school. They are looking for the same kind of inner-reality response we give so easily to other adults, but find so hard to give to our kids.

As in the earlier situations, with the boy whose father had abandoned him, and the girl whose block creation had been destroyed, parents and teachers report again and again that when they manage to keep to the inner-reality response, and resist the temptation to start rescuing and giving advice, they can see a visible, physical sense of relief, as the tension from the negative feelings melts away. By listening in a quiet and compassionate way, you let children know they are respected, that their feelings are normal and human. When they reveal their inner selves to you, by your quiet example you can let them know there is nothing "wrong" about their feelings. Consequently, there is no need for them to slam their inner door tight against your words or to close their ears to your voice. The child's integrity and dignity can remain intact.

Many of us find it frightening to accept and listen when a child expresses extreme anger over a perceived or real problem: "I'd like to kill him!" or "I hate her!" Teachers often tell how they are able to listen to a student's feelings, but have a difficult time listening to the negative feelings of their own children. It is especially hard for parents to allow their children to experience negative feelings because we feel so protective of our own kids. Sometimes we want so much to protect our children from the pain we ourselves experienced as children, we deny their pain even exists. We often think we are failures as parents when our children are feeling friendless or discouraged or jealous; at these times we cannot even admit to ourselves that our children feel this way, much less allow them to feel it. Sometimes the old tapes play from our own childhoods: "Nice children do not say these things, good children do not feel these feelings. Shame on you. What a bad boy you are to feel like that." Such a simple thing, to allow a child to feel his or her own feelings, yet so hard for a loving parent to do.

If Gloria says she would like to kill somebody, it is tempting to leap in with a lecture on outer-reality and talk on and on about why we cannot even think of killing people and what the Bible says about killing and on and on. But of course Gloria already knows that. She is not really planning to kill anyone. The truth is that children who are allowed to express all their emotions, including anger, will not need to act out their anger in aggressive ways. Children who are not allowed to talk honestly about their inner-reality feelings are most likely to hurt themselves or others. People who bury their feelings are the ones who will ultimately take out their pent-up rage on others. When feelings are listened to and accepted, they lose their power to create the anger which prompts us to lash out and hurt ourselves or the people around us.

It may help you to accept a child's anger if you understand that anger is a secondary emotion which gives us the strength to survive the pain of some deeper first emotion. Was the child humiliated? Is the child afraid of failure? Does the child feel unloved? Rejected? Stupid? Helpless? As has been mentioned earlier, emotions which are experienced first are what fuel the secondary emotion of anger.

Here is an example from my own experience of how anger arises from primary, underlying emotions: Several years ago, my husband and I were both working long hours. We were both exhausted. At one point it seemed to me we were just eating and sleeping together, living together in a house as mere acquaintances. One evening I came home and found him sitting in the living room reading the paper. I felt such a longing to be playful and carefree and intimate again; I went over and tickled him. He jerked my hand away and said angrily, "Can't you leave me alone when I'm reading?"

Imagine my feelings. I went into the kitchen and stood by the sink. I experienced powerful feelings of anger. I was about ready to go storming back into the living room and tell him what I thought of his insensitivity when I suddenly thought, "Wait a minute. What did I feel *before* I felt the anger?" You have probably guessed most of my primary feelings: rejection, loneliness, and fear. The fear was that our relationship was disintegrating. In verbalizing to myself the primary feelings, my anger faded somewhat, although the pain of the first feelings seemed to hit even harder.

I went back into the living room and sat down beside my husband, "I've got to talk to you. I'm scared and I'm lonely." Immediately the paper came down and my husband's concerned eyes looked out at me. "What is it?" The paper was forgotten. He listened to me tell of my fear that our relationship was crumbling. I listened to him explain how he was resentful of having so many people to deal with at work, and how he had looked forward to coming home to peace and solitude. He felt I had not respected his need to be alone for awhile. (Tickling is an extremely demanding kind of touching, by the way.) At this point, I was finally able to imagine *his* feelings. We talked about how the stresses of time and energy were creating a barrier between us. We sat for a long time saying nothing, holding each other. Intimacy was restored. Not only did the anger evaporate, the fear and the loneliness also melted away. If I had gone back into the living room and confronted him with the secondary emotion of my anger, even if I had put it in a polite form of "I feel so angry at you," instead of "How can you be so uncaring, you louse?" we might have had a major problem build between us for days or even weeks. Most likely we both would have taken our unresolved anger back to hurt, not only ourselves, but also the children and adults we worked with.

Children are usually not going to be able to verbalize their primary emotions for you. Many adults are also not able to verbalize the primary emotions which cause their own anger to flare. As a young adult, I certainly did not know how to share my primary feelings. Unfortunately, many adults and children have this in common: The emotion they can share most easily with others is the secondary emotion of anger.

Most people think of anger as a negative, or a "bad" emotion, but anger also has a positive face. Anger is an expression of a human being's strength and energy. Anger gave me the energy to walk back into the living room and confront my husband with my pain. Without the anger, I might have been able to do nothing about dealing with my pain. Without anger, children too, might give up, lose their inner integrity, wither emotionally, maybe even physically die, as has happened to so many children in orphanages. Anger gives each human being the energy to go forward, to change things, to get what he or she needs.

The reason so many of us are afraid of anger is because we have so often witnessed the power of anger to hurt ourselves or other people. Alice Miller's book, *For Your Own Good*, is well worth reading if you would like to understand just how devastating and far reaching are the consequences for all of human culture when the primary emotions of children are not heard and accepted. Dr. Miller has documented in convincing detail the reasons for allowing children to be honest about their feelings.

When children express deeply felt and negative emotions, they often just want to be listened to. Usually, they do not expect any thing else from you. The very act of airing their emotions lessens the need for taking any other action. On the other hand, there are times you can sense a child needs some help in problem-solving the situation. Resist the temptation to leap in and take control by giving outer-reality advice. Listen and let the child take the lead. Ask his or her permission to help find solutions, for example:

1. "Is there something I can do to help?" (Only agree to do what you feel good about doing. You do not have to agree to anything which would whittle away at your own inner core of integrity.)

2. "Do you have any ideas for making things go better?"

3. "Do you want me to think of some ideas for you to try?"

At first it will be hard not to slip back into the outer-reality response. After the first successful two minutes of inner-reality listening, you may find yourself falling back into saying the same old things. Habits die hard. Do not be discouraged if this happens to you. Keep at it and you will gradually feel more comfortable at not leaping in to solve the child's problems. If you cannot think of anything to say, just keep quiet. Look sympathetic, and pay close attention. You can even try telling the truth, "Gosh, I just don't know what to say."

Use the inner-reality response only when children express a deep and troubling emotion which is tied to a real problem in their lives. *Do not use the inner-reality response when you are carrying out a correction for a self-indulgent misbehavior.* It is up to you, as a sensitive adult, to decide whether the child is really having a difficult time coping with his or her emotions, or whether the child is engaging in a self-indulgent, attention-getting misbehavior. If you are not sure, first try an inner-reality response. You will be able to see from the child's reaction whether this is a real problem for the child or whether it is just an habitual self-indulgent misbehavior. Many well intentioned and caring C adults have sabotaged themselves by giving lots of listening attention to a child who used feelings as a smokescreen for self-indulgent behavior.

Eight-year-old Beth could always deflect her parents' demands for responsible behavior by using feeling language she had learned would trigger their reflective listening skills. One noteworthy example was for her to furrow her brow and say sorrowfully, "I feel very sad when you make me do the dishes all alone in the kitchen." This would divert her parents attention from the task of getting her to do the dishes while they had a long discussion with her about her feelings and their feelings. The parents came away from these encounters with Beth feeling frustrated and angry, but not exactly sure why. No wonder they were upset. Their own inner sense of integrity was threatened. They felt outwitted and manipulated by their eight-year-old daughter. In fact, Beth had no deep troubling feelings in this matter other than she definitely did not like to do the dishes. She had learned to use the language of feelings to manipulate her parents into discussing emotions instead of her chores. When these parents learned to ignore the self-indulgent behavior of feigned sadness, and concentrate on some creative consequences for dishwashing, everyone was happier.

Finally, there is no formula you need to memorize, no correct word pattern you need to remember. The key to really being able to listen to human beings express deep and hurting feelings, whether child or adult, is to believe they have a right to feel what they are feeling, and to believe that they are strong enough to bear the pain.

EXERCISE:

> *Study the charts on the following two pages.* Using the first "Inner and Outer-Reality" chart as a guide, use the second chart to write down any inner or outer-reality responses you give to your children during the coming week.

INNER AND OUTER-REALITY /
HELPING THE CHILD COPE WITH PAINFUL EMOTIONS

Child's Opening Remark	Outer-Reality Response	Inner-Reality Response
"Jane gets to go everywhere! I never get to do anything good!" (Stamps her foot.)	"Jane didn't get to do all these things either when she was your age. When you are her age you will get to do all the things she does. Anyhow, I think you get to do *more than Jane got to do at your age!*"	" I bet you wish you were the oldest one in this family..." (Spoken with understanding, not as a put-down) or just a sympathetic look, and "Hmmm," or "Gosh!"
"I don't want to go to school anymore! I hate this dumb school!" (Throwing school books on the floor.)	"But everyone has to go to school. It's the law! You just have to learn that everything in life isn't fun. *I* have to go to work, even when I don't want to!"	"Gosh, what a tough day you must have had!" or just a sympathetic look, and "Hmmm," or "Gosh..."
"I can't do it . . ." (Slumped shoulders and downcast eyes.)	"Of course you can! You are just as smart as anyone in this class. I'm sure you can get it. Just keep trying. Maybe you just need to work harder."	"You're feeling pretty discouraged today...." or just a sympathetic look, and "Hmmm," or "Gosh..."
"I'm never going to play with that stinky Ginny again!" (Frowning, with hands on hips.)	"Well, you might be angry right now, but you'll get over it. Remember the argument you had with John last week? And now you are friends again."	"Something happened between you two that was really upsetting..." or just a sympathetic look, and "Hmmm," or "Gosh..."
"There's nothing to *do* around here." (Drooping head and whining voice.)	"Have you thought about making something with the Legos? Or maybe you could see if Jimmy wants to come over. Or...how about helping clean up that garage?"	"One of those boring days..." or just a sympathetic look, and "Hmmm," or "Gosh..."

Characteristics of Outer-Reality Response	Characteristics of Inner-Reality Response
1. Closes the door to two-way communication.	1. Opens the door to two-way communication.
2. The adult does lots of talking (advising, analyzing, moralizing, criticizing, consoling, judging, ordering, questioning . . .)	2. The adult does lots of quiet listening along with short verbal responses which clarify the child's feelings.
3. Insists on logic, reason, rationalization.	3. Accepts the fact that feelings often seem irrational or illogical.
4. Argues the child out of his or her feelings and makes judgments about those feelings.	4. Accepts the child's feelings—does not judge them.
5. Assumes the adult must take away the child's pain. The nonverbal message to the child is, "You aren't very strong. You aren't very capable."	5. Trusts the child to deal with his or her own pain. Nonverbal message to the child is, "You are a strong and capable person."

PRACTICING INNER-REALITY RESPONSES

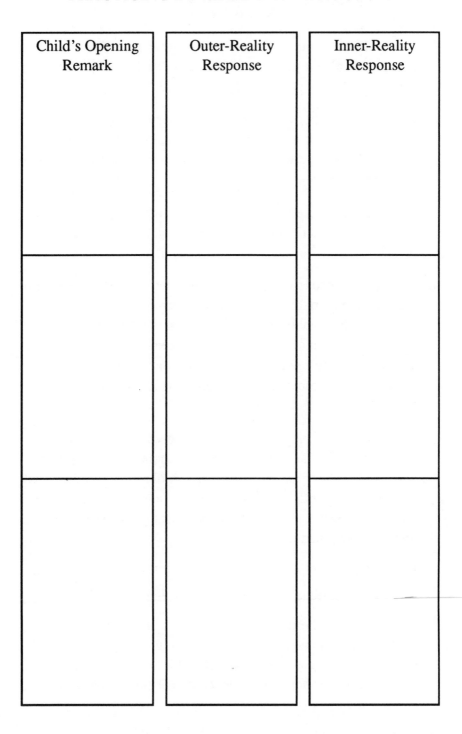

Child's Opening Remark	Outer-Reality Response	Inner-Reality Response

DISCUSSION IDEAS: CHAPTER 9: LISTENING TO INNER-REALITY

1. Using the "Practicing Inner-Reality Responses" chart, share the stories about your inner and outer-reality responses this week.

2. Do you remember a time you were angry as a child? Do you remember a time your parents were angry? What happened? Can you identify the primary feelings which came before the anger erupted?

3. Think about a recent time, as an adult, when you were angry. Can you identify the primary emotions which gave rise to your anger?

4. Divide into groups of three. Have each person take a turn playing the part of the child, the part of the adult, and an observer. Have each "child" choose either a situation from the chart or use a situation from real life. Remember, *do not use a situation where the adult is carrying out a correction for a misbehavior.* It must be a situation in which the child is trying to cope with painful emotions.

   Have the person playing the adult role give (1) the outer-reality response. Then start the situation over again and have the adult give the (2) inner-reality response. The observer can then lead the discussion with the "child" and the "adult" to explore what happened between the two people during the outer and the inner-reality interactions.

   Do this three different times so each adult has the opportunity to experience being the child, the adult, and the observer.

5. Check back to the discussion guidelines at the end of the first chapter. Is your group still following the guidelines? Is everyone getting a chance to talk? Does each member of the group feel his or her own inner-reality is being listened to?

10 Describing Outer-Reality

Human beings are verbal beings. Our rich use of language sets us apart from all other species. Talking and listening is a major way we learn from one another and is one of the ways we bond emotionally with other human beings. For most of us, conversation is a large part of the joy of living. We have already talked about the fact that talking and listening is most productive and fun during times of positive and neutral behaviors; during positive and neutral times, grownups and kids can all just go with the flow and enjoy each others company.

USING DESCRIBING LANGUAGE IN POSITIVE AND NEUTRAL SITUATIONS:

Occasionally though, when talking in a friendly way to a child at a positive or neutral time, the adult realizes that the child has suddenly withdrawn. For example, have you ever had the experience of giving praise to a child when the child suddenly drew inward or ran away? Sometimes the child will respond with a negative behavior, leaving the adult bewildered and wondering, "Well, what brought *that* on?" A common example of this is the child who has drawn a picture. The adult looks at it and says, "Oh, what a beautiful picture." The adult really thinks the picture is beautiful; the adult is honestly telling the child what he or she thinks. But the child grabs the picture from the adult's hand, scrunches it up and throws it into the wastebasket. The child says, "No, it isn't!" and runs from the room, slamming the door behind him. This is so common a situation, in fact, that many parents and teachers never comment at all on a child's picture but instead make it a rule to ask, "Do you want to tell me about it?" In this way, the adult avoids misinterpreting, and possibly offending the child.

Asking children's opinions about their artistic creations is certainly a much better way to react than belittling by asking, "Is it a horse?" while turning to another adult in the room and giving a laugh. Or, in an attempt to be helpful, some adults will take the drawing and begin improving on it, "That's a very nice house but look, I can show you how to make it even better. See, if you add these lines, it looks three dimensional." One little boy gave up drawing by the time he was five years old because his father, who was a loving, concerned parent, kept improving on his son's drawings in an attempt to teach him how to do it even better. The message to the child in both of these situations is, "You are not a competent person." The same applies in every facet of life. We have all known daughters of good cooks who were afraid to cook for fear they would make a mistake, and carpenter's sons who refuse to even own a hammer. Without meaning to, each parent convinced his or her child that the child was incompetent in the very area the parent most wanted the child to succeed.

But back to our first example, in which the adult only said, "What a beautiful picture." Now how on earth can sincere praise cause a child to become upset enough to crumple up his or her own picture? The answer has something to do with that same inner core of integrity which we talked about in the last chapter. The child needs to feel true to his or her inner self. If the inner self believes that the picture is not beautiful, then the child cannot accept the adult's praise. From the child's point of view the picture is *not* beautiful. The child crumples the picture and throws it away because inner honesty demands that the child not accept praise for something he or she does not deserve.

Martin, a new sixth-grade-student to our school, is a memorable example of the strength of a child's inner integrity. Martin was in continual trouble with his teacher, the playground personnel, and the principal because he was frequently involved in fights with other children. After getting to know him better, his teacher tried to work out as many ways as he could to begin to supply Martin with some of the emotional needs Martin yearned for; security, belonging, Being-Love and competency/respect. Without the help of Martin's troubled parents, the teacher could not supply much, but even the little he could do seemed to help because the incidences of fighting went way down. One day at the end of lunch period, the teacher brought Martin to my counseling office to visit. "I want to tell you how good Martin has been this week," the teacher said. "He has been just wonderful." Martin was sitting on my desk chair (all the kids liked sitting on my desk chair which had rollers on the legs.) He began to move nervously back and forth. The more the teacher praised him, the more frantic Martin's movements became until finally he and the rolling chair were practically bouncing off the walls of the room. The bell mercifully rang and they walked off down the hall. After school this exasperated teacher told me, "Do you know what Martin did after we left your office? He walked into the room just ahead of me and the very first kid he met, he doubled up his fist and punched him in the face. The other kid never even looked cross eyed at him."

Martin was a boy who had come to believe in his inner self that he was not good, that he was a bad person. We could not have known all of Martin's behaviors that week. Only Martin knew all of his behaviors. Maybe that very morning at the bus stop Martin had taunted a little fat girl and made her cry. How could Martin remain true to himself and accept the verdict that he was good when he was convinced he was "bad"? Martin chose to hit the first child he saw to show the teacher the truth, to prove to the teacher that he, Martin, was not really a good kid. "See, this is how I really am! This is the *real* me!"

Here is that inner core of integrity again, driving us to make our own honest and independent judgments. Perhaps our inner integrity is a survival instinct. How could human beings have survived for over a million years without the ability to make reality based and independent decisions? Individuals or nations who consistently deceive themselves about their situation will not survive. Wherever the urge toward inner integrity comes from, it is especially strong in children because they have not yet learned to repress it.

Martin obviously needed some kind of praise, some kind of recognition for his new positive behaviors. What could the teacher have said that Martin could have accepted? Martin could have accepted a *description* of what he had done, a *describing praise*. The teacher could have said, "Martin has not been sent to the office one time this week for fighting. Not even during lunch period. Mrs. Jones told me she has not had to get after him once on the playground all week." Martin's inner integrity can accept these statements because they cannot be argued with. Even Martin has to admit that all these statements are true. The pleased tone of the teacher's voice, his arm on Martin's shoulder, make the process of describing warm and caring. There is nothing clinical or cold about describing praise.

As a teacher or a parent, you can help strengthen each child's self-esteem staircase by providing pure descriptive bits of positive information. Remember Maslow's staircase of needs? You cannot help a child build his or her self-esteem staircase by making evaluations or judgments, such as, "You are good," or "You are smart." Children must build their own staircase, brick by brick, a small piece of information at a time. They need to make their own judgments about being capable and smart before they can accept your opinion that they are capable and smart. A brick at a time is how each of us, whether child or adult, builds our own stairway to self-esteem and independence.

An adult can evaluate children every day by telling them they are good artists, or that they are beautiful, good, or loveable. Children will refuse to accept this kind of evaluating praise unless they believe in their honest inner selves that the statement is true.

Children will not believe the evaluating statement, or feel good about it, until they themselves make a long series of independent judgments based on factual information from the world around them. Only after children make a positive evaluation about themselves can they accept the same evaluation from you. Only when Martin believes he is smart, can he accept it when you tell him he is smart. Only when Martin believes he is good, can he accept it when you say he is good.

Even when children agree with you that they are smart or good or beautiful, evaluating has another pitfall. Evaluating causes rivalry between children and sometimes even a belief that they must be perfect in whatever they do. The following incident is an example not only of the power of describing praise, but is also an example of how evaluating praise can cause children to think they must be perfect:

Jacob was a four-year-old boy who willingly took his turn painting at the preschool easel. But each day Jacob took the painting which he had done, wadded it up into a ball, and stuffed it as far down as possible into his take-home tub. Jacob's mother always retrieved Jacob's cast off paintings, smoothed them out, exclaimed at how beautiful they were and said, "It's beautiful. Let's take this home and hang it up." The mother's praise and entreaties were to no avail. Jacob stubbornly continued to stuff his finished paintings into the basket and refused to take them home. To all of us adults who worked at the preschool, Jacob's paintings were indeed beautiful, radiant with varied forms and colors. Jacob, however, obviously believed they did not measure up. His mother evaluated his paintings by pronouncing them to be beautiful and he, being in touch with his inner integrity, could not in all honesty accept her evaluation. He had a seven-year-old sister who had been praised for her beautiful paintings for many years prior to his artistic attempts. Jacob was convinced his sister's paintings were beautiful and that his were not.

The preschool director finally suggested that everyone, teachers and parents alike, stop evaluating Jacob's, or any other child's paintings by saying they were "nice" or "beautiful" or "super" and stick strictly to describing what we saw. No interpreting and no evaluating. Describing praise is harder than evaluating praise because you have to really pay attention to whatever is being described. Describing simply cannot be done in an off-hand manner. It requires total attention. Some examples: "You're using reds and blues today." "A big, big, circle over there and lots of lines below." "Three boxes in the corner." "Lots of red dots." "You mixed that blue and that yellow to make green." Describing Jacob's paintings gave him outer-reality information that could not be argued with. Everything the adults described was acceptable to Jacob's honest inner self.

Finally, the day came when Jacob proudly held up a finished painting for his mother to see, "Look, Mother." It had taken two months, but Jacob had finally made his own independent decision that his paintings were worth admiring. Brick by brick, he had come to some independent conclusions. Jacob now believed his paintings were interesting, that the process of painting was a fascinating one, and that he was a capable person who was able to control and play with the process of making patterns on paper. The idea of whether or not his paintings were beautiful or not beautiful as compared to his sister's paintings no longer made any sense to Jacob. By describing what he was doing, we had helped him to focus on the *process* of painting instead of the final product. Earlier, we had unwittingly compared his completed paintings with his sister's completed paintings, (and with all the other children's completed paintings) by evaluating them as "beautiful" or "pretty." Without meaning to, we had pushed Jacob into the scary situation of thinking he always had to produce a perfect and praise-worthy product.

You can probably remember something in your own life you never tried because you were afraid you might fail. Juan's brother, who was five years older than Juan, was a model student. Juan decided very early that he could never be as successful in school as his big brother. Feeling the need to be competent at something, Juan gave up on schoolwork and learned to be the best baseball player in the neighborhood. Competing with his older brother was too scary. Many a perfectionistic child refuses to try anything they think will not have a praise-worthy outcome, whether it be going out for a sport (one of the most intensely evaluated activities in our schools) or signing up for a class they might not get an "A" in. The child assumes, "If I am not good at it, then people will think *I* am not good." In this way, many doors are closed at an early age because of the fear of being evaluated.

Describing focuses on process. Nobody fails at process. You do one thing and then you do another thing. This thing works and this other thing does not work. Learning how things work is interesting. Sometimes the process is frustrating. Sometimes the process is exciting. Sometimes the process gets boring. Sometimes the process is fun. Process is just the way things work.

Evaluation, on the other hand, is intimidating. Evaluation means there is a right way to do things. Evaluating means there is an end product and a standard which we must measure up to. Things must turn out good, or beautiful, or right, or even perfect. Evaluating means some people are better than others, smarter, more capable. Evaluating means if he is the best, then I am worse than he is. If she is beautiful, than I am less beautiful. If he is the smartest, then I am dumber than he is.

You may remember some examples given in Chapter Three, during the discussion about negative scripting as a self-sabotage. If you will look back and reread the examples which were given, you will see that each of the positive scripts *described* one specific incident. Each is a description, not an evaluation. Because each positive message is a description of a fact, the child has to accept the statement as true. Even the example of the father saying, "This morning when I woke up I thought to myself, 'I'm so happy they were born,'" is a description of fact. That *was* how he felt when he woke up that morning. Each of these statements is one more solid brick which the children can use to build their self-esteem staircase. In this way, a description is much more helpful to the child than a positive evaluation. If you evaluate a child in any way, even if you use the words "good," "wonderful," "beautiful," or "smart," you have put yourself, and not the child, in control. You do not want the child to be always dependent on your opinions about him or her. Children who do not have to depend on other people's opinions will grow up with the inner confidence to be able to think for themselves. Our goal as adults should be to help children learn to make their own positive decisions about themselves.

Even though some evaluating labels can at first sound very positive, children may still feel trapped by them, powerless to be any different than what the adult has given them permission to be. An example of how restrictive even a positive evaluation can be was told by fifty-two-year old Amanda. Amanda's parents had decided almost from the moment of her birth that she was the "lucky" child. Her older sister had been severely crippled from polio two years before she was born. Amanda often heard that script, "She is so lucky." Amanda agreed she was lucky not to be crippled by polio, but unfortunately, all through her childhood, she never dared ask for help nor does she remember ever expressing any negative feelings to her parents. She tried to live up to her lucky script by smiling on the outside and keeping any pain she may have felt totally to herself. "I never thought I had the right to ask for anything or to feel badly about anything. It was very lonely sometimes," she told us. Or, consider Maria, whose family and friends gave her the evaluating script of, "She is such a beauty." As Maria grew into old age, she desperately tried everything to hold on to her youthful beauty. Without it, she felt she had nothing left. Her old age was robbed of the contentment she might otherwise have experienced partly because of her almost frantic attempts to hang on to her childhood script of being outwardly beautiful.

DESCRIBING IN NEGATIVE SITUATIONS:

Describing language can also be used to lower stress in negative situations between people. For example, take a situation where a teacher steps in to stop a fight and help two children problem-solve a disagreement. If the teacher starts out by evaluating or judging the situation and says, "Which one of you started it *this* time?" both kids will slam shut their inner doors. From that point on, they will try to close out whatever the teacher says. But if the teacher begins by describing the situation, without blaming or evaluating, the children will be able to keep on listening. The teacher might say, "I see two boys both wanting a turn on the swing." By describing the situation, using no evaluating words, the teacher is giving accurate outer-reality information which both children can accept as true and inarguable, therefore they are more able to listen to their teacher as he leads them through the problem-solving process.

Another negative situation was that of a mother who was trying to put an end to the power struggle between herself and her rebellious eighteen-year-old daughter, Sara. On the night of her high school graduation, Sara came home from a graduation party at 11:30 p.m. She ran into the living room where her mother was still up waiting for her to come home, and said, rather defiantly, "I'm going to the beach with some of the other kids so don't wait up for us. We'll probably have breakfast down there."

The beach was a two-hour drive over mountain roads. Some of her friends had probably been drinking. The mother wanted to scream, "It's not safe. You are not going and that's that!" but she knew she could not tell her eighteen-year-old daughter what to do forever. So she focused on describing her own inner-reality. "I would be so worried about you, I don't think I could sleep." For a moment, Mother and daughter looked into each other's eyes, then Sara turned and ran down the walk to the waiting car, talked with her friends awhile then came slowly back into the house. "I don't really need to go. Some of the guys have been drinking anyway."

The mother had given her daughter an important piece of information and trusted her to make her own evaluation of the situation.

The mother took a risk. The daughter might have said, "Oh, don't be such a worry wort," and driven away with her friends. But she did not. The same inner integrity which would have compelled Sara's inner door to shut, had her mother evaluated the situation and made the decision that Sara could not go, now compelled the daughter to make her own honest evaluation.

Not all situations turn out so happily. Children do not always make the same judgment we adults would make. But it is true just the same, that we cannot tie an eighteen-year-old, or a three-year-old for that matter, to the bedpost. We cannot control another person's inner self. At the inner core, each child is his or her own person and needs to have opportunities to make decisions about his or her own life.

If you will think back to Chapter Five and the section on how to give commands to the child, you will see that *describing what needs to be done* is one of the main ingredients of giving a command. Describing outer-reality in this way lessens the chance that the child will refuse to do the task. Describing allows the child to honestly appraise the situation. The inner integrity of a child will often prompt him or her to carry out the command if the child can see it is a reasonable one.

As a general rule, whenever you get into a difficult situation while trying to communicate outer-reality to a child, use describing language. Consider the mother who comes home from work and finds her school age children have strewn books, toys and coats all around the living room and dining room. She is exhausted and dinner needs to be prepared. She experiences feelings of being discouraged and unappreciated. Her anger flares. She thinks, "What do they think I am? A slave?" But she keeps from evaluating the situation; she avoids demeaning and blaming the kids. Instead she tries to describe the situation. She lets her tone of voice sound as exasperated as she feels and says, "I see coats and hats all over the living room and toys all over the dining room floor. And books, books, books, everywhere!" Then she goes to the kitchen to start dinner. She has given them basic outer-reality information and trusts that their inner integrity will help them make an honest independent decision of what to do about it. In this case, the kids did pick up their mess before they came out into the kitchen to visit and share the events of the day. Mom remembered not to sabotage herself. She did not mention the messy house again except to say, "I really appreciate that you straightened things up."

You can also use describing statements whenever you need to share your own inner-reality feelings with someone you love. Do you remember the situation in Chapter Nine when I described my primary feelings of loneliness and fear to my husband? "I feel lonely and I'm scared." My inner-reality was at that moment part of my husband's outer-reality world. He needed information about the condition of my inner self in order for his own inner integrity core to make a decision. He could not have listened to me if I had started the conversation by evaluating him by saying, "You are constantly ignoring me. I don't think you even care about my feelings anymore." From my husband's point of view, these evaluating statements would not have been true. He did care about me, and he did not perceive himself as constantly ignoring me. His inner integrity would not have allowed this judging, evaluating message in. Because I used describing language, he did not withdraw from me but instead put down his paper and listened to what I had to say.

Because describing is such a pure language form, it is a powerful and effective method of communicating with another human being, no matter what age that other human being happens to be. Whenever you are in doubt, and wonder what on earth you can say to get through to the other person, try using describing language. Other people may not make the decision you want them to make, but they will be able to listen. And very often, if other people are at all in touch with their own inner selves, their inner core of integrity will impel them to a fair decision.

EXERCISE:

Study the charts on the following pages. Using the "Describing Praise" chart as a guide, use the practice chart to write down any evaluating or describing responses you observe or participate in during the coming week.

DESCRIBING PRAISE

Situation	Examples of Evaluating Praise	Examples of Describing Praise
Mother to her 5-year-old who has just wiped up his spilled milk:	"What a good boy!"	"You wiped up all the milk!"
First grade teacher to one of her students who is showing her his picture:	"What a beautiful picture!"	"Look at that! You used greens, blues, and reds. And lines that curve and squiggle!"
Music teacher to her girls' choir:	"That's the best job any class in this school has ever done on that song!"	"I especially like how your voices blended while you sang. I couldn't hear one single voice louder than the others."
Mother to Dad, who has just come home from work and is holding three-year-old Johnny in his arms:	"Johnny was super good today!"	"Johnny helped me feed the baby and change her pants, and he put the lunch dishes in the sink, too!"

Characteristics of Evaluating Praise	Characteristics of Describing Praise
1. Implies that one child has performed better than another. Tends to encourage rivalry and jealousy between children.	1. Accepts each child where he is and encourages cooperation among children.
2. Emphasizes the end product of learning.	2. Emphasizes the process of learning.
3. Temporary: Even if adults give a positive evaluation today, they can take it away tomorrow with a negative evaluation.	3. Permanent: No one can take away from the child the fact of what he or she has done.
4. Encourages dependence on the opinion of other people for a sense of self-worth.	4. Gives children the basic building bricks to build their own competency and self-esteem stair steps.
5. Is open to honest argument: If children think your judgment is in error or is an attempt to manipulate them, their inner-integrity will not allow them to believe your evaluation.	5. Is inarguable because it is a statement of fact.
6. Behavior may worsen if children feel compelled to prove to you that they are not as good as your evaluation of them.	6. Behavior is likely to improve. Children do not have to defend their inner-integrity by proving to you that you are wrong.

PRACTICING DESCRIBING PRAISE

Situation You Observed or Participated In	Example of Evaluating Praise	Example of Describing Praise

DISCUSSION IDEAS: CHAPTER 10: DESCRIBING
OUTER-REALITY

1. Share the examples of the evaluating and describing praise exercise which you did this week. Is the difference between evaluating and describing clear to you?

2. Has one of your students or children ever refused to accept evaluating praise from you? What happened?

3. Do you remember a time as a child when your inner integrity was threatened causing you to close your inner door on an adult? Will you share that with the group?

4. When you are finished with this book, your group might enjoy discussing *How to Talk So Kids Will Listen, How to Listen So Kid's Will Talk* by Adele Faber and Elaine Mazlish. They have also written an excellent book on reducing sibling rivalry called, *Siblings Without Rivalry: How to Help Your Childre n Live Together So You Can Live Too.*

5. Has anyone had a chance this week to help a child by listening to his or her inner-reality? Were you able to continue to listen and be quiet, or did you revert to the old habit of jumping in with outer-reality information? If you could not continue to listen, be patient with yourself. It takes time to change old habits.

6. Does anyone want to talk about a misbehavior and a correction they are having problems with?

7. How are the self-sabotages coming? Would anyone like to talk about a self-sabotage that is particularly causing a problem?

11 The Family and Classroom Meetings

If you have experimented your way through this book, trying out each new concept as you went along, you have acquired some new and effective tools for dealing with discipline. By now you are beginning to feel "in charge," at least some of the time. If you are like most parents and teachers, you are probably also feeling relieved at knowing that you can take charge in a way which encourages each child to blossom as a strong and unique individual. On the other hand, most adults would like children occasionally to share in the responsibility for managing the family and the classroom. It is an energy drain to have to be the one in charge all of the time.

This final chapter will show you how to involve your children in making responsible decisions about their own behavior through participation in classroom and family meetings. The value of meetings are two-fold: First, meetings provide children the opportunity to learn the art of negotiation and compromise, thereby lifting some of the burden off the adult of having to be the only one responsible for deciding what is to be done; second, meetings will not only help strengthen your children's self-esteem, they also help strengthen the family or classroom group to which they belong.

You are probably already familiar with the concept of the family or classroom meeting. Sometimes, parents and teachers have the idea that the major purpose of the family or classroom meeting is to find a solution to a specific problem. They believe that if the members of the family or class cannot agree, then the group should choose a solution by voting. After all, if the family and the classroom are democratic institutions (as Rudolf Dreikurs had convinced many of us it is) then the democratic way must be to vote and let the majority decide. Consequently, many adults refuse to hold meetings with children because of their fear of being outvoted by the kids.

Understandably, adults are nervous about giving children an equal vote. The thought of being outnumbered by their children and students is too scary. As one father said, "It's crazy to give a five-year-old an equal vote with a parent. Kids don't have the background or the responsibility that adults do. We don't let anybody vote in this country until they are eighteen. No five-year-old is going to have an equal vote in this family."

Fortunately, voting is not necessary for a successful family or classroom meeting. In fact, voting at family or classroom meetings is not appropriate for any age. While the custom of voting is an admirable idea for a nation, voting in the more intimate family or classroom setting can tear the group apart. Whenever there is a vote, someone wins and someone loses. People who lose are likely to feel misunderstood and put down. The losing minority group often resists the will of the majority, sometimes in very subtle ways. The result is that the original group begins to fracture and split into factions. For example, suppose 28 sixth graders vote 20 to 8 for a new classroom rule. The outcome is likely to be 20 people who obey the rule and 8 people who continue to resist, either openly or behind the teacher's back. Even worse, the next meetings are likely to become forums for argument in which one section of the class tries to persuade the rest of the class to vote for one particular point of view. The outcome is that hardly anyone is able to really listen to other ideas; they are too busy thinking of what to say next and how to convince the other side to vote for their idea. As a result, very few members of the group will feel their views have been given a respectful hearing.

The most difficult and most important concept to keep in view as you lead any family or classroom meeting is this: *The process of searching for a solution is more important than actually finding a solution.* The major task for the leader of a family or classroom meeting is to keep alive the process of giving each person a chance to speak and to be heard. In other words, even if the group does not agree on a solution to the problem, the meeting will have been a success if the process of speaking and respectful listening is encouraged. Remember Maslow's staircase of needs; the opportunity to talk, and be listened to, gives each person the emotional support needed to build his or her self-esteem staircase. People of all ages who have their needs met for belonging, security, Being-Love, and competency/respect, are much more likely to be cooperative and able to trust other members of the group. By providing for at least some of the emotional needs of its individual members, the meeting will help both the group and the individuals in it stay vital and strong. In marriages which break apart, in families where children run away, in schools where students drop out, the bonds that held the group together have been weakened. When the group is somehow no longer supplying the basic emotional needs for each individual, members will withdraw, either physically or emotionally.

Following are two examples of meetings which took place in response to crisis situations. The first was a home meeting, the second took place in a middle-school. Both meetings had an adult in charge who managed to concentrate on the *process* of solving the problem, rather than persuading everyone to agree on a specific solution. No solution was forced on any group member, and yet the problem was resolved, or it might be more accurate to say, the problem no longer seemed like such a problem anymore.

To paraphrase John Dewey, "We don't usually solve our problems so much as we just get over them."

FAMILY MEETING EXAMPLE

A mother had two sons, ages four and six. The six-year-old stayed home from school one day, with a cold and a slight fever. When it was time for her to take the four-year-old to his preschool class, she told her oldest son, Bobby, "Go put your coat on so we can take Ricky to school." Bobby protested, "I don't need a coat. I'm hot. I'm *real* hot."

As you can imagine, an argument followed, with the mother trying to reason with Bobby about how she did not want him to go out in the rain with a fever and no coat. Finally, in desperation, she used the physical assist and forcibly put the coat on her son while he screamed and cried. Once in the car, Bobbie kept taking off his coat causing her to stop several times to put it back on. By the time they returned home, they were both angry. Bobbie was difficult all the rest of the day. He sulked and complained about everything. Finally, in the late afternoon, Bobbie approached his mother and demanded, "I want a family meeting!"

Mother agreed that a family meeting would be a good idea. They decided to have the meeting after dinner when Dad would be home. After dinner, they popped some popcorn, divided two cans of coke and sat down around the table. Bobby started out by telling them he was "old enough to know whether or not to wear a coat and it's nobody else's business anyway." Mother again explained why she could not let a sick child go out without a coat. Bobby insisted he had the right to decide whether or not he had to wear a coat. After all, it was his body. Everyone got a turn to give an opinion, even four-year-old Ricky who was mostly interested in munching on the popcorn. Mother and Dad tried their best to listen to Bobby's inner-reality by looking at him intently as he talked and saying, "Gosh," and "Hmm."

But there was no way Mom or Dad could ever agree that Bobby had the right to go out in a rainstorm with a fever and no coat. Dad tried describing the situation, "So you didn't think it was fair for Mom to force you to wear the coat. And Mom, you didn't dare let him go without the coat because you were afraid he would get even sicker." Both Bobby and Mom shook their heads in agreement. Dad finally threw up his hands. "I don't have any ideas. It just seems like two people who have entirely different points of view." There was a long silence while they sipped their cokes and ate their popcorn. Finally Mother said, "Well, I don't know what to say. I can't change my mind and I guess Bobby can't either. Let's just quit talking about it for awhile. Maybe one of us will get an idea for something to do about it later on." Dad said, "Does anybody want to play Chutes and Ladders before it is time for bed?" In this way, the meeting adjourned. No solutions were found. Mother and Bobby still disagreed about a proper course of action.

The interesting outcome of this meeting was that Bobby's disposition immediately returned to his normal, sunny self. Bobby never mentioned the incident again. The next day, when it was time to take Ricky to preschool, Mother said, "Time to get ready to go." And Bobby, still sniffling from his cold, got his coat on without complaint.

By listening to Bobby's inner-reality, by using describing words to talk about a negative, high stress situation, and by not insisting that all parties come to an agreement and find a solution to the problem, both Bobby's and Mother's emotional needs were met. Even Dad's and Ricky's needs for belonging and competency were met. Were not their opinions asked for and respected?

CLASSROOM/SCHOOL MEETING

A middle-school principal gave a school counselor an urgent morning phone call asking her to spend a day at his school. The regular counselor was unable to come to school because of illness and the principal needed someone to try to prevent a student from being badly hurt by some of the other students.

Joe, a ninth grade student, had been killed in an automobile accident several days earlier. The endangered boy, David, had been overheard to say, "It's no big loss to the world that Joe got killed. He was a son-of-a-bitch anyway." David's remark was overheard by some indignant students who spread it throughout the school. David's comment was eventually reported to Joe's friends and to Joe's seventh grade sister. The girl was devastated. The remark added cruelly to the pain she was already feeling over the death of her brother.

Joe's friends were upset and angry. They decided to take revenge. They made a plan to catch David when he got off the bus after school that day and "kill him." This plan was in turn reported to the principal, who got on the phone to call the counselor for help. The principal did not think Joe's friends would actually kill David, but was convinced they were angry enough to seriously hurt the boy when they caught him alone off the school grounds.

The principal spent considerable amounts of time that morning going into classrooms, and bringing back various groups of students to meet with the counselor. The major groups were the dead boy's friends, a group of neutral but sympathetic students, and David and his friends. Joe's sister was not included in any of the groups since she asked not to be involved. All that morning, the counselor met with small groups of students, asking them to state the problem, listening to feelings, asking for ideas.

When the counselor first met with Joe's friends early in the morning, they were in no mood to think of ideas to make things better, so she totally concentrated on listening to their inner-reality feelings of pain and anger. Later, someone in the neutral student group came up with the idea that David could write Joe's sister a note of apology and also spend his own money to buy her a teddy bear for her stuffed animal collection. The group agreed this was a good idea because it would be similar to bringing flowers to a funeral and would mean more than just a note of apology. When the counselor presented the idea to David, who was by now very sorry and extremely frightened, he eagerly agreed.

Next, the student group who had come up with the idea met with the counselor and the dead boy's friends. They presented the teddy bear idea as a possible solution. All Joe's friends but one, Lee, the leader of the group, thought the teddy bear idea was a good one. As in earlier meetings, Joe's friend Lee sat sullen and withdrawn, refusing to participate. The counselor asked him, "Would it be okay with you if I told David you think giving Joe's sister a stuffed animal and a letter of apology would be a good idea?"

Lee looked straight at the counselor, with hard eyes, and said, "You can tell him anything you want."

The counselor shook her head. "No, I don't want to say anything that isn't true. How about if I just tell him you are so hurt and angry you don't even want to talk to him at all?"

Suddenly, tears welled up in Lee's eyes. The hard look was gone. He did not speak, perhaps he could not have spoken without crying, but he nodded his head in agreement.

Joe's other friends went to Joe's sister and told her what David was planning to do as an apology to her. She felt supported and protected by her brother's friends and was relieved they had tried to find a peaceful solution. The counselor again met with David to tell him that most, but not all, Joe's friends had agreed to the idea, and that Lee in particular was still so hurt and angry he did not even want to talk to David. David said he would write the apology and buy the teddy bear that evening.

When the kids got on the bus that afternoon, no one knew for sure whether the situation had been defused. After all, Lee was a key leader of the group and he had not agreed to any solution. Lee had only agreed that the counselor could tell David he was so hurt and angry he did not want to talk to him. There was great relief on the school staff when the two adults who had volunteered to monitor David's bus stop reported that there were no unpleasant incidents that afternoon. Nothing violent happened to David that day, or for the rest of the school year.

As in the earlier situation involving Bobby and his coat, we see the healing power of respecting every person's emotional needs. No solution was imposed on the group. Nobody voted for or against the teddy bear/apology idea. There were no winners and no losers. The adults hoped things would be all right for David at the end of that school day but had no way to know for certain. Lee had made no promises to leave David alone. What the counselor did know was that in each group which met that morning, everyone, including David and Lee, had a chance to talk and be listened to. Each person's inner-reality had been respected. Doors to communication which had been slammed tight were reopened. Undoubtedly, the turning point came when the counselor respected Lee's inner-reality feelings by saying, "I don't want to tell him anything that isn't true. How about if I just tell him you're so hurt and angry you don't even want to talk to him at all?"

GUIDELINES FOR HOLDING
FAMILY OR CLASSROOM MEETINGS

Here is a basic list of guidelines for setting up and leading a meeting. Keep in mind the importance of not having to persuade anyone in the group to accept any particular solution. As leader of the meeting, you will have plenty of opportunities to use the skills learned in earlier chapters, especially listening to inner-reality feelings, using describing language in negative situations, and not sabotaging yourself by talking, talking and more talking.

1. *Schedule a regular meeting time.*

Most families and elementary classes have time for at least one weekly meeting. High school classrooms, in which students meet for only an hour a day, will probably have to meet less often. For example, some high school classes hold a meeting every other Friday. The main idea is that the meeting times be regular and predictable.

As a child, Larinda hated family meetings. Meetings in her family were held only during crisis times. Usually, by the time her father called the meeting, he was drunk and angry at his wife. He would start the meeting by yelling at everyone to get into the living room. He would then proceed to lecture his assembled children in a loud and angry tone of voice on why he was right and why their mother was wrong. The father's goal was to persuade his children to take his side against the mother. Mother rarely got a chance to speak because Dad would shout her down. "Who do you think is right? Your mother or me?" No child wants to be torn between taking sides with Dad against Mother, or with Mother against Dad. No wonder Larinda remembers her family meetings with such anguish. These were not family meetings at all. *The primary purpose of a family meeting is to strengthen the family group and the individuals in it, and secondarily, to look for solutions to problems.* The meetings Larinda described were political meetings designed to defeat and humiliate her mother.

Waiting for a crisis time to call a meeting always increases the possibility that the stresses of the immediate situation will turn the meeting into a negative experience for everyone. Weekly meetings held on a regular basis help insure a calm and supportive atmosphere in which differences of opinion are more likely to be listened to. Before your first family meeting, ask each member of the family when would be the best time to meet. From the very beginning, each person needs to know that this is their meeting and they will have a say in deciding when the meetings are held. Thereafter, before the closing of each meeting, ask the family, "Shall we meet at the same time next week? Will this be a good time for everyone?" Then write the date on a calendar which you display in a prominent place, such as the refrigerator door. It is best to keep a regular, predictable meeting date, but given the busy schedules of some family members, a firm schedule will not always work.

Classroom meeting times are more easily structured because the total school schedule is more predictable than the ordinary family situation. But even in a school situation, you need to be flexible. For example, if one child is unexpectedly scheduled into a special reading class during the regular Friday meeting time, the teacher can discuss the need for a change, "From now on, Eric will be going out of the room during our regular class meeting time. We'll need to change the time so everyone can be here. How about meeting just before lunch on Friday? Does anybody see a problem with that?" In this way, the teacher shows respect for her student's opinions regarding a new meeting schedule, while at the same time she emphasizes the idea that each individual is essential to the meeting.

A family in which the father was expected to solve most of the family problems started holding regular family meetings after the father got a job driving a long distance truck. With the father gone over half of the time, the mother and grandmother turned to a weekly meeting as a way to involve the whole family in providing the discipline which they had earlier expected the father to give. To their pleasant surprise, the meetings turned out not only to provide the means by which they could deal with the problems of living together, but also enriched the relationships between the generations. The grandmother used the opportunity to begin sharing her experiences, of growing up in Mexico, with her daughter and grandchildren. As a result, the children became well acquainted with their family history in a personal way they might never have realized without the leisurely and regular meetings their mother and grandmother provided. The father also began to participate in the meetings when he was home and seemed quite comfortable with this new way of dealing with family problems.

Ruth, who grew up in a Jewish family, remembers regular family meetings from her childhood. These meetings always opened with a reading from the Bible. (The practice of opening the family meeting by teaching a value system could by adapted to any faith. Any religious or secular philosophy could be used according to each parent's belief system.) After the opening reading, each child was asked to tell about something interesting that had happened in school that week or some award they had earned. Family problems were then discussed with each child being asked their opinion. Ruth recalls that she looked forward each week to the family meetings and that they made her feel very important. She remembers the meetings with great affection and now holds regular family meetings with her own children.

2. *Establish a relaxed and upbeat atmosphere for the meeting.*

Talking and listening flows better when people are feeling relaxed. In the classroom, a favorite relaxing technique for younger students is to allow them to draw pictures at their desks while they are participating in the discussion. In smaller groups, children can choose whether they would like to color or work with clay while they talk and listen. Any adult who is part of the group should choose, too. (Clay may be the best choice for the adult because children are often intimidated when adults draw pictures beyond the ability level of the child. By the same token, never make anything special with the clay. Only roll it and squish it to establish a relaxed atmosphere.) If anyone chooses just to sit, that is okay. If your room has a carpeted floor or pillows in a reading corner, children could choose whether to stay at their desks or sit on the floor. This might be the time to give a popcorn treat. Turn off those bright fluorescent lights. The dimmer, natural light has a calming effect on many children. In the upper grade classroom, arranging the desks in a circle helps establish an atmosphere of equality and informality.

At home, a special treat like popcorn, pop, or a popsicle sets a friendly mood. One family lit a fire in the fireplace on cool evenings just before the meeting began. You could light candles. Do any simple thing which helps convey the idea of a relaxing, friendly time.

3. *Involve everyone in setting the agenda.*

An agenda is a list of the things to be done at a meeting. It is crucial for the success of the family or classroom meeting that every individual be encouraged to suggest items for the agenda. If teachers and parents are the only people to decide what gets talked about, the children will very quickly decide they do not want to participate. This is why so many children resist the idea of a family or classroom meeting when they first hear about it. They assume the adults will set the agenda items and that all topics of discussion will center on the adults telling the child what to do. Since no one likes to be a captive audience and have to set through a lecture telling how to live a life, the normal kid says, "No thank you."

The simplest method for getting everyone involved in setting the agenda for the family meeting is to use a blank sheet of paper. Title the paper, "Topics for Discussion." Fasten it to a clipboard or to the refrigerator door. Tell everybody, "Here is where you can write down anything you want to talk about at the next family meeting." Sometime during the week, if there is something you want to talk about, write it on the list also. During the week, if anyone comes to you with a complaint about someone else, you can listen to their inner-reality feelings by saying, "Hmmm," or "Gosh, what a problem." You could also suggest, "If that's something you'd like to talk about at the next family meeting, you could write it down on the list." If people are using the list for name calling or other inappropriate language, be sure to immediately write down on the list, "What shall we do about people who do name calling when they write down topics to discuss?" and then, if the problem continues, make the name calling issue a high priority topic for discussion at the next meeting. If the children are only writing down problems, be sure you always include one fun topic to discuss, for example: Where shall we go on vacation this summer? or "Does anyone want to tell about something that happened in school this week that made them feel happy or proud?"

As the meeting begins, you can pass around the list of suggested topics for discussion and ask if anyone wants to cross any topic off the list. Probably some of the topics will no longer be a problem to the person who wanted to discuss it earlier in the week. "Oh, that. You can cross that one off. We settled it already." Sometimes, in both the classroom and family settings, there will be several difficult topics which need more time than you can give in one session. The group may have to decide which topic to talk about first, and how much time to give each topic. If need be, get out the timer to see that each topic gets equal time.

Setting the agenda for the classroom meeting can be accomplished by setting up a covered shoe box with a slot in the top. Encourage your students to fill out a simple form to be deposited in the box whenever they have an idea for something to discuss. The form should have three parts: (1) "A Topic I Would Like to Discuss," (2) a line for the name of the student; and (3) a line for the date.

Asking students to sign their notes has several advantages. It allows the teacher to know who is having the problem. Sometimes the teacher may decide it is a problem best discussed privately. The signed note will give the teacher enough information to know who to go talk with about the problem. The signed note also encourages accountability for any statements made about another person. The privacy of the notes in a box also prevents children in the classroom from having their feelings hurt over any name calling which might take place on a more public agenda. On the day of the classroom meeting, the teacher can take the agenda suggestions out of the box and decide how to present them to the class. In this way, the teacher can act as a buffer to insure that any particular child is not attacked by others in the room.

4. *Keep focused on the general problem:*

Sometimes there will be many specific individual problems which are related. Take, for example, a fourth-grade classroom in which six children write down six different incidents about someone teasing them. The teacher can ignore the specific names of who was teasing whom, and state the problem as a general one. For example, instead of saying, "Mattie said Geoff pushed her in the lunch line, and Craig said Nancy ran off with his coat during recess, etc.," the teacher can lump these related problems together by saying, "There are quite a few people who had a problem with someone bugging them this past week." The problem then becomes the general problem of "bugging" and not Craig, Nancy, Mattie, or Geoff. Emphasizing specific names of people makes it easy to end up with the meeting turned into a blaming session, where the "good" guys blame the "bad" guys and the "bad" guys blame everybody else. Throughout the discussion, you can help by refusing to focus on specific names and instead respond by always coming back to the more general problem, for example, when Craig says, "I don't know why Nancy is so mean," you can turn this statement back to the general problem by saying, "It's hard to understand why some people do so much teasing." Try to keep the group focused on the problem, rather than on any particular individual.

At home, where you are dealing with fewer children, you are freer to use names more often, but the principle is the same: Try to downplay focusing on any particular individual in favor of focusing on the general problem.

5. *Watch out for your hidden agenda.*

As leader, you need to be aware that frequently there is an unwritten, or hidden, agenda. This hidden agenda is the list of items no one actually writes down but which people instead carry around in their heads. Hidden agendas happen when people come to the meeting determined to either find or prevent a particular solution. For example, the mother who wants to discuss the problem of people leaving their coats and books all over the living room when they come home from school may have a hidden agenda of trying to persuade her children to adopt the solution to the problem which she has already decided would work the best. (Her solution is to fine everybody five cents for every coat or book she picks up.) If Mother comes to the meeting convinced she has already found the correct solution, it will be almost impossible for her to listen her children's ideas. Since children are smart, they will soon realize their mother is not able to listen to ideas other than her own. The children will then develop a hidden agenda of their own, "Why should I have to lose my allowance? It's not such a big deal to leave a few books around. I'll be darned if I'll agree to her idea."

The hidden agenda item which children often bring to a meeting is to avoid being blamed for anything. By focusing on avoiding blame, they also effectively sabotage the process of finding a solution. "I'm not going to admit it's my fault. Other people do it all the time. I'm not going to take part in this dumb meeting."

The need for hidden agendas tends to disappear as everyone, both adults and children, begin to have faith in the power of the group to respect the rights of every individual as it searches for solutions to problems.

6. *Use Brainstorm techniques to think about possible solutions:*

The following is a three-step process you can use with any group to look for a solution to any problem. Remember, do not expect a solution to come out of the process. Neither you or the group is a failure if no solution is found. The group meeting will be successful if every individual's inner integrity (including your own) is respected.

Step 1. Describe the problem.

Give each person a chance to state the problem as he or she understands it. First, describe what you think the problem is. For example, in the classroom teasing problem you could say, "Six different people had a problem with being teased. So it sounds like the problem to talk about is--what can you do when someone teases you?" Then, open it up to the group by saying, "Does anybody else have another way to state the problem?" This gives the people who have the problem a chance to clarify or change the focus of the problem. In the small family group, you will have time to go around the group and ask each person specifically to state the problem. In the large classroom group, you will have to limit it to only those who volunteer.

Expect that some members of the group, especially those who are fearful of being blamed for the teasing, will at first try to sabotage the process. The person who has been doing much of the teasing may make outrageous statements like, "*She* calls it teasing, but she's just a big cry baby!" or "*I* get bugged all the time and *I* don't whine about it!" Try some inner-reality listening. Even the person who teases gets teased sometimes, too. You can try saying, "You hate to get teased, too, but you keep quiet about it." Or, if you cannot think of anything to say, just nod your head and say, "Hmm." Make frequent friendly eye contact with the persons in the group who are fearful of being blamed. Assume that no one in this entire group likes to be teased. Assume that even teasers get teased sometimes.

When everyone agrees on what the problem is, restate it, and write it down so that during the subsequent discussion you can refer back to it. At the family meeting, someone can act as secretary and write it on a piece of paper. At the classroom meeting, you or a class secretary can write it on the chalkboard. Do not go on to the next step until everyone agrees as to what the actual problem is.

Step 2. Brainstorm possible solutions.

Now invite everyone to come up with possible solutions to the problem. Make a list of each of the ideas on the chalkboard (or the secretary can keep a list on a piece of paper.) Expect that a few people are going to come up with outrageous solutions like, "Send them to a different school," or "Make them stay home for two days every time they make someone cry." *All* ideas, no matter how silly, must be written down on the list. This is not the time to find flaws in the ideas presented. If someone argues, "Well, that won't work. The principal won't let us send anybody to a different school," you can interrupt and say, "Next we'll talk about whether or not the ideas will work. Right now, all ideas are welcome."

The list can be written in shortened form but should contain the major idea; for example, "different school," and "stay home." Some of these outrageous ideas will be offered as a joke, so, if you recognize the humor, be sure to grin a little as you write it down. The rest of the group will see your smile and begin to learn that brainstorming is a creative process which can be fun.

Include your own ideas on the list, for example, "Maybe it would work if the person being teased would try to pretend the teaser was invisible." You will be amazed at the creative ideas a group of children can engender. Feel free to offer your ideas as long as you, and the children, recognize that your idea is just one more piece of the brainstorming process, no more and no less important than any other person's idea.

When you and the group are satisfied you have a fairly complete list, go on to the last step.

Step 3. Attempt to choose a solution.

Start at the top of the list. Take each idea in turn and ask the group, "What about this one? Do you think this would work?" Your leadership role for this part of the process is to help the group think out loud about their various options. You do not have to make the decision. The entire group must make the decision whether or not to choose a particular solution. *Every single person in the group has the power to veto any one of the solutions.*

Some children are accustomed to having adults make all major decisions for them. They will often come up with solutions which shift all responsibility to the parent or teacher, for example, "We could come tell the teacher when someone teases us and she could make him stay in for recess." Even though you may be inwardly thinking there is no way you would ever agree to this idea, go ahead and list it on the chalkboard. But during this third step in the process, as you come to the idea that the teacher should be the judge, you can say, in a thoughtful way, "I wouldn't feel comfortable having to be the judge who everyone comes to about being teased. I wouldn't know who started it. I can't go along with this idea." If you do not want to be the judge, say so. Respect your own inner integrity and feelings just as you would respect those of any other member of the group.

After the group has gone down the list crossing off any ideas which would not work and circling the ideas which seem to have possibilities, go back to all the circled items and one by one, ask, "If we do choose this one, what could go wrong?" Things usually do go wrong with almost any new proposal. It is a valuable lesson in planning to try to anticipate as many glitches as possible. A fourth-grade group which I led in a similar brainstorming discussion finally selected out two possible solutions to the problem of being teased: The first was to play in a different area of the playground from the person who teased you. Not everyone agreed that playing in a different area of the playground was a good idea for them personally. Many students felt they had the right to play wherever they wanted. They were not going to let some teaser scare them away. But, and this was the point of universal agreement, they did agree it would be an okay solution for anybody who wanted to try it. When I asked, "What could go wrong?" someone immediately said, "The teaser might just follow you everywhere on the playground."

If the teaser did follow them around, they decided to use the second solution, which was to try to pretend the teaser was invisible. That way, people who teased would not get any enjoyment out of seeing they were making you miserable. When the group was asked what could go wrong with this solution, many children said they did not know how long they could keep up pretending when the other person was being really mean to them. Everyone agreed it is really hard to ignore teasing. Then, a third proposal surfaced. Someone said, "If that happens, how about going over to talk with the grown-up on recess duty. You wouldn't have to tattle, you could keep on pretending the other person was invisible and just talk to the grown-up about other things. Then I bet the teaser would go away." Everyone agreed that might work. The meeting ended with an agreement to talk about the teasing problem at a later time if these three ideas did not help.

This discussion took a long time, almost forty-five minutes. But the incidents of teasing, or at least the complaints about being teased, dropped way off after this meeting. Even if the group had not found a single acceptable solution, it is possible the result would have been the same. It is the thoughtful and respectful process of involving every person in the group in looking for a solution which raises self-esteem and changes behavior.

7. *Practice the skills you learned from the chapters on listening to inner-reality and describing:*

The family or classroom meeting provides a perfect situation for practicing listening and describing skills. In fact, without your listening and describing skills, you risk being baited into a futile and endless argument with at least one of the group participants.

Naomi had four children who left their clothing and books strewn all over the house when they came home from school. Naomi hated coming home from work each day to this mess. Usually, she could not stand to look at the clutter so she would pick everything up and then scold her children about it at dinner time. Naomi decided to discuss this problem at the family meeting which she and her husband had recently begun to hold on a regular basis. She presented the problem to her kids, using good describing language, "When I come home from work, I see coats and books in the living room and dining room and after school lunch snacks left out on the kitchen counter. I'm tired at the end of the day. I get even more tired when I come home to a messy house. I need some help in figuring out a plan for keeping things picked up."

Her twelve-year-old daughter said, "Why can't the baby sitter pick things up? She's getting paid for taking care of us." And Naomi's ten-year-old son added, "Why should I have to work on this problem? I never leave my stuff around." Imagine Naomi's feelings. She ended up giving an outer-reality lecture to her daughter on the need for everyone to be responsible for their own things, while the son got another outer-reality lecture from the father on the obligations of being a member of a family where everyone should be concerned for everyone else. All doors to communication slammed shut. The meeting deteriorated into heated argument and ended with a pair of discouraged parents who began to question the value of family meetings.

If the mother and father had been able to bite their lips for just a moment and think of a describing or inner-reality response, the meeting might have gone differently.

EXAMPLE A (Daughter's comment): "Why can't the babysitter pick things up? She's the one getting paid!"

Describing response: (Describe what the daughter said by repeating her exact words.) "You think the babysitter should pick things up." Try to look thoughtful and keep calm. Turn to the rest of the group and ask, "Anybody else have any ideas?"

or

Inner-reality response: "Hmm." Be quiet for a few moments while you try to think about it from her point of view. Turn to the rest of the group and ask, "Anybody else have any ideas?"

EXAMPLE B (Son's comment): "Why should I have to work on this problem? I never leave my stuff around!"

Describing response: (Describe what the son said by repeating his exact words.) "You never leave your stuff around so you think you shouldn't have to work on the problem." Try to look thoughtful and keep calm. Turn to the rest of the group and ask, "Anyone else have any ideas?"

or

Inner-reality response: "Hmmm." Be quiet a few moments while you try to think about it from his point of view. Maybe you could add, "You don't think it's fair." Then turn to the rest of the group and ask, "Anyone else have any ideas?"

You can use either the describing or the inner-reality response. Both approaches work fine to help you sidestep the child's attempts to disrupt the meeting.

Naomi's parenting group role-played this situation with Naomi playing the part of her twelve-year-old daughter. At first, Naomi played her daughter's role as an extremely hostile child. But after she experienced the inner-reality and describing response from the person playing the adult, she couldn't keep up her hostility. "It's amazing," she said, "but I don't feel like arguing anymore. I think I'm ready to start problem-solving."

The hardest part about using the describing and outer-reality responses is that when a child makes some apparently outrageous remark, the indignant adult can hardly resist giving the child a logical, outer-reality response in return. Even though it is tempting to tell the child how the real world actually works, talking about outer-reality during negative times of high stress closes the door to any further meaningful communication. Often, the child's outrageous statement is an attempt to sabotage the group process by deflecting blame away from himself. In any case, keep calm and describe what the child said, or just say, "Hmm," then go right on and turn your attention to the next person. In this way, you can effectively ignore the child's behavior if it is self-indulgent. On the other hand, if the child's comments are based on troubling inner feelings, at least you will not have tried to argue him or her out of their feelings. Your goal is to ignore any self-indulgent behaviors while still respecting the inner integrity of the child. This is not an easy balancing act to pull off, but you can do it with a little practice.

The only way to learn how powerful the inner-reality and describing responses are is to practice them. The family and the classroom meetings provide a safe, regular way to increase your listening and describing skills. Reading about them will only give you a clue. You must dare to risk. You must dare to practice. That is how I learned to use them, and that is how you will learn to use them, too.

8. *Rotate leadership of the meeting when children request it or when you think they will benefit from it.*

Probably the most efficient use of the limited school day is to stick with the teacher as leader. Yet, it is a valuable experience for each child to have a turn learning to use this type of problem-solving leadership style. If you decide to try student leadership of classroom meetings, wait until your students are familiar with the way you conduct the classroom meeting before you begin to rotate their leadership turns.

Parents, too, should wait before suggesting that their children take turns being the group leader. Children need to become familiar with the way the meeting is conducted before they try it. If a child asks to be the leader the very first time you hold a meeting (as one-six-year old put it, "*I* want to be President,") tell the child yes, he or she can have a turn being leader. Make it clear to the child that adults will have the first turns since they are the people who have been studying how to do it. Children can learn how to lead the meeting by watching how Mother and Dad do it. After the first two meetings you will have established some kind of meeting framework. The children will learn, for example, that the first thing the family does is to open the meeting with a reading, and the second thing the family does is to talk about the Topics for Discussion list. You will also have had time to set a tone of friendliness and respect for each person's ideas. By the time a child's leadership turn comes along, he or she will have at least some idea how to proceed.

If you rotate leadership, rotate the leader each week. Do not elect the leader. There should be no voting for any reason. If you need some way to select which person starts the rotation process, toss a coin or draw a name out of a jar. As children grow into their middle-school years, the regular experience of having been a group leader, and of having learned interpersonal relationship and problem-solving skills by observing how you participate in the group, will be invaluable in their personal lives.

Of course, the parent or the teacher will have to continue to exercise informal leadership in all the areas mentioned in this chapter which are beyond the capabilities of a child. Whether or not you rotate formal leadership of the group, you will be amazed at how much your children will learn from observing and copying your behavior in the group. If you are able to listen to their inner-reality, they will begin to listen to yours. If you demonstrate how to brainstorm ideas, they will learn how to do it, too. How you interact with the group will be how they think a group leader should interact. Children learn from everyday experiences of living with adults and observing how they interact with other people. By watching how you participate in the group, children will learn effective leadership and human relationship skills without ever having to read a book like this one.

EXERCISE:

Study the "Taking Charge Overview" chart on the following page before going to your next discussion group. Do you see how family and classroom meetings fit into the "Child Has A Problem" box? Do you see how all the major concepts you have learned in *Taking Charge* fit into this over-all pattern?

TAKING CHARGE OVERVIEW

Child's Staircase of Needs*

Self-esteem
"I like myself. I like other people. I like learning new things."

Competency
"I have skills and abilities. People respect me."

Being-Love
"I am loved just because I exist."

Belonging
"This is where I belong. This is my place."

Security
"I feel safe. The world is a trustworthy place.

Physical
"I have food, shelter and someone to hold me."

* Adapted from A. Maslow

The Child's Behaviors: Behaviors you pay attention to will continue

Positive	Neutral	Negative
1. Adult gives non-verbal attention (eye contact, touching, smiles)	1. Adult gives non-verbal attention (eye contact, touching, smiles)	1. Not-minding (Physical assist, broken record)
2. Adult gives verbal attention (describing praise)		2. Self-indulgent (Ignore and either/or choice)
		3. Routine-not-minding (Choices and consequences)
		4. Aggressive (Time-out)
Pleases you—a joy for you	Child doing his or her own thing	Angers or irritates you —a problem for you

The Four Self-Sabotages

1. Procrastination

2. Talking and talking about the misbehavior: Act, don't talk. Carry out the correction and do not mention it again.

3. Forgetting to give 4-1 attention (4 parts positive to 1 part negative)

4. Negative scripting

Child Has Problem

Adult helps by:

1. Adjusting the environment

2. Teaching problem solving and assertiveness skills

3. Listening and accepting the child's inner reality

~ ~ ~ ~ ~ ~ ~ ~ ~ ~ ~ ~ ~ ~ ~ ~ ~

ANGER

Hidden Unmet Needs of the Adult ⟶ Primary Feelings ⟶ Shame
Helplessness
Inadequacy

DISCUSSION IDEAS: CHAPTER 11: THE FAMILY OR CLASSROOM MEETING

1. Before you try leading a meeting at home or at school, try practicing with your discussion group:

    a. Write out a "Topics for Discussion" list for your pretend family or classroom. Choose a couple of topics which are presently a problem for your real family or class.

    b. Decide who will play the role of parent (or teacher) and who will be the children. When you play the part of a child, choose to be a child you know well. Try to get into the feeling of how you think that child would behave and feel in a similar situation. If you only have two people in your group, that is enough. Two people make a family.

    c. First, choose one of your topics and use it to practice the three-step brainstorming technique described in this chapter. If the "adult" gets stuck, he or she should call for a break while the group re-reads the material and discusses what happened. Then back to the role-play.

    d. After you have gone through all three steps, stop and discuss what happened during the role-playing. What was the hardest part about the brainstorm session for the "parent" (or "teacher")? Did the "children" feel listened to? Did anyone catch themselves having a hidden agenda? Did anyone use a describing or inner-reality response?

    e. Practice a family meeting from beginning to end. This time, change roles so that the person who played a child role has a chance to play the part of the adult.

    f. Keep practicing with your discussion group until you feel comfortable enough to start holding meetings at home or in the classroom. Remember, the only way to learn this is to do it. The discussion group is a safe place to learn by making lots of mistakes. If you do not make mistakes, you will not learn much.

2. Look at the "Taking Charge Overview" chart on the preceding page. Does everyone understand how each of the child's behaviors and each adult's responses fit into the chart? Which of the concepts illustrated on the chart are most confusing to you? Which have been most helpful? Which idea is the hardest for you to put into practice? Has anyone noticed whether any of these ideas also work for grownups?

3. Do members of the group want to continue meeting on a regular basis to review the material and to lend support to one another? If yes, decide if there are any changes you want to make in the way the group is organized.

   Many ongoing Taking Charge discussion groups allow at least one half-hour each meeting for helping each other solve specific misbehavior problems as they arise at home or school. "The Taking Charge Overview" review sheet can be used as a quick reference to help you pinpoint just how the problem fits into the overall Taking Charge pattern.

4. At the end of this chapter is a list of books (and tapes) you may want to read and discuss, either on your own, or as you continue to meet with your discussion/support group. Each offers helpful insights into how to provide kids with loving discipline. The ideas in these materials will reinforce the concepts which you have learned in *Taking Charge.*

May all your dedicated efforts at learning the Taking Charge approach to discipline be rewarded with rich and loving relationships between you and your children.

REVIEW: Guidelines for Conducting a Family or Classroom Meeting

1. Schedule a regular meeting time.

2. Establish a relaxed and upbeat atmosphere.

3. Involve everyone in choosing topics for discussion.

4. Keep focused on the general problem.

5. Watch out for your hidden agenda.

6. Use Brainstorm techniques to think about possible solutions:

   Step one: Describe the problem;

   Step two: Brainstorm possible solutions;

   Step three: Attempt to choose a solution.

7. Practice your listening and describing skills.

8. Rotate leadership of the family meeting after the children become familiar with how the meeting is conducted.

9. You do not have to come up with a solution. It is the thoughtful and respectful process of involving every person in the group in looking for a solution which changes behavior.

REMEMBER NOT TO SELF-SABOTAGE

Reading List

Bradshaw, John. <u>On the Family</u>. Health Communications, Inc.; Pompano Beach, Florida, 1988.

Discusses the hidden unmet needs of the adult. Needs that were unmet as a child leave "gaping holes" which can cause rage directed at our own children. Bradshaw describes the dysfunctional family patterns which give rise to the problem and discusses ways these wounds can be healed. Bradshaw's video tapes are also available from your public library or from: Bradshaw Cassettes, P.O. Box 980547, Houston, Texas, 77098.

Cline, Foster and Fay, Jim. <u>Discipline With Love and Logic</u>. 4 audio tapes. Available from your public library or from: Cline/Fay Institute, 2207 Jackson St., Golden, Colorado, 80401

Excellent ideas for logical consequence planning. The talks are highly entertaining and informative, but watch out for possible self-sabotage in the speaker's tone of voice.

Dreikurs, Rudolf and Grey, Loren. <u>A Parent's Guide to Child Discipline</u>. Hawthorn Books; New York, N.Y., 1970.

Dreikurs was the first and best known advocate of using logical consequences to deal with misbehaviors. This book has numerous case histories. Dreikurs also emphasized the idea that parents should act instead of talking so much.

Elkind, David. <u>The Hurried Child</u>. Addison-Wesley; Reading, Mass., 1983.

Shares concerns about children growing up too fast, too soon. Both schools and families demand things of children before they are ready to do them. Hurried children are stressed by the fear of failure--of not achieving fast enough or high enough.

Faber, Adele and Mazlish, Elaine. Liberated Parents, Liberated Children. Avon; New York, N.Y., 1976. How to Listen so Kids Will Talk and Talk so Kids Will Listen. Avon Books; New York, N.Y., 1988. Siblings Without Rivalry. Norton; New York, N.Y., 1987.

All three books are easy reading. How to Listen So Kids Will Talk and Talk So Kids Will Listen focuses on communication skills: for example, how to give commands; how to use describing words for praise and sharing how you feel; and how to listen to feelings. Tells how to avoid power struggles. Siblings Without Rivalry has good tips on how to deal with the new baby, fighting, and ways to promote co-operation between children. Liberated Parents, Liberated Children emphasizes why these techniques work.

Fraiberg, Selma. The Magic Years: Understanding and Handling the Problems of Early Childhood. Scribner; New York, N.Y., 1959.

Explores the age of magical thinking when children believe their thoughts can cause things to happen, for example, when they take responsibility for a divorce or even a death in the family.

Gardner, Richard A. The Boys and Girls Book About Divorce. Bantam Books; New York, N.Y., 1971.

Excellent book for older children whose parents are going through a divorce. Also good for a parent and younger child to read and discuss together.

Ginott, Haim. <u>Between Teacher and Child.</u> Avon; New York, N.Y., 1972. <u>Between Parent and Child</u>. Avon; New York, N.Y., 1976. <u>Between Parent and Teenager</u>. Avon; New York, N.Y., 1982.

Haim Ginott's teachings were the foundation on which Mazlich and Faber built in their writings. Ginott's books are especially good for his discussion of using descriptive language.

Gordon, Thomas. <u>P.E.T.: Parent Effectiveness Training</u>. Peter Wyden; New York, N.Y., 1970. <u>Teacher Effectiveness Training</u>. David McKay; New York, N.Y., 1974.

Stresses communication skills-active listening, "I-messages" not "you-messages." Discusses how adults undermine their own discipline in what he calls roadblocks to communication (you will recognize the "talking and talking" self-sabotage here.) Tells how to modify the environment to solve problems.

Hayden, Torey L. <u>One Child</u>. Avon; New York, N.Y., 1981.

Reads like a novel. A true story of one teacher's work with an emotionally disturbed child. Illustrates how discipline can be healing for children when, at the same time, it also helps build their emotional needs staircase. The teacher uses strategies like time-out, physical restraint, routines, ignoring, giving choices, paying attention at positive and neutral times, listening to feelings, and many others you will find familiar.

James, Muriel, and Jongewar, Dorothy. <u>Born To Win: Transactional Analysis with Gestalt Experiments</u>. Addison-Wesley; Reading, Mass., 1971.

Based on the ideas of Transactional Analysis which were presented earlier by Eric Berne in <u>Games People Play</u>, this book is easier to read and is valuable for any group focused on exploring their own hidden, unmet needs. Contains many usable exercises and discussion topics at the end of each chapter. Chapter Four is especially good for its comprehensive explanation of how children are unwittingly scripted for certain types of behavior.

Keirsey, David and Bates, Marilyn. <u>Please Understand Me: Character and Temperament Types</u>. Prometheus Nemesis; Del Mar, Calif., 1984.

An explanation of the basic four personality types and their combinations; based on the writings of Jung, the Myers-Briggs Type Indicator test, and the authors' considerable experience. Includes a self-test. This book would be helpful for any discussion/support group to use as a way of gaining more understanding and respect for one another's basic personalities. It also offers insights into the difficulties involved when the adult's personality type clashes with that of the child.

Liedloff, Jean. <u>The Continuum Concept: Allowing Human Nature to Work Successfully</u>. Addison-Wesley; Reading, Mass., 1977.

A look at the way the Tauripan Indians of South America raise their children. The Tauripan people keep young children close to an adult's body, even when sleeping, until the child no longer wants to be there. Logical and natural consequences are widely used with no scolding or other talking about the misbehavior. Punishment is unheard of and young children receive much nurturing from adults. The author is convinced these child-rearing practices must be the reason she saw so many happy, strong people in this society.

Maslow, Abraham. <u>Toward A Psychology of Being</u>; 2nd ed. Van Nostrand Reinhold; New York, N.Y., 1968.

Not especially easy reading, but well worth the effort for a look at Maslow's original concept of a hierarchy of needs which has been adapted in this book as a stairway of needs. An optomistic and caring look at the enormous potential of human beings.

Mayer, Mercer. <u>Little Critter's Bedtime Stories</u>. Western; New York, N.Y., 1987. <u>Little Critter's: This Is My School</u>. Western; New York, N.Y., 1990.

These two titles are only a recent sampling from this prolific author. Many of Mayer's stories tell about Henry, the rascally critter who is frequently getting into trouble and is loveable all the same. Conveys the message to young children that they are not bad persons even if they sometimes need to go sit in a quiet corner.

Miller, Alice. <u>For Your Own Good: Hidden Cruelty in Child-rearing and the Roots of Violence.</u> Farrar Straus Giroux; New York, N.Y., 1980.

Makes a convincing case that emotional and physical child abuse causes violence in later life. She illustrates how cruel child-rearing tactics caused the destructiveness of an Adolph Hitler. Alice Miller's works are an important element in John Bradshaw's teachings.

Mitchell, Grace. <u>A Very Practical Guide to Discipline</u>. Telshare; 1982.

Focuses on discipline of young children. Good tips on how to manipulate the environment, discussion of spanking, what to do about behavior that bugs you. Easy reading. She shares her mistakes with you.

Stevens, Barry, Rogers, Carl, et. al. <u>Person to Person: The Problem of Being Human.</u> Simon and Schuster; New York, N.Y., 1971.

A wise Barry Stevens shares her very readable and personal responses to seven articles written by professionals in the mental health field. In the words of Carl Rogers, "This book helps me to understand myself a little better, so now I understand the other a bit better, and to this degree I am a little less baffled by both of us."

Wholey, Dennis. Becoming Your Own Parent: The Solution for Adult Children of Alcoholic and Other Dysfunctional Families. Bantam; New York, N.Y., 1990.

Written by an adult child of an alcoholic, this is a collection of personal stories by numerous adults who grew up in dysfunctional family situations. Describes the problems faced by these adults and offers solutions. A readable book which can help you discover your own unmet, hidden needs, and give you clues as to what you can do to begin to satisfy them.

Index

praise **210-214**
pregnancy, teenage 122, 128
problem-solving **57-67** (See also negotiation and assertiveness)
procrastination **29-35**, 162, 173
quiet corner 108-110, 255
rage 175-178 (See also anger)
reality check 186
reinforcers, positive 156-169
    negative 165
Ritalin 60
Rogers, Carl xiii, 255-256
role-play 69-70, 90, 94, 174, 176, 180, 206, 248
routine not-minding behavior 55-56, **119-169** (review 150)
safety and security needs 19-20, 112, 175, 177, 180,
sassing 83, 86, 93, 96, 112, 134, 191-192
school
    extra-curricular activities 140-141
    getting there on time **135-138**, 144-145
    grades 156-157
    Saturday school 145-146
schoolwork 119, 122, 143-144, 145, **156-169**
scolding and yelling 94, 111, 112
scripting **41-45**, 214, 254
security and safety needs 19-20, 112, 175, 177, 180
self-esteem 7, 17-18, 22-24, 45, 190, 214, 220 (See also staircase of needs)
self-indulgent behavior 55, 78, 83, 85, **93-117**,
    difference from expressing painful emotions 201-202
self-sabotage **29-51**, 78-79, 81-82, 105, 136, 137, 139 (chart 50)
    forgetting to give positive attention 40-41, 87-88, 155-156, 167, 177, 187 (See also neutral behavior)
    hidden, unmet needs **45-48**, 256
    negative scripting **41-45**
    procrastination **29-35**, 162, 173
    talking and talking **35-40**, 76, 80-88, 119-120, **128**, 130, 131, 134, 136-139, 174

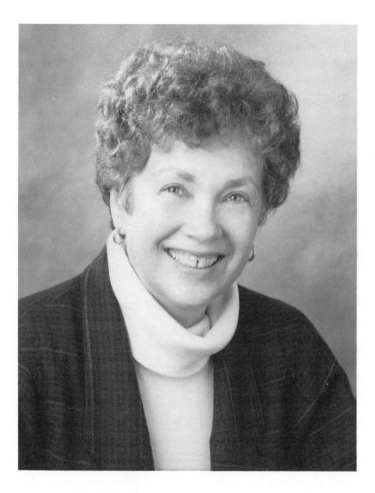

Jo Anne Nordling, M.S., M.Ed., is a teacher, parent, counselor and workshop leader. She is co-founder of Parent Support Center in Oregon state, where she teaches effective discipline techniques to parent groups in cooperation with Washington County Community Action Organization, and has served in an advisory position with the Domestic Violence Resource Center in Hillsboro, Oregon. She also conducts seminars and graduate level classes for teachers and school support personnel.

Jo Anne and her husband, George, have 4 sons and 5 grandchildren.

More Quality Books from R & E Publishers

TAKING CHARGE: A Parent and Teacher Guide to Loving Discipline by Jo Anne Nordling. At last, here is a book that shows both parents and teachers everything they need to know to discipline children effectively and fairly.

This easy-to-understand action guide will show you how to handle the most critical disciplinary issues in teaching and raising children.

$11.95	LC 91-50985	ISBN 0-88247-906-7
Trade Paper	6x9	Order #906-7

THE GOAL BOOK: Your Simple Power Guide to Reach any Goal & Get What You Want by James Hall. Would you like to be able to turn your dreams into realities? You can if you have concrete goals. This book is based upon a unique goal achievement technique developed by a high school teacher and career counselor in California's Silicon Valley. "Action Conditioning Technology" (ACT) will help you convert your dreams and wishful fantasies into obtainable goals. With this new achievement technology, you will be able to decide exactly what you want, what steps you need to take and when you will reach your objective.

$6.95	LC 91-50675	ISBN 0-88247-892-3
Trade paper	6 x 9	Order #892-3

FOR TEACHERS ONLY: Personal and Confidential by William Sorrells. Teachers are the most poorly treated, and poorly paid professionals in this country. *For Teachers Only: Personal and Confidential—The Secret Files of a Veteran Teacher* exposes the shocking treatment that leads to low self-esteem and job burnout among this nation's educators. Author William Sorrells has issued an emancipation proclamation for teachers that will help them to reclaim their power and restore the vision that originally lead them to become teachers. His book offers specific actions that every teacher must take to increase their own self-worth. Only in this way, Sorrells tells us, can we reverse the trends that are undermining the very fabric of our educational system.

$9.95	ISBN 0-88247-889-3	LC 91-52960
Trade paper	Order #889-3	6 x 9

THE SOLUTION STRATEGY: Your Handbook for Solving Life's Problems by Phil McWilliams. If you didn't have any problems, what would you do? You'd probably be reading *The Solution Strategy* by Phil McWilliams. He has written the one book you need to solve *any* problem. Now you can stop relying on luck or guesswork to handle difficult situations. With this step-by-step technique you'll be able to determine where your problems come from, how to identify them and then—eliminate them. You'll learn how to overcome problems through the integration of emotions and intellect. Once you learn these techniques, you'll be able to accomplish any goal. *The Solution Strategy* is not Pop Psychology or Religion. It is a new kind of self-help book that really works!

$9.95	LC 91-61309	ISBN 0-88247-875-3
Trade paper	6x9	Order #875-3

ADVENTOURING: A Sourcebook for Adventure and Special Interest Travelers by Shirley Deeter. Americans are on the GO...and this book will help get them going on 1000's of exciting trips. Essential and hard-to-find facts on close to 200 specialty tour operators, newsletters and more. Whether its trekking to Timbuktu or cycling through Scotland, Shirley Deeter reveals what outfits go there, who they take, what they charge. This one volume can replace a stack of tour brochures and save hours of time and hundreds of dollars.

$8.95	ISBN 0-88247-866-6
Perfect Bound	Order #866-6

YOUR ORDER

Please rush me the following books. I want to save by ordering three books and receive FREE shipping charges. Orders under 3 books please include $2.50 shipping. CA residents add 8.25% tax.

ORDER #	QTY	UNIT PRICE	TOTAL PRICE

SHIP TO:

(Please Print) Name:_____

Organization:_____

Address:_____

City/State/Zip:_____

PAYMENT METHOD

Enclosed check or money order

MasterCard   Card Expires _____   Signature_____

Visa

R & E Publishers • P.O. Box 2008 • Saratoga, CA 95070 (408) 866-6303 FAX (408) 866-0825

More Quality Books from R & E Publishers

TAKING CHARGE: A Parent and Teacher Guide to Loving Discipline by Jo Anne Nordling. At last, here is a book that shows both parents and teachers everything they need to know to discipline children effectively and fairly.

This easy-to-understand action guide will show you how to handle the most critical disciplinary issues in teaching and raising children.

$11.95	LC 91-50985	ISBN 0-88247-906-7
Trade Paper	6x9	Order #906-7

THE GOAL BOOK: Your Simple Power Guide to Reach any Goal & Get What You Want by James Hall. Would you like to be able to turn your dreams into realities? You can if you have concrete goals. This book is based upon a unique goal achievement technique developed by a high school teacher and career counselor in California's Silicon Valley. "Action Conditioning Technology" (ACT) will help you convert your dreams and wishful fantasies into obtainable goals. With this new achievement technology, you will be able to decide exactly what you want, what steps you need to take and when you will reach your objective.

$6.95	LC 91-50675	ISBN 0-88247-892-3
Trade paper	6 x 9	Order #892-3

FOR TEACHERS ONLY: Personal and Confidential by William Sorrells. Teachers are the most poorly treated, and poorly paid professionals in this country. *For Teachers Only: Personal and Confidential—The Secret Files of a Veteran Teacher* exposes the shocking treatment that leads to low self-esteem and job burnout among this nation's educators. Author William Sorrells has issued an emancipation proclamation for teachers that will help them to reclaim their power and restore the vision that originally lead them to become teachers. His book offers specific actions that every teacher must take to increase their own self-worth. Only in this way, Sorrells tells us, can we reverse the trends that are undermining the very fabric of our educational system.

$9.95	ISBN 0-88247-889-3	LC 91-52960
Trade paper	Order #889-3	6 x 9

THE SOLUTION STRATEGY: Your Handbook for Solving Life's Problems by Phil McWilliams. If you didn't have any problems, what would you do? You'd probably be reading *The Solution Strategy* by Phil McWilliams. He has written the one book you need to solve *any* problem. Now you can stop relying on luck or guesswork to handle difficult situations. With this step-by-step technique you'll be able to determine where your problems come from, how to identify them and then—eliminate them. You'll learn how to overcome problems through the integration of emotions and intellect. Once you learn these techniques, you'll be able to accomplish any goal. *The Solution Strategy* is not Pop Psychology or Religion. It is a new kind of self-help book that really works!

$9.95	LC 91-61309	ISBN 0-88247-875-3
Trade paper	6x9	Order #875-3

ADVENT*OU*RING: A Sourcebook for Adventure and Special Interest Travelers by Shirley Deeter. Americans are on the GO...and this book will help get them going on 1000's of exciting trips. Essential and hard-to-find facts on close to 200 specialty tour operators, newsletters and more. Whether its trekking to Timbuktu or cycling through Scotland, Shirley Deeter reveals what outfits go there, who they take, what they charge. This one volume can replace a stack of tour brochures and save hours of time and hundreds of dollars.

$8.95	ISBN 0-88247-866-6
Perfect Bound	Order #866-6

YOUR ORDER

ORDER #	QTY	UNIT PRICE	TOTAL PRICE

Please rush me the following books. I want to save by ordering three books and receive FREE shipping charges. Orders under 3 books please include $2.50 shipping. CA residents add 8.25% tax.

SHIP TO:

(Please Print) Name: _____

Organization: _____

Address: _____

City/State/Zip: _____

PAYMENT METHOD

Enclosed check or money order

MasterCard   Card Expires _____   Signature _____

Visa

R & E Publishers • P.O. Box 2008 • Saratoga, CA 95070 (408) 866-6303 FAX (408) 866-0825